1/15/13
$25.00

FEAR

FEAR

*Essays on the meaning and
experience of fear*

Kate Hebblethwaite & Elizabeth McCarthy

EDITORS

FOUR COURTS PRESS

Set in 11 on 14 point AGaramond for
FOUR COURTS PRESS LTD
7 Malpas Street, Dublin 8, Ireland
e-mail: info@fourcourtspress.ie
http://www.fourcourtspress.ie
and in North America by
FOUR COURTS PRESS
c/o ISBS, 920 N.E. 58th Avenue, Suite 300, Portland, OR 97213.

ISBN 978-1-84682-070-0

A catalogue record for this title
is available from the British Library.

Printed in England
by Antony Rowe Ltd, Chippenham, Wilts.

Contents

PART II

Illustrations

Acknowledgments

We would like to thank the Trinity College Dublin Association and Trust for their kind financial assistance in support of the *Fear* conference, which took place in Dublin on 19 May 2006 and contributed towards this book's subsequent development. We would also like to thank all those who were involved in the organization and running of the conference itself, most particularly Darryl Jones, co-ordinator of the MPhil in Popular Literature at the School of English, Trinity College Dublin.

Introduction

KATE HEBBLETHWAITE & ELIZABETH McCARTHY

> 'Neither a man nor a crowd nor a nation can be trusted to act humanely
> or to think sanely under the influence of a great fear.' – Bertrand Russell

Fear is endemic. At once a primary emotion, yet also curiously nebulous, fear's
manifestation and manipulation has become a persistent feature of modern culture. From news reports to scary movies, it would seem as though life in the
twenty-first century is underscored by a vein of fear that nourishes social activity,
from political policy to box-office takings. While a seemingly epoch-specific emotion, fear, in fact, is what most pervasively links modern culture to its historical
past: the primary causes of fear remain largely constant across generational, geographical, and political divides. Psychologists such as John B. Watson and Paul
Ekman have argued that fear, along with a few other basic emotions such as joy
and anger, is innate in all human beings. Fear of attack, pain, death and loss are
the fundamentals which have impelled both individual and state endeavour from
the earliest times to the present day. A study of fear, above all things, shows that
the motivating factors behind modern events are not as distant from historical
ones as we may imagine.

Although the experience of fear may be influenced by social norms and values,
fear itself is an innate response. In his study of the comparability of human and
animal behaviour, *The expression of the emotions in man and animals* (1872),
Charles Darwin remarked that, 'fear was expressed from an extremely remote
period' in the development of humans and remains an emotion not only shared
by both man and beast, but expressed in remarkably analogous ways: 'trembling,
the erection of the hair, cold perspiration, pallor, widely opened eyes, the relax-
ation of most of the muscles, and by the whole body cowering downwards or held
motionless.'[1] An emotion shared by all sentient life, fear is fundamental to the

---

[1] Charles Darwin, *The expression of the emotions in man and animals.* Introduction, afterword and commen-
taries by Paul Ekman (London, 1999), p. 356.

biological makeup of all animals. Likewise, in prompting a largely *physical* reaction to an emotion *mentally* perceived, fear reveals *Homo sapiens* at its most visceral. Thus, in controlling or manipulating one's own fear – or indeed another's fear – one also has the potential to control a central aspect of human behaviour.

Of course, the term "fear" has many connatations, most of them negative. In the modern age – which may be termed post-Enlightenment as readily as post-Modern – concepts of the nature and effects of fear have remained surprisingly consistent. Edmund Burke's assertion that 'No passion so effectually robs the mind of all its powers of acting and reasoning as fear'[2] remains a predominant reaction to fear as a personal psychological experience. In light of fear's function as a basic tool of self-preservation it seems ironic that it should be pitted so readily against action and reason. Yet, it is fear's apparently elemental nature, its connections to a primal sense of self, which makes it seem such a threatening breach of the "productive" individual's status within a society that views itself as thoroughly modern and inherently progressive. Of course, this is just one of many examples of how fear – both as a psychological experience and a theoretical concept – raises conflicting and seemingly incompatible possibilities. The aim of this book is to explore these possibilities further.

In the early part of the twenty-first century we have become increasingly aware of the psychological and social manifestation of fear as a major force in people's lives and, indeed, their deaths. The "specter of the terrorist" is one of these fears, as is its inevitable and necessary corollary, fear of increasing state-control and surveillance in the individual's everyday life and the threat this poses to civil liberties. Of course this "climate of fear" is nothing new in the socio-political history of the West. Balancing between threats to personal freedom on the one hand and the terror of sudden and indiscriminate death on the other, the middle of the twentieth century, for example, witnessed the dual fears of communism and the atomic bomb.

However, such fears (with the ever-present aid of the media) have, undeniably, taken on a greater sense of global significance today than ever before. Since 9/11, terrorism has become the West's fear nucleus and the dark-skinned, Middle-Eastern fundamentalist the ultimate symbol of fear and loathing. The figures of Saddam Hussein and Osama bin Laden have been consistently represented as global terrorists, the rulers of terrorist nations whose primary political aim is simply to invoke terror. They represent a fear which is provoked from outside, from the Other.

Yet, far from acceding to the counsel that mass-panic merely plays into terrorism's hands, the reportage of terrorist violence is drawn out by a media machine

---

2 Edmund Burke, *A philosophical enquiry into the origin of our ideas of the sublime and beautiful* (1757) (Oxford, 1998). Pt. 2 Sections 3–6.

which itself is largely influenced by sales targets and the drive for greater viewing figures. In anticipation of attack, both America and Britain now accord Threat Levels corresponding to the evaluated intensity of fear *anticipated*. Pre-crime, once the stuff of Philip K. Dick novels, is now a chargeable offence as pre-emptive accusations of "attempting to conspire" are brought against those Others considered to be dangerous: incarceration without evidence – or trial – has become a terrifying reality in the West, and remains a stark example both of the power of fear and the fearful power of authority itself.

Heightened security and surveillance likewise, while intended to monitor the minority of people who would seek to harm us, at the same time advances a mood of mistrust and omnipotent observation that creeps inexorably closer to an Orwellian vision of society ruled by fear under the guise of paternalistic love. As Joanna Bourke argues in *Fear: a cultural history*, 'fear has become the emotion through which public life is administered':[3] fear is now used to drive out fear itself in the attempt to endorse social cohesion and the repression of violence.

As well as these widespread images of the "global terrorist", more localized figures of fear also abound in contemporary media reports. As Jacques Derrida argues in his discussion of terrorism with Giovanna Borradori:

> Terror is always, or always becomes, at least in part, "interior". And terrorism always has something "domestic", if not national, about it. The worst, most effective "terrorism", even if it seems external and "international", is one that installs or recalls an interior threat, at home [...] and recalls that the enemy is also always lodged on the inside of the system it violates and terrorizes.[4]

Indeed, the existence of "domestic terrorists" such as the Oklahoma City bomber Timothy McVeigh and the Right Wing political extremists suspected of engineering the anthrax scare of 2001, along with the distinctly Western backgrounds of many Muslim terrorists, testifies to the veracity of these observations. Of course this notion of the unavoidable "interior", "domestic", even "homely" nature of the threat of terrorism is itself a conspicuous aspect of fear. Narratives of fear have continually put forward the likely origins of the experience as interior and domestic. Unsurprisingly, such narratives are far more likely to be fictional and at an appreciable remove from the "sensitive" issues surrounding current events.

In fact, a discernable feature of many turbulent social and economic periods in history is the increase in fictional narratives whose focus is on the fantastic and terrible destructive possibilities within the *individual*. The economic and social

3 Joanna Bourke, *Fear: a cultural history* (London, 2006), x.   4 Jacques Derrida, 'Autoimmunity: real and symbolic suicides – a dialogue with Jacques Derrida' in Giovanni Borradori, *Philosophy in a time of terror: dialogues with Jurgen Habermas and Jacques Derrida* (Chicago, 2003), p. 188.

upheavals experienced in France in the wake of the French Revolution, the religious turbulence of the 1798 Irish rebellion, the Great Depression of post-World War I and the social repressions of post-World War II, have all left their indelible mark on the writers and artists of these times. At such apparently pivotal periods in human history, when society itself seems to be on the verge of some frightening change or mutation, the fictional narratives emerging from this milieu have made these moments of cultural convulsion visible. Rosemary Jackson's assertion that such fantastic literature, 'traces the unsaid and the unseen of culture: that which has been silenced, made invisible, covered over and made absent'[5] highlights this literature's tendency to disclose, reveal and make visible that which is deemed best hidden from view. Whether these taboo subjects take the form of the discontents or anxieties of a given class, race or gender, or whether they involve other related issues of economic, religious or scientific origin, writers such as Marquis de Sade, Matthew Lewis, Mary Shelley, Bram Stoker, Robert Louis Stevenson, Franz Kafka, M.R. James, H.G. Wells, Joyce Carol Oates, Richard Matheson, Stephen King and Thomas Harris have developed fictional narratives which focus on the destabilizing threat of otherness, while simultaneously intimating that the greatest object of fear is in fact the self.

In popular culture, the archetypal images of Frankenstein's monster, Dracula, and Mr Hyde are still some of our strongest signifiers both of the fear of otherness and of ourselves. Similarly, more recent cinematic recreations of zombies and psychopathic killers remind us of the frightening possibility that what we understand as the self may be both physically and psychologically altered and twisted out of all recognition. Time and again such fictional images and scenarios are utilized as a means of describing actual events. In a curious doubling back and forth, socio-cultural fears, apparently too sensitive to be addressed overtly, are "dealt" with in fictional narratives which are then used by commentators as a means of depicting similarly sensitive socio-cultural events. In other words, that which is unthinkable and unsayable in a social "real life" context is given form in the realm of fiction, which is then used to describe and comprehend actual events and situations. From the images of the Irish Land Reform movement as the Irish Frankenstein and Jack the Ripper as the degenerate Mr Hyde, to descriptions of Saddam Hussein as a sociopathic serial killer and 9/11 as a real-life *Towering inferno* or *Independence day*, threatening social occurrences are continually figured in terms which rely on the fictional.

Indeed, the imaginative manipulation of images of fear has become, in the twenty-first century, almost as much a commodity as the search for fear's panacea itself. For as much as modern media coverage of national and international disasters draws inexorably closer to a Hollywood-style of reportage with sensational

5 Rosemary Jackson, *Fantasy: the literature of subversion* (London, 2003) p. 2.

footage and lurid details, Hollywood itself increasingly seeks to make its horror movies as "realistic" as possible: another example of art imitating life imitating art. The plethora of horror movies which have been released since the turn of the millennium, including the remake of *The Texas chainsaw massacre* (2003, dir. Marcus Nispel) and the brutally violent *Hostel* (2005, dir. Eli Roth) would seem to indicate that, even in a world saturated by violent images, the public's appetite for fictionalized brutality remains high.

This predilection for fear and trembling, however, is not necessarily a modern phenomenon. Slasher movies in glorious Techni-, Eastman- and Metrocolor were predated by Phantasmagoria, a pre-cinema projection ghost show, invented in France in the eighteenth century, which gained popularity throughout Europe. In these shows, a modified type of magic lantern was used to project frightening images such as skeletons, demons and ghosts on to walls, smoke or a semi-transparent screen. Likewise, the Gothic novel's upsurge in popularity during the late-eighteenth century, and its continued success throughout the nineteenth century, drew heavily upon contemporary fears for its up-to-the-minute chilling appeal. Matthew Lewis' *The Monk* (1796) was as much an embodiment of the traditional English mistrust of Roman Catholicism, with its intrusive confessional, its political and religious authoritarianism and its cloistered lifestyles, as it was a hyperbolic role call of bleeding nuns, ruined castles, rape and incest. Almost a century later, Bram Stoker's *Dracula* (1897) played upon late-Victorian fears of disease contamination, reverse-invasion and the sexually rampant New Woman to achieve a similarly bloodcurdling effect.

By the same token, certain works of fiction have regularly been adapted to appeal to the fears of new audiences. First published in 1898, H.G. Wells' *The war of the worlds* not only tapped into current theories on the inhabitants of Mars as expounded by Percival Lowell's canal hypothesis, but also provided a searing commentary on late-Victorian imperial enterprise, political hypocrisy and human egotism. The destruction of English middle-class suburbia by the restive foreign Other emphasized the complacency into which humanity had seemingly fallen, while the rout of civilization that follows underscores the essential incivility lying behind polite society. It is little wonder, therefore, that Wells' story has subsequently resurfaced at flashpoints of political tension and cultural anxiety – notably in 1938 by Orson Welles, in 1953 by George Pál, and in 2005 by Stephen Spielberg. Welles' version employed the medium of radio and a news-bulletin style format to achieve an element of credibility that led to widespread panic across a country poised on the brink of war. Moving away from the form of Wells' narrative – with its appeal to the single reader – Orson Welles exploited radio's facility to reach a large audience simultaneously. This in turn exploited fear's wider ability to maneuver within a larger social network, wherein personal fears are synergetically compounded as mass hysteria.

In like manner, utilizing increasingly sophisticated developments in mass-entertainment, the 1953 film adaptation of *The war of the worlds*, moved the location from the environs of London to southern California. World War II stock footage was spliced into the film to produce a realistic montage of destruction which viewers may have readily (and fearfully) identified with, while the ineffective employment of an A-Bomb against the invading aliens manipulated contemporary fears about communist aggression and the Cold War. In 2005, less than four years after the attacks on New York's World Trade Centre, Spielberg created his own image of the apocalyptic invasion of the Unites States of America by a group whose physical, cultural and ideological cohesion juxtaposes the relatively alienated, individualistic and divided nature of Western society. In Spielberg's version of Wells' novel, moreover, the aliens are never identified as being resolutely Martian; they remain throughout technologically advanced, emotionless super-beings of unknown origin, further playing on modern concerns about the nebulous, invading, foreign Other. Aside from highlighting the tendency to link fear to concerns about racial otherness, these two films also characterize a consistent second theme of fear as identified by Peter Stearns in his study *American fear* (2006): a recurring 'apocalyptic strain'.[6] In 1953, the threat of communists with a bomb, atomic or hydrogen, capable of obliterating life in a single act, easily fits this apocalyptic premise. The theme is also comparable with the rhetoric of 2005 that suggested an apocalyptic end, not to life on earth, but to the American way of life, destroyed by terrorist violence.

However, despite the fact that fear is primarily perceived as a negative emotion, the commercial success of these two films appears to confirm George Slusser's view that Americans 'seem to revel in mass destruction'.[7] Catastrophic events involving aliens, global devastation or mass murder are now the mainstay of the summer box office as millions of moviegoers experience fear that, as Peter Stearns speculates, allows 'people to display courage in essentially controlled environments'.[8] Indeed, such an inclination for shocking news footage, scary movies, horror novels or even extreme sports, highlights an interesting aspect of our relationship with fear. We like being scared. Or, rather, we like being counselled to "feel the fear and do it anyway", so long as the fear we feel is controllable. Being able to shut a book, turn off the television or close the newspaper gives us an element of control regarding the levels of fear to which we are exposed which, in turn, allows us to experience a false sense of security regarding our own particular situation. In being able to control our levels of fear and to walk away from its source we also leave the characters in the book/movie/newspaper trapped in their

6 Peter N. Stearns, *American fear: the causes and consequences of high anxiety* (New York, 2006), p. 63. 7 George Slusser, 'Pocket apocalypse: American survivalist fictions from Walden to the Incredible Shrinking Man' in *Imagining apocalypse: studies in cultural crisis*, ed. David Seed (New York, 2000), p. 124. 8 Stearns, *American fear*, p. 5.

own cycle of fear to which, for a short time, we have been voyeuristic observers but non-participants. In returning to our own relatively non-fearful lives thereafter, an inversely proportionate level of security is experienced. We feel safe when others are scared. In a wider dimension, as Bourke points out, '[w]e now use terror speak to justify terrorizing others'.[9] Inflating the levels of fear perceived may validate a reaction disproportionate to the actual hazard; however it also commensurately increases feelings of security. A successful overreaction, in other words, is more likely to subdue fear than a merely adequate rejoinder. We hurt in order not to be hurt; we cause fear in order not to feel afraid.

There is undoubtedly something of this disturbing equation at work in numerous instances of violent assault and murder. Delving into the background of brutal and seemingly motiveless crimes, cycles of abuse are often discovered, abusers are revealed to have been the victims of abuse who re-enact this abuse in an attempt to eradicate their own feelings of powerlessness. The serial killer and the mass murderer are among the most potent figures associated with this fatal cycle, creating a sense of their own selfhood through violent scenarios of revenge. The Boston Strangler, Albert De Salvo, and serial rapist and killer of 33 boys, John Wayne Gacy, are among the numerous examples of multiple murderers known to have been seriously abused as children.

Many commentators have drawn comparisons between these personal psychodramas and much broader socio-political circumstances, even to the extent of aligning individual psychology with national character and vice versa. Robert Tracinski's comments on the Virginia Tech shootings are a noteworthy example of this commingling of psychoanalysis and political commentary. Paralleling Seung-Hui Cho's murder of 32 students and faculty members of Virginia Tech on 16 May 2007 with the terrorist activities of the 'Jihadis', he writes, 'The Virginia Tech killer is, in effect, a terrorist without a cause [...] His killing spree is meant to protest the narrow fact of his own sense of failure in life. This kind of mass murderer has the mentality of a terrorist, but without a wider political cause to give his murderous scheme a sense of moral or religious legitimacy.'[10] Alerting his readers to the "real" threat the West faces Tracinski invokes a nightmare vision of whole religious and political systems which help feed a similarly violent psychological dysphoria:

> What of those who have a theory that transforms mass murder into a holy war – a *jihad* – which, in turn, allows them to recruit followers and organize an international movement with many sympathizers among the "moderates" in the general population? That is precisely what we face in the

9 Bourke, *Fear*, x. 10 Robert Tracinski, 'The killers we should really worry about are the Jihadis', *Rear Clear Politics* 18 Apr. 2007. www.realclearpolitics.com/articles/2007/04/the_killers_we_should_ really_ w.html, accessed 22 Apr. 2007

Middle East in the War on Terrorism: the mentality of the mass murderer or serial killer, but projected into a religious and political *system* that threatens us with mass death on a scale far greater than any disaffected loner with a handgun could ever dream of.[11]

Such a reduction of complex cultural, religious and economic unrest between East and West enables the wholesale marketing of fear. In doing so it bypasses troublesome issues regarding international and domestic polices and instead represents terrorism as a quantifiable threat based on the wrongheaded disaffection of the Other. Thus fear becomes a commodifiable force not only justifying but fuelling its own existence.

A similar commodification of domestic and personal fear has become big business in contemporary Western culture. Threats to personal health, be it mental or physical, have resulted in a therapy culture in which individuals can be taken seriously, and treated, for almost every phobia imaginable – from agoraphobia to zoophobia. Potentially large-scale health-scares such as avian bird flu, meanwhile, regularly receive significant news coverage, despite their relatively insignificant incidence. Fear appeals are often used in marketing and social policy as a method of persuasion – intentionally shocking anti-tobacco and anti-speeding advertisements being just two examples of this. Noam Chomsky, among others, has suggested that such appeals to fear also play a role in social oppression on a large scale. According to this line of argument, political institutions and the mass media deliberately manufacture a culture of fear to foster conformity and maintain the status quo.[12]

In a less extreme, but equally pervasive way, a culture of fear may be seen to have crept into everyday situations. "Fear, uncertainty and doubt" (or FUD) is a recognized term in sales or marketing, in which a company disseminates negative (and vague) information on a competitor's product. The term originated to describe misinformation tactics in the computer hardware industry and has since been used more broadly to refer to implicit coercion by any kind of disinformation used as a competitive weapon. Consumers are manipulated to purchase by brand, regardless of relative technical merits, in the belief that by doing so, fear levels will be commensurately reduced. In many ways fear's inverse, the state of happiness, has meanwhile become a veritable holy grail with a multitude of handbooks and manuals dedicated to its attainment. Undoubtedly inspired by the lessons of aromatherapy, there even exists a perfume called *Happy* (Clinique), as though one can distil the emotion in a bottle and unleash it upon demand. Paradoxically, this elevation of happiness to a near-transcendental state actually serves

11 Ibid. 12 Noam Chomsky, 'The culture of fear' in Javier Giraldo, *Colombia: the genocidal democracy* (Monroe, ME, 1996). www.chomsky.info/articles/199607—.htm, accessed 2 May 2007.

to increase levels of *anxiety* as we are persuaded to pursue ever more nebulous ideas of pleasure. Daniel Gilbert's *Stumbling on happiness* (2006) even argues that we actually do not know what makes us happy, the limitations of the human imagination essentially working against true fulfilment. The insinuation is evident: buy the book and discover *real* happiness. In effect, Gilbert is using the marketing principles of "fear, uncertainty and doubt" against happiness itself.

Although encompassing a plethora of auxiliary sensations such as anger, awe, dread, excitement, terror, horror, guilt, shame and jealousy (to name but a few), the inherently complex emotion of fear itself defies ready simplification to a basic cause. From the writing of children's novels to international political policy, fear, it can be argued, is one of the key motivational factors in the human psyche. Dealing with a variety of topics from goblins and ghosts to advertising propaganda and horror movies, the aim of this book is to examine how fear's manifestation and manipulation has influenced human endeavour.

The majority of essays in this collection are based on papers given at an interdisciplinary conference, entitled *Fear*, held at Trinity College Dublin on 19 May 2006. Run in association with Trinity College's MPhil in Popular Literature and kindly supported by the TCD Association and Trust, the conference sought to explore and engage in the subject of fear from multiple historical viewpoints and genre perspectives. Such an interdisciplinary approach allowed for participants to engage in dialogue above and beyond the remit of their own particular fields and thus to work towards a broader understanding of the cause and effects of that most primary of emotions, fear. It is this ethos of comparative study that this volume hopes to further promote.

This collection opens with Frank Furedi's essay on the modern culture of fear, and then moves chronologically through a series of essays which examine literary concepts of fear in an historical and political perspective. Although each tackling widely differing subject material, Shanahan, Glover, McCarthy, Ó Donghaile, Colgan, Jones and Durodié's essays nevertheless reveal that the forces which impelled topics as historically and politically diverse as the 1798 Irish rebellion and American neo-Nazism are nevertheless inextricably connected, and driven, by discourses of fear. Marking a conceptual transition in the volume, Part II deals with fear on a more personal, psychological and imaginative level. The essay by the award-winning author Mark O'Sullivan's explores ideas about fear as a fundamental factor in his own childhood experience. Piesse's essay continues this examination of fear, with a consideration of its place and importance in the childhood imagination and children's literature. Finally, essays by Downey, Hebblethwaite, Murphy and Frayling examine the influence of fear on the artistic and literary imagination – Henry Fuseli, M.R. James, Mark Z. Danielewski and the modern horror film being among the topics discussed.

Towards a sociology of fear

FRANK FUREDI

Fear represents an important dimension in twenty-first century consciousness. It is a form of consciousness that explicitly engages with specific issues through a narrative fear. Symptoms of this trend are visible in the past century, which was frequently characterized as the Age of Anxiety.[1] In recent decades, however, this sensibility has gained greater definition and focus through the cultivation of specific fears. Numerous catch phrases – politics of fear, fear of crime, fear of the future – are testimony to its significance as a cultural idiom for interpreting experience. Fear is not simply associated with high profile catastrophic threats such as that of terrorism, global warming, AIDS or a flu pandemic. Social scientists have also drawn attention to the quiet fears of life. Phil Hubbard claims that ambient fear 'saturates the social spaces of everyday life'[2] and Brian Massumi echoes this approach with his concept of 'low-grade fear.'[3] In recent years the question of anxiety and fear has been considered in relation to a wide variety of phenomena: the ascendancy of risk consciousness; fear of the urban environment; the fear of crime; fear of the Other, and its amplification through the media; as a distinct discourse; its impact on legal norms; its relationship to politics; as a culture; and, whether it constitutes a distinctive cultural form.[4]

Although fear is often explored as a problem associated with the subject under discussion it is rarely considered as a sociological problem in its own right. Elemér Hankiss argues that the role of fear is 'much neglected in the social sciences'. He

---

1 R. May, *The meaning of anxiety* (New York, 1950).   2 P. Hubbard, 'Fear and loathing at the multiplex: everyday anxiety in the post-industrial city', *Capital & Class* 80 (2003), 32.   3 B. Massumi (ed.), *The politics of everyday fear* (Minneapolis, 1993), p. 24.   4 For specific arguments pertaining to these ideas, see: P. Slovic, 'Perception of risk', *Science* 236 (1987); N. Ellin, 'Thresholds of fear: embracing the urban shadow', *Urban Studies* 38:5–6 (2001); D. Garland, *The culture of control: crime and social order in contemporary society* (Oxford, 2001); D.L. Altheide, *Creating fear: news and the construction of crisis* (New York, 2002); S. Grupp, *Political implications of a discourse of fear: the mass mediated discourse of fear in the aftermath of 9/11*, (unpublished paper, Berlin, 2003); C.P. Guzelian, *Liability and fear* (Stanford, CA, 2004); F. Furedi, *The culture of fear: risk taking and the morality of low expectations* (London, 1997); C. Robin, *Fear: the history of a political idea* (New York, 2004); B. Glassner, *The culture of fear: why Americans are afraid of the wrong things* (New York, 1999).

claims that fear has received 'serious attention in philosophy, theology and psychiatry, less in anthropology and social psychology, and least of all in sociology.'[5] The under-theorization of fear is particularly striking in relation to the ever-expanding literature on risk. Fear has become the invisible companion of risk. Although sometimes used as a synonym for risk, fear is often treated as an afterthought in the literature. Yet the idea that fear is risk's companion is continually acknowledged in the literature. As Lupton notes, risk 'has come to stand as one of the focal points of feelings of fear, anxiety and uncertainty.'[6] This point is echoed by Cohen, who writes that 'reflections on risk are now absorbed into a wider culture of insecurity, victimization and fear.'[7] A study of New Labour's economic discourse claims that it is characterized by the 'language of change, fear and risk'.[8] Fear is never far behind risk in Luhman's analysis of the subject, *Risk: a sociological theory* (2005).[9] Indeed the terms fear and risk are used virtually interchangeably in many contributions on the subject. However, whereas the sociology of risk has become an important field in the discipline, the theorization of fear exists in an underdeveloped form.

Probably the most significant contribution to the sociology of fear is to be found in the work of Norbert Elias. Elias' account of the civilising process conceptualizes fear as one of the most important channels 'through which the structures of society is transmitted to individual psychological functions'. His argument that the 'civilized character' is constructed in part through the internalization of fears provides important insights into the historical dimension of this subject.[10] Unfortunately Elias' insights about the historical sociology of fear have not been developed in relation to contemporary experience. Indeed fear is frequently used as a "taken for granted" concept that requires little elaboration.

The aim of this essay is to examine the components of what constitutes the experience of fear in contemporary society. Its focus is on how fear works and to isolate the key dimension of today's fear culture. As Garland notes in relation to fear of crime, 'our fears and resentments, but also our common sense narratives and understandings – become settled cultural facts that are sustained and reproduced by cultural scripts.'[11] A cultural script has a lot to say about emotions such as fear. It is broader than the concept of emotional climate discussed by Jack Barbalet which refers to the emotional experience of individuals in the context of group interactions.[12] As a socially constructed phenomenon, a cultural script is to

---

5 E. Hankiss, *Fears and symbols: an introduction to the study of western civilisation* (Budapest, 2001), pp 1, 8. 6 D. Lupton, *Risk* (London, 1999), p. 12. 7 S. Cohen, *Folk devils and moral panics* (3rd ed. London, 2002), p. 4. 8 M. Raco, 'Risk, fear and control: deconstructing the discourses of New Labour's economic policy', *Space and Polity*, 6:1 (2002), 25. 9 N. Luhman, *Risk: a sociological theory* (New Brunswick, NJ, 2005), p. xxxii. 10 N. Elias, *The civilizing process, vol. 2: state formation and civilization* (Oxford, 1982) pp 300, 326. 11 Garland, *Culture of control*, p. 163. 12 J. Barbalet, 'Introduction: why emotions are crucial' in J. Barbalet (ed.), *Emotions and sociology* (Oxford, 2002), p. 5.

some extent independent of specific individuals and groups. It transmits rules about feelings and also ideas about what those feelings mean. Individuals interpret and internalize these rules according to their circumstances and temperament but express them through culturally sanctioned idioms. As Elias notes, 'the strength, kind and structures of the fears and anxieties that smoulder or flare in the individual never depend solely on his own "nature".' They are 'always determined, finally by the history and the actual structure of his relations to other people'.[13]

Fear is situational and is to some extent the product of social construction. It is constituted through the agency of the self in interaction with others. It is also internalized through a cultural script that instructs people as to how to respond to threats to their security. That is why the specific features of the fear experience are most likely to be captured through an assessment of the influence of culture. Fear gains its meaning through the mode of interpretation offered by the narrative of culture. An orientation towards meaning and the rules and customs governing the display of fear can help take the discussion beyond the stage of merely treating it as a self-evident emotion. Sociologists need to ask the question of 'what may be the meaning of emotional events' such as fear to a community.[14] One of the most perceptive studies of the history of emotions, Lewis and Stearns' *An emotional history of the United States* (1998), points to the need for distinguishing between the 'collective emotional standards of a society' and subjective feeling of the individual.[15] While the emotional experience of the individual is an important dimension of the problem, our attempt to conceptualize fear as a social phenomenon requires that we analyse the prevailing cultural narrative of fear. Cultural norms that shape the display and management of emotions influence the way that fear is experienced.

Experience shows that fear and the intensity with which it is felt is not directly proportional to the objective character of a specific threat. Adversity, acts of misfortune and threats to personal security do not directly produce fear. The conversion of a response to specific circumstances is mediated through cultural norms that inform people about what is expected of them when confronted with a threat and how they should respond and feel. Hochschild, in her ground-breaking study of the sociology of emotions, characterizes these informal expectations of what constitutes an appropriate emotional response to situations as "feeling rules".[16] These feeling rules influence behaviour in stressful circumstances and instruct us how and what we ought to fear. According to Giddens, 'people handle dangers and the fears associated with them in terms of emotional and behavioural formulae which have come to be part of their everyday behaviour and thought.'[17] But

---

13 Elias, *Civilizing process*, p. 327.   **14** D.L. Scruton (ed.), *Sociophobics: the anthropology of fear* (Boulder, 1986), p. 15.   **15** P. Lewis & J. Stearns (eds), *An emotional history of the United States* (New York, 1998), p. 7.   **16** A.R. Hochschild, 'Emotion work, feeling rules, and social structure', *American Journal of Sociology*, 85 (Nov. 1979).   **17** A. Giddens, *Modernity and self-identity: self and society in the late modern age* (Cam-

the transformation of anxious responses into fears also requires the intervention of social actors, of fear entrepreneurs. The sociologist David Altheide argues that 'fear does not just happen; it is socially constructed and then manipulated by those who seek to benefit.'[18] While this formulation of the social construction of fear may inflate the role of self-interest, its emphasis on the role of human agency provides a useful counterpoint to the naturalistic and psychological representation of fear.

The meaning and experience of fear is subject to cultural and historical modifications. The historic fear of famine is very different to the 'powerful fear' of being fat.[19] The meaning a society attached to the fear of God or the fear of Hell is not quite the same as the fear of pollution or of cancer. Fear does not always convey negative connotations. The sixteenth-century English philosopher Thomas Hobbes regarded fear as essential for the realization of the individual and of a civilized society. For Hobbes and others, fear constituted a dimension of a reasonable response to new events. Nor does fear always signify a negative emotional response. As David Parkin argues, as late as the nineteenth century the sentiment of fear was frequently associated with an expression of "respect" and "reverence" or "veneration".[20] From this standpoint the act of "fearing the Lord" could have connotations that were culturally valued and affirmed. In contrast today, the act of fearing God is far less consistent with cultural norms. Matters are also complicated by the fact that the words and expressions used to describe fear are culturally and historically specific. The language we use today represents fear through idioms that are unspecific, diffuse and therapeutic. Bourke in her key study of the cultural history of fear points to the importance of the 'conversion of fear into anxiety through the therapeutic revolution' today.[21] Anxieties about being "at risk" or feeling "stressed", "traumatized" or "vulnerable" indicate that an individualized therapeutic vocabulary influences our sensibility of fear.

Contemporary fear culture

In an important discussion on how culture is used, Ann Swindler observes that 'people vary greatly in how much culture they apply to their lives.' But in the very act of using culture, people 'learn how to be, or become, particular kinds of persons'. Swidler claims that such 'self-forming' continually utilizes the symbolic resources provided by the wider culture. 'Through experience with symbols, people learn desires, moods, habits of thought and feeling that no one could

bridge, 1991), p. 44.   **18** D. Altheide, *Terrorism and the politics of fear* (Lanham, MD, 2006), p. 24.   **19** A. Beardsworth, *Sociology on the menu: an invitation to the study of food and society* (London, 1997), p. 173.   **20** D. Parkin, 'Toward an apprehension of fear' in Scruton (ed.), *Sociophobics*.   **21** J. Bourke, *Fear: a cultural history* (London, 2005), p. 191.

invent on her own', she observes.[22] These habits of thought and feeling influence the way individuals make sense of their experience, how they perceive threats and how they respond to them. As Elias stated, the strength and form of 'shame, fear of war and fear of God, guilt, fear of punishment or of loss of social prestige, man's fear of himself, of being overcome by his own affective impulses' depend on 'the structure of his society and his fate within it'.[23]

Threats are mediated through cultural norms that instruct us how to respond. Arguably, the role of culture is more significant today than in previous times. According to Grupp, individual fears are cultivated through the media and less and less an outcome of direct experience. 'Fear is decreasingly experienced first-hand and increasingly experienced on a discursive and abstract level' she concludes, and she suggestively notes that 'there has been a general shift from a fearsome life towards a life with fearsome media.'[24] This point is echoed by Altheide who claims that 'popular culture has been the key element in promoting the discourse of fear.'[25] This trend appears to be understood by Osama bin Laden who, in an interview in October 2001, was asked 'why is the Western media establishment so anti-humane' and replied 'because it implants fear and helplessness in the psyche of the people of Europe and the United States.'[26] According to an important contribution by the legal theorist Christopher Guzelian, it is this indirect dimension of fear that represents the distinctive feature of contemporary fear culture. He believes that 'most fears in America's electronic age' are the results of 'risk information (whether correct or false) that is communicated to society'. He concludes that it is '*risk communication*, not personal experience' which 'causes most fear these days'.[27]

The influence of the discourse of fear is not a direct outcome of the power of the media. The dynamic of individuation has encouraged fear to be experienced in a fragmented and atomized form. That is why fear is rarely experienced as a form of collective insecurity along the lines of previous generations. This development is well captured by Ellin, who argues that the fear that we sense today is no longer the fear of "dangerous classes", or vice versa, and that fear has 'come home' and become privatized.[28] The sensibility of fear is internalized in an isolated form as a fear of crime or as a routinized sense of apprehension towards everyday life, what Hubbard characterizes as 'ambient fear'. He notes that this is 'fear that requires us to vigilantly monitor every banal minutia of our lives' since 'even mundane acts are now viewed as inherently risky and dangerous'.[29] Outwardly it is the flourishing of low grade fears and risks that captures the imagination. But the real

22 A. Swidler, *Talk of love: how culture matters* (Chicago, 2001), pp 46, 75. 23 Elias, *Civilizing process*, p. 328. 24 Grupp, *Political implications*, p. 43. 25 Altheide, *Creating fear*, p. 177. 26 Bruce B. Lawrence, 'In Bin Laden's Words', *Chronicle of Higher Education*, 4 Nov. 2005. 27 C.P. Guzelian, 'Liability and fear', *Ohio State Law Journal* 65:4 (2004), 712, 767. 28 N. Ellin, *Postmodern urbanism* (New York, 1999), p. 149. 29 Hubbard, 'Fear and loathing at the multiplex', p. 72.

significance of this development is the highly personalized – even customized – way that fear is experienced. Or as Zygmunt Bauman argues, postmodernity has privatized the fears of modernity: 'With fears privatized […] there is no hope left that human reason, and its earthly agents, will make the race a guided tour, certain to end up in a secure and agreeable shelter.'[30] Keane has drawn attention to another manifestation of the privatization of fear, which is the growing tendency to transform private fears into public ones.[31] The privatization of fear encourages an inward orientation towards the self. People interviewed about the personal risks they faced tended to represent 'crisis, fears and anxieties as self-produced and individual problems, the products of a "personal biography"'.[32]

Fear as a problem in its own right

One of the questions raised in public debates and sociological reflections on contemporary risk consciousness is whether society today is more fearful than previously and whether fear has become a defining feature of contemporary times. Some believe that the 'magnitude and nature of fear' is different to the past since 'it seems that fear is everywhere.'[33] The growth of fear as a dimension of everyday life is a theme discussed in contributions on the fear of crime. Ellin, for example, argues that:

> The fear factor has certainly grown, as indicated by the growth in locked car and house doors and security systems, the popularity of gated or secure communities for all age and income groups, and the increasing surveillance of public space […] not to mention the unending reports of dangers emitted by the mass media.[34]

However, an increase in the quantity of fear is difficult to measure since its very meaning is itself subject to continuous alteration. That is why, as Tudor argues, 'simply to document the considerable range of fears given currency in our cultures is not enough.' As a result, we would 'also have to demonstrate that late modern conceptions of fear are distinctive in their fundamental character when compared with other periods and societies'.[35] An emphasis on the quality and meaning of fear is the starting point for gaining insight into its specific socio-cultural dimensions.

30 Z. Bauman, *Intimations of post-modernity* (London, 1992), p. xviii.   **31** J. Keane, 'Fear and democracy' in K. Worcester, S.A. Bermanzohn & M. Ungar (eds), *Violence and politics: globalization's paradox* (New York, 2002).   **32** J. Tulloch & D. Lupton, *Risk and everyday life* (London, 2003), p. 38.   **33** Altheide, *Creating fear*, p. 175.   **34** N. Ellin, *Architecture of fear* (New York, 1997), p. 26.   **35** A. Tudor, 'A (macro) sociology of fear?' *Sociological Review*, 51:2 (2003), 254.

An interesting dimension of contemporary culture is the pervasive character of the discourse of fear. Fear is frequently represented as a defining cultural mood that dominates society. Of course the institutionalization of a discourse of fear through the issuing of health warnings, risk management or media alerts should not be interpreted as proof that the quantity of fears has increased. It possibly has. Nor can we conclude on the basis of existing evidence that people fear more intensely than in the past. The prominent role assumed by the narrative of fear merely indicates that it serves as a frame through which we interpret a variety of experiences. It also suggests that fear works as a problem in its own right. Through its association with the narrative of risk, fear has become objectified. Hunt has noted that 'risk discourse transposes anxieties into an objectivist problematic'.[36] As a result, increasingly fear is perceived as an autonomous problem. Consequently 'fear becomes a discourse' which 'expands beyond a specific referent and is used instead as a more general orientation'.[37]

One of the distinguishing features of fear today is that is appears to have an independent existence. In this respect it resembles the way in which social anxiety was conceptualized in the 1940s and 1950s. But whereas anxiety was represented as a diffuse intangible condition, fear exists in an objectified form as a clearly identifiable social problem. Fear itself, rather than what it responds to, is a distinct problem of our times. It is frequently cited as a problem that exists in its own right disassociated from any specific object. Classically, societies associate fear with a clearly formulated threat, for example the fear of death, the fear of a specific enemy or the fear of hunger. In such formulations, the threat was defined as the object of such fears. The problem was death, illness or hunger. Today we frequently represent the act of fearing as a threat itself. A striking illustration of this development is the fear of crime. Nowadays, this is conceptualized as a serious problem that is to some extent distinct from acts of crime. As Garland observes; 'fear of crime has come to be regarded as a problem in and of itself, quite distinct from actual crime and victimization, and distinctive policies have been developed that aim to reduce fear levels, rather than reduce crime.'[38] Indeed it seems that the fear of crime is 'now recognized as a more widespread problem than crime itself'.[39]

It is far from clear what is measured when statistics point to an increase or decrease of the fear of crime. As Hale suggests, what is measured is not so much the fear of crime but 'some other attribute which might be better characterized as "insecurity with modern living", "quality of life", "perception of disorder" or "urban unease".'[40] However through quantifying a cultural mood, the fear of

36 A. Hunt, 'Risk and moralization in everyday life' in R.V. Ericson & A. Doyle (eds), *Risk and morality* (Toronto, 2003), p. 174. 37 Grupp, *Political implications*, p. 18. 38 Garland, *Culture of control*, p. 10. 39 J. Bannister & N. Fyfe, 'Introduction: fear and the city', *Urban Studies*, 38:5–6 (2001), 808. 40 C. Hale, 'Fear of crime: a review of the literature', *International Review of Victimology*, 4 (1996), 84.

crime becomes objectified and can acquire a force of its own. Its objectification may turn it into a "fact of life" that legitimates – if not encourages – the fear response.

Frequently, public anxiety and concern are represented as a material factor that can have a decisive impact on people's health. Contemporary medical culture contends that stress and fear are likely to increase the risk of heart disease, cancer and chronic lung disease. In the UK the conclusion of an enquiry held into alleged health effects from cell phones is now regarded as a model for how to respond to contemporary health fears – particularly related to environmental health. The Independent Expert Group on Mobile Phones (IEGMP) set up "to keep ahead of public anxiety" concluded that there was no known health threat posed by mobile telephony. At the same time, the report stated that anxieties created by the simple presence of mobile phone masts need to be taken seriously since public fear by itself could lead to ill health. There is always a potential for people's health anxiety to turn into a major problem. The medical sociologist Phil Strong writes of an 'epidemic of suspicion' that can cause serious public health problems.[41] However it is only recently that fear has been represented as an autonomous cause of illness.

With the autonomization of fear the issue is not simply its cause but the potential negative consequences of this emotion. This perspective often encourages the strategy of managing feelings of fear rather than locating the source of the problem. If people feel that their health is at risk then this fear is often seen as a risk to people's well being. The legal system in the US and the UK has also internalized this trend and there is a discernible tendency on the part of courts to compensate fear, even in the absence of a perceptible physical threat. As Guzelian noted, in the past, 'fright' (i.e. a reaction to an actual event) was compensated, whereas now the fear that something negative would happen is also seen as grounds for making a claim.[42]

The autonomization of fear is also associated with a growing tendency to conceptualize risk as an independent variable. Risk communication is informed by a perspective that believes that 'fear itself is a risk and must be part of risk-management policy making'.[43] The transformation of fear into a risk is paralleled by the tendency to represent risk as a negative experience. Terms like a "good risk" enjoy little cultural affirmation. Even the representation of risk as neutral appears inconsistent with the temper of our time. Instead, risk is associated with negative outcomes that people are expected to fear. Through risk management the performance of fear is both institutionalized and culturally encouraged.

41 P. Strong, 'Epidemic psychology: a model', *Sociology of Health & Illness*, 12:3 (1990), 253.   42 Guzelian, 'Liability and fear', 771.   43 M. Gray & D.P. Ropeik, 'Dealing with the dangers of fear: the role of risk communication', *Health Affairs*, 21:6 (2002), 106.

The unstable, free-floating and raw character of fear

The volatility of the discourse of fear is conceptualized by Parkin as a shift from a concept of fear that 'encompassed that of respect' to what he calls 'raw fear'. The former is described as an 'institutionally controlled fear' whereas 'raw fear' has more of a free-floating and unpredictable character.[44] Bourke claims that this shift towards more 'nebulous anxiety states' is due to the decline of the tangible threats to corporeal existence that are occasioned by war.[45] However as noted previously, it is likely that it is the privatization of fear that endows it with an arbitrary and fluid dimension.

This volatility is enhanced by fear's unstable and unfocused trajectory. In contemporary times, fear migrates freely from one problem to the next without there being a necessity for causal or logical connection. When the Southern Baptist leader Reverend Jerry Vines declared that Mohammed was a 'demon possessed paedophile' and that Allah leads Muslim to terrorism in June 2002, he was simply taking advantage of the logical leaps permitted by the free-floating character of our fear narratives.[46] This arbitrary association of terrorism and paedophilia can have the effect of amplifying the fear of both. In the same way constant claims that this or that hurricane, flood and other natural disasters are symptoms of global warming has the effect of altering perceptions and fears of such events.

Fear today can attach itself to a wide variety of phenomena. The fear of terrorism illustrates this trend. Since 11 September 2001, this fear has drifted into an ever-expanding territory. Deliberations on this subject have acquired a phantasy-like character. 'Corporations must re-examine their definition of risk and take seriously the possibility of scenarios that only science fiction writers could have imagined possible one year ago' argues a leading economist.[47] Fear expands into new territory because since 9/11 normal hazards can be turned into exceptional threats by associating them with the action of terrorists. As a result we do not simply worry about the hazard posed by a nuclear power station; we also fear that it may turn into a terrorist target. The fact that an ever-expanding phenomenon can be perceived as a target is less an outcome of an increase in the capabilities of terrorists than in the growth of competitive claims about what to fear.

The free-floating dynamic of fear is promoted by a culture that communicates hesitancy and anxiety towards uncertainty and continually anticipates the worse possible outcome. The culture which has been described as the culture of fear, or as precautionary culture, encourages society to approach human experience as a potential risk to our safety. Consequently every conceivable experience has been

---

44 Parkin, 'Toward an apprehension of fear', pp 158, 159. 45 Bourke, *Fear*, p. 293. 46 D.M. Filler, 'Terrorism, panic and paedophilia', *Journal of Social Policy and the Law*, Spring Issue (2003), 345. 47 D. Hale, 'Insuring a nightmare', *Worldlink* (19 Mar. 2002), 11

transformed into a risk to be managed. The leading criminologist, David Garland, writes of the 'Rise of risk' – the explosion in the growth of risk discourse and risk literature. He notes that little connects this literature other than the use of the word risk.[48] However, the very fact that risk is used to frame a variety of otherwise unconnected experiences reflects a "taken for granted" mood of uncertainty towards human experience. In contemporary society little can be presumed other than an apprehensive response towards uncertainty. Arguably fear, like risk, has become a "taken for granted" idiom – even a cultural affectation – for expressing confusion and uncertainty. The French social theorist Francois Ewald believes that the ascendancy of this precautionary sensibility is underwritten by a cultural mood that assumes the uncertainty of causality between action and effect. This sensibility endows fear with a privileged status. Ewald suggests that the institutionalization of precaution 'invites one to consider the worst hypothesis (defined as the "serious and irreversible" consequence) in any business decision'.[49] The tendency to engage with uncertainty through the prism of fear, and therefore anticipate the worst possible outcome, can be understood as a crisis of causality. Riezler, in his early attempt to develop a psychology of fear, draws attention to the significant influence of the prevailing system of causality on people's response to threats. 'They have been taken for granted – and now they are threatened' is how he describes a situation when '"causes" are hopelessly entangled'.[50]

The question of causation is inextricably bound up with the way communities attempt to make sense of acts of misfortune. The way people interpret such events – an accident or a catastrophe – is processed through the prevailing system of meaning. Questions like "was it God" or "was it nature" or "was it an act of human error" have important implications in how we understand acts of misfortune. Confusion about causation encourages speculation, rumours and mistrust. As a result events often appear as incomprehensible and beyond human control.

Identity of vulnerability

'Whom and what we fear, and how we express and act upon our fearing, is in some quite important sense as, Durkheim long ago realized, constitutive of who we are.'[51] That is why the autonomization of fear has important implications for the constitution of identity. The consciousness of being subjected to threats that possess an independent existence is clearly formulated through the recently con-

48 D. Garland, 'The rise of risk' in *Risk and morality*, p. 52.   49 F. Ewald, 'The return of Descartes' malicious demon: an outline of a philosophy of precaution' in T. Baker & J. Simon (eds), *Embracing risk: the changing culture of insurance and responsibility* (Chicago, 2002), p. 284.   50 K. Riezler, 'The social psychology of fear', *American Journal of Sociology*, 49:6 (1944), 497.   51 R. Sparks, E. Girling & I. Loader, 'Fear and everyday urban lives', *Urban Studies*, 38:5–6 (2001), 885.

structed concept of being *at risk*. The emergence of the "at risk" concept ruptures the traditional relationship between individual action and the probability of some hazard. To be at risk is no longer only about what you do or the probability of some hazard impacting on your life – it is also about who you are. It becomes a fixed attribute of the individual, like the size of a person's feet or hands. When public officials categorize groups of people who are at risk they can literally visualize the objects of their labelling. At the same time, the perception of being at risk encourages the emergence of a fearful subjectivity. According to Beck, 'the movement set in motion by the risk society [...] is expressed in the statement I am afraid!' He adds that therefore the 'commonality of anxiety takes the place of the commonality of need.'[52] This sensibility suggests that fear has become an identity-endowing experience.

To be at risk assigns to the person a passive and dependent role. Increasingly, someone defined as being at risk is seen to exist in a permanent condition of vulnerability. The belief that people exist in a state of vulnerability informs the way that we are expected to make sense of the threats we face. As a cultural metaphor, vulnerability is used to highlight the claim that people and their communities lack the emotional and psychological resources necessary to deal with change, make choices and possess the emotional resources to deal with adversity.

The term "vulnerability" is habitually used as if it is a permanent feature of a person's biography. It is presented and experienced as a natural state of being that shapes human response. It is a label that describes entire groups in society. That is why it has become common to use the recently constructed concept of vulnerable groups. The term "vulnerable group" does not simply refer to groups of the psychologically distraught or to a small minority of economically insecure individuals. All children are automatically assumed to be vulnerable. A study of the emergence of the concept of vulnerable children shows that in most published literature, the concept is treated as 'a relatively self-evident concomitant of childhood which requires little formal exposition'. It is a taken for granted idea that is rarely elaborated and 'children are considered vulnerable as individuals by definition, through both their physical and other perceived immaturities'. Moreover, this state of vulnerability is presented as an intrinsic attribute. It is 'considered to be an *essential* property of individuals, as something which is intrinsic to children's identities and personhoods, and which is recognizable through their beliefs and actions, or indeed through just their appearance'.[53] However, it is not just children who are defined as a vulnerable *en masse*. So are women, the elderly, ethnic minorities, the disabled and the poor. Indeed, if all the groups designated as vul-

52 U. Beck, *Risk society: towards a new modernity* (London, 1992), p. 49.   53 R. Frankenberg, I. Robinson & A. Delahooke, 'Countering essentialism in behavioural social science: the example of the "vulnerable child" ethnographically examined', *Sociological Review* (2000), 588–9.

nerable by experts and policy makers are added together it would appear that they constitute nearly one hundred per cent of the population!

The sense of vulnerability is so deeply immersed in our cultural imagination that it is easy to overlook the fact that it is a relatively recent concept. The term "vulnerable group" came into usage in the 1980s. One study notes that the tendency to frame children's problems through the metaphor of vulnerability became visible in the late eighties but actually took off in the 1990s.[54] According to the authors of this study the tendency to outline children's problems through the frame of vulnerability is also a comparatively new development. Their search of a major bibliographical database, BIDS, revealed over 800 refereed papers between 1986 and 1998 which focused on the relationship between vulnerability and children. They noted that 'whilst in the first four years of this period there were under 10 references each year to vulnerability and children, an exponential increase to well over 150 papers a year occurred from 1990 onwards.'[55] They believe that this figure underestimates the tendency to interpret children's lives through the prism of vulnerability since it ignores the substantial non-academic literature on the subject.

Our survey of the *LexisNexis* database of newspapers confirms the findings of this study. It indicates that the term "vulnerable group" is a relatively recent concept.[56] An analysis of articles in the *New York Times* suggests that this term began to be used in the 1980s. Between 1973 amd 1979 there were no references to vulnerable groups in *New York Times* articles. A similar pattern is evident in the UK; before the mid-1980s, citations of this term were rare. It began to be widely used in the years 1985–7, however. More significantly it appears that in the late 1980s the meaning of "vulnerable" was transformed to signify people's intrinsic identities. From this point onward, the term not only signifies a person's relation to circumstances, for example to poverty, but to the inherent condition of an individual. This shift is best captured by the newly emerging term, "the vulnerable". This shift from the idea of "vulnerable to …" to the noun "*the* vulnerable" solidifies powerlessness as a state of existence.

The emergence of vulnerability as an identity is associated with the objectification of fear that occurred in the 1980s. A heightened consciousness of threat is 'experienced as an ordeal of unexpected vulnerability' argues Ewald.[57] Ewald's characterization of the expression "to be vulnerable" as a newly constructed "sacred term" captures an important moment in the formation of contemporary

---

54 Ibid.   55 Ibid., p. 584.   56 The earliest reference to a vulnerable group uncovered through *Lexisnexis* (1960–2004) was in June 1969 in connection with the appointment of a Presidential Consultant charged with organizing a conference on food and nutrition by the Nixon White House. At a press briefing, Nixon stated that this conference would seek to develop new survey methods to keep track of malnutrition levels and improve the nutrition of the nation's 'most vulnerable groups', *New York Times*, 12 June 1969.   57 Ewald, 'The return of Descartes' malicious demon', p. 282.

fear identity. From this point onwards, fear ceases to be just an emotion; it also serves as an important dimension in the construction of identity. This sensibility is admirably expressed by an International Labour Union report warning about 'fear in the workplace'. Guy Standing, one of the authors of the report, stated that 'unless this is reversed, the vulnerable will become more vulnerable'.[58] Consequently supporters of trade unions self consciously describe their members as vulnerable.

Through the paradigm of vulnerability, the sense of fear is cultivated as part of the normal state of being. The converse of this deflation of the status of human subjectivity is the inflation of the threat that external circumstances represent to the integrity of the individual self. The vulnerability and impotence of the individual stands in sharp contrast to the formidable powers attributed to the everyday challenges that people confront. Through the constant amplification of the risks facing humanity – pollution, global warming, catastrophic flu epidemic, weapons of mass destruction, large variety of health scares etc – even the limited exercise of individual choice appears to be restricted by the harsh regime of uncertainty. The identity of vulnerability is the flip side of the autonomization of fear.

Conclusion

A sociological conceptualization of fear requires further research into the way that this emotion is mediated through the prevailing cultural script and system of meaning. It needs to address not simply the emotion of fear and the threats to which it responds but the crisis of causality that shapes the fearful subject. As indicated previously, twenty-first century fear culture possesses several distinct characteristics that work towards its normalization as a force in its own right. In such circumstances, fear is endowed with authority for responding to, and making sense of, the world. This orientation stands in sharp contrast to the approach adopted by President Franklin D. Roosevelt's inaugural address in 1933, when he stated that the 'only thing we have to fear is Fear itself'. Roosevelt's statement sought to assure the public that it was both possible and necessary to minimize the impact of fear. His was a positive vision of a future where fear would be put in its place by a society that believed in itself. Today politicians are far more likely to advise the public to fear everything and not simply fear itself. Moreover fearing fear has assumed the character of a naturalized problem that is detached from any specific experience. In this form, it is not so much a response to a threat but a perspective on life.

---

58 'Fear infects flexible workplaces', *Guardian*, 2 Sept. 2004.

Fearing to speak: fear and the 1798 rebellion in the nineteenth century

JIM SHANAHAN

The rebellion that broke out in Ireland in the summer of 1798 was the bloodiest single event in modern Irish history. Perhaps 100,000 people were involved on the rebel side, and as many as 30,000 may have died during the course of the rebellion itself and in the mopping-up activity afterwards. The rebellion provided an excuse, if one were needed, for the incorporation of Ireland into the British state with the subsequent Act of Union in 1801. It occurred at the end of a decade in Ireland that had seen an increase in sectarian tension, political disillusionment and instability in agricultural prices, as well as increased competition for land. In addition, the spirit of the patriotic Volunteer movement of the 1780s had, at its extremes, bifurcated into militant revolutionary activity and ultra-conservatism. The rising was largely concentrated in three main theatres of action, with the most serious and bloody activity taking place in south Leinster, particularly in Wexford and the surrounding counties. There was also a short-lived, mainly Presbyterian rising in the counties of Antrim and Down in Ulster and, later in the summer, the landing of a small French force in Mayo inspired a rising in the west. Each of these theatres had its own particular dynamic. While there was no doubt that the republican United Irishmen had intended a rebellion, the key question that still divides historians today is to what extent the actual rebellion that occurred was their rebellion, and how much of it was due to other factors. Was it, in fact, a rebellion inspired by the French and American revolutions, or a sectarian *jacquerie* uprising? To what extent were the rebels politicized or politically motivated? Was 1798 something new, breaking with the old sectarian past, or was it merely another in a long succession of Irish rebellions? While most modern historians would accept that the actual (as opposed to any intended) rebellion was a complex mixture of different elements, and that the key areas of difference lie in the weight to be applied to these factors, early attempts to provide simple and straightforward answers to these questions invariably pandered to peoples' prejudices and fears.

The famous line, 'Who fears to speak of ninety-eight?', from Richard Kells Ingram's ballad, 'The memory of the dead' (1843), remains for many people the most memorable literary allusion to the 1798 rebellion. Some variation on this line has provided the title inspiration for innumerable books, articles and essays about the rebellion – including this one. Ingram's famous phrase is particularly pertinent here both as a title and as a starting-point for an investigation into the relationship between the concept of fear and the 1798 rebellion. The use of the word "fear" by Ingram highlights an important distinction to be made in this essay. The first four lines of the ballad – 'Who fears to speak of ninety-eight?/Who blushes at the name?/When cowards mock the patriot's fate/Who hangs his head for shame?'[1] – suggest the fear implied was that one might be thought some kind of monster or fanatic for daring to consider the rebellion as anything other than a savage and brutal outrage. Ingram's fear was that the rebellion was seen as something shameful rather than as a glorious national movement for independence by committed and courageous people, and, as the last verse of the ballad makes clear, an important component of the glue that keeps the Irish nation together. That such a ballad could be written in the mid-1840s by a man who was a professor and later vice-provost of Trinity College Dublin, is a testimony both to the enduring attraction of the non-sectarian ideals of the United Irishmen and the complex nature of the legacy of the 1798 rebellion. Ultimately what it demonstrates is that fears about 1798 related as much to the way the rebellion was remembered as to any anxiety about the recurrence of a similar event. In the context of the nineteenth century, therefore, it is more correct to talk about the "fears" of 1798, rather than the "fear".

It is also important to recognize that fear was one of the reasons for the rebellion itself, and it is clear that some distinction needs to be made between the different kinds of fears associated with 1798. As a general definition, fear can be taken to mean the experience of apprehension, particularly in relation to potentially evil or threatening outcomes. The psychologist Stanley Rachman makes a distinction between fear – a feeling of apprehension about tangible and predominantly realistic dangers – and anxiety, which he defines as apprehensions 'that are difficult to relate to tangible sources of stimulation'.[2] Rachman argues that the three 'pathways to fear' are conditioning (including the actual experience of fear-inducing conditions), vicarious acquisition (the direct or indirect observation of people displaying fear) and the transmission of 'fear-inducing information'. In addition, he states:

> we now have to incorporate the novel idea that fears can be enhanced or inflated by events that occur well after the fear is established, and even by

---

1 Terry Moylan (ed.), *The age of revolution: 1776 to 1815 in the Irish song tradition* (Dublin, 2000), p. 102.
2 S.J. Rachman, *Fear and courage*, 2nd ed. ([1978]: New York, 1990), p. 3.   3 Ibid., p. 4.

events that are not directly related to the fear. These new findings, which suggest that a fearful connection can be formed between events that are separated in time and space, are compatible with a radically revised and expanded conception of conditioning.[3]

This last point is particularly relevant when we consider the portrayals of 1798 as both another 1641 by Protestant loyalist writers, or as an analogue of the French Revolution by anti-Jacobin writers, or indeed the different ways that the 1798 rebellion itself was used and portrayed in the nineteenth century.[4] It is here that the concept of 'political fear' becomes useful. Described as 'a people's felt apprehension of some harm to their collective well-being',[5] political fear allows us to consider a corporate feeling of apprehension as fear. Political fear is often a determinant of public policy, a vehicle by which certain groups come to power and other groups are excluded, and the reason why laws are enacted or overturned. The penal laws of the eighteenth century, for example, which attempted to legislate the Catholic religion out of existence, can be seen as a product of political fear. Therefore, a range of different types of fear can be discerned in relation to the 1798 rebellion, both corresponding to the occurrence of the rebellion itself and the way that it was subsequently remembered and represented. These are, broadly speaking, the fear that provoked the rebellion in the first place; the identification and use of iconic fear "moments" from the rebellion (these usually depended on the political sympathies of the user); the various uses to which the associative fear of the rebellion itself was put; and, the one that alarmed Richard Kells Ingram most, the fear that the more noble actions, aims and intentions of the rebellion would be forgotten or misrepresented. Although this last fear may seem to be the least important, it actually spawned one of the most significant literary approaches to representing the rebellion in the nineteenth century: the "alternative rebellion" strategy. This essay will examine to what extent 1798 came to be a trope for fear, and what uses were made of this trope by writers in the nineteenth century.

Whatever about the ideals of the United Irishmen, a widespread fear of extermination was a major contributor to the rebellion that actually occurred in 1798. Even William MacNeven, one of the United Irish leaders arrested in the months before the rebellion, stated in evidence to an investigating committee that the rebellion was the result of the 'house-burnings, the whippings to extort confessions, the torture of various kinds, the free quarters, and the murders committed upon the people by the magistrates and the army'; sentiments echoed by another prominent United Irishman, Thomas Addis Emmet.[6] Those looking to justify the

4 In 1641 the killing of many Protestants in Ulster by Catholic rebels was often portrayed as part of a Europe-wide campaign to extirpate "heresy" (and to recapture confiscated land in the process).   5 Corey Robin, *Fear: the history of a political idea* (New York, 2004), p. 2.   6 William J. MacNeven, *Pieces of Irish*

actions of the rebels could point to the unchecked activities of the Orange Order and the military as provoking the population into rebellion. The county of Armagh, one of the principal areas of tension in the 1790s, had a population that was divided almost equally between Catholics, Protestants (that is, members of the established Anglican church) and Presbyterians, and had been riven by sectarian strife. This had reached a peak in 1795, culminating in the famous 'battle of the Diamond' and the founding of the Orange Order. Those Catholics driven out of the county brought tales of their treatment to other parts of Ireland, and contributed to the spread of the Defenders, a largely agrarian society initially set up to "defend" Catholics from Protestant and state aggression, but which quickly developed into a body with a conscious, if ill-defined political agenda, that ranged from the redress of local grievances right up to the bringing-down of the existing social order. The activities of certain notorious militias, such as the North Cork and the Ancient Britons, together with the widespread use of torture, half-hangings and the pitch-cap, increased levels of fear and paranoia among Catholics. Loyalists in turn could cite as justification for the "pacification" tactics of the military in 1797 and early 1798 their fear of another 1641, the nocturnal tactics of the Defenders and the fear of another attempted French invasion, following the one which almost landed at Bantry Bay in December 1796. Levels of fear on both sides were heightened by the cynical – and ultimately disastrous – circulation of bogus Orange and Defender oaths for propaganda purposes. These oaths suggested that the express purpose of those organizations was to exterminate all those of the opposite faith. By 1798, therefore, many on either side of the potential conflict were convinced that their opponents were merely waiting for the right opportunity to strike and wipe them out, and the evidence for this lay both in what had happened in the past and what was occurring in the present.

***

The sophisticated and intense propaganda battle that followed the rebellion has been well outlined elsewhere, most notably by Kevin Whelan.[7] In the aftershock, the question of blame was the paramount concern. Immediate textual responses were, not surprisingly, mainly reactionary in nature. To a large extent the rebellion in Wexford and south Leinster served – perhaps unfairly – as an analogue for the entire rebellion. Early "histories" of the rebellion, such as Sir Richard Musgrave's *Memoirs of the different rebellions* (1801), and eye-witness accounts such as George Taylor's *A history of the rise, progress and suppression of the rebellion in the County of Wexford, in the year 1798* (1800) painted a picture of a rampaging Catholic sec-

history (New York, 1807), p. 241.   7 See ''98 after '98', in Kevin Whelan, *The tree of liberty: radicalism, Catholicism and the construction of Irish identity, 1760–1830* (Cork, 1996), pp 133–75.

tarian *jacquerie* whose desire was not some kind of modest constitutional change, or even a republic along the lines of the French model, but the total and utter extermination of the Protestant people of Ireland. This chilling prospect was given some credence by portraying 1798 as a re-run of the 1641 rebellion, in which many Protestants had been massacred by Catholic rebels. Rather than emphasizing the activities of the military, they stressed instead the "unnatural" tranquillity of the country in the run-up to the rebellion, which was seen as proof of a nationwide Catholic conspiracy. Indeed, dread of another 1641 remained an essential component of Protestant fear.[8] Although the actual total number of Protestants massacred in 1641 was somewhere between two and four thousand,[9] a substantial figure in itself, there was a widespread belief among Protestants of the time – a belief still promoted in some quarters today – that hundreds of thousands were killed. Anything even tangentially associated with 1641 was bound to provoke a determined response from the Protestant population of Ireland and Britain, and provide a justification for swift and decisive countermeasures. Fear of another 1641 provided the justification for the policy of severe repression before, during and after the rebellion. In this regard, the title of Musgrave's book stressed the idea that 1798 was merely another in a long line of rebellions and his use of sworn affidavits as evidence was a clear echo of the approach of Sir John Temple in his influential history of the 1641 rebellion. Temple's *History of the Irish rebellion* (1646) was regularly reprinted in times of Protestant crisis, and served as a barometer of Protestant anxiety. It was republished nine times by 1812.

The perception of Irish history as a recurring cycle of rebellion and repression resulted in a culture of fear on both sides of the sectarian divide, and drew strength and vigour from the ability of historians from either tradition to point to historical precedents. With regard to 1798, three events in particular were seared into the Protestant memory: the killing of perhaps as many as 400 prisoners at the rebel camp at Vinegar Hill; the burning to death of between 100 and 200 people – almost all of whom were Protestants – in a barn at Scullabogue, Co. Wexford; and the piking to death of between 70 and 100 loyalist prisoners on Wexford Bridge. These events were to pass into loyalist and Protestant folklore as examples of the savage and sectarian nature of the rebellion, and Scullabogue became its iconic "fear" moment. Musgrave, giving the number of people burned in the barn as 184 with a further 37 shot in front of it, recounts eye-witness testimony that told how the fingers of people endeavouring to escape from the barn were cut off, and how a young child, escaping under the door, was piked and thrown back into the flames. The rebels also reportedly 'took pleasure in licking

---

8 For an extensive review of this mentality and the "atrocity literature" that sustained it, see James Kelly, '"We were all to have been massacred": Irish Protestants and the experience of rebellion' in Thomas Bartlett, David Dickson, Dáire Keogh & Kevin Whelan (eds), *1798: a bicentenary perspective* (Dublin, 2003), pp 312–30. 9 R.F. Foster, *Modern Ireland, 1600–1972* (London, 1988), p. 85.

their spears' after piercing the bodies of those they killed outside the barn.[10] Quoting the evidence of 'respectable persons' who witnessed the pikings on Wexford Bridge, Musgrave writes: 'The manner, in general, of putting them to death, was thus: two rebels pushed their pikes into the breast of the victim, and two into his back; and in that state (writhing with torture) they held him suspended, till dead, and then threw him over the bridge into the water.'[11] Not all the accounts of the rebellion were quite so graphic. More liberal accounts were largely conciliatory and stressed the relative decency of the rebels and the essential loyalty of the vast majority of the Catholic population. These accounts, although in the majority, did not have quite the same effect on the public imagination.[12] Catholic writers like Edward Hay and Francis Plowden portrayed the rebellion largely as a spontaneous reaction to oppression and intolerable provocation on the part of the Irish government and its agents. In other words, a product of fear.

As such, the memory of massacres was not just confined to one side. In the early years of the nineteenth century, accounts of outrages perpetrated on the people by government forces and their agents were kept alive not just in folk ballads and broadsheets but in the pages of Walter ('Watty') Cox's *Irish Magazine*. This publication ran from 1807 to 1815 and specialized in recounting the deeds of informers, and selected hate figures like Hepenstal, 'the walking gallows', and his henchman Jemmy O'Brien; Major Sirr, who had captured Lord Edward Fitzgerald; and prominent 'class traitors' like Francis Higgins, the so-called 'Sham Squire'; as well as promoting the cult of the dead United Irish leadership. Aggressively Catholic and anti-unionist in tone, in an attempt to provide some kind of parity of atrocity the *Irish Magazine* gave special attention to accounts of outrages by government forces, and continued to stoke sectarian animosity in the decades following the rebellion and union. An illustration in the *Irish Magazine* of militiamen hanging old men and women, printed with the ironic caption 'dedicated to the Ancient and Modern Britons, by their dutiful servt. W. Cox' (with the deliberate emphasis on 'Ancient *and* Modern') and one of Captain Richard Swayne, of the City of Cork militia, pitchcapping seemingly innocent civilians, made the point that Protestants had no monopoly on suffering in 1798.

Although Protestant fears of Catholic power and intensions were, if anything, increasing in the 1820s and 1830s, the effect of the publication in the period between 1826 and 1863 of a series of memoirs by prominent United Irish leaders (including Tone, Teeling, Holt and Miles Byrne, as well as a controversial biogra-

---

10 Sir Richard Musgrave, *Memoirs of the different rebellions in Ireland*, 2 vols, 3rd ed. ([1801]: Dublin, 1802), i, p. 529.   11 Ibid., ii, p. 17.   12 [Joseph Stock], *A narrative of what passed at Killalla, in the County of Mayo, and the parts adjacent, during the French invasion in the summer of 1798. By an eye witness* (Dublin, 1800); Revd James Bentley Gordon, *History of the rebellion in Ireland in the year 1798* (Dublin, 1801); Edward Hay, *History of the Irish insurrection of 1798* (1803); Francis Plowden, *An historical review of the state of Ireland, from the invasion of that country under Henry II to its union with Great Britain* (1803).

phy of Lord Edward Fitzgerald by the poet Thomas Moore) was to put a heroic and patriotic slant on the rebellion. Even more significant, perhaps, in this regard, was Richard Madden's eleven-volume collection *Lives of the United Irishmen,* published between 1842 and 1860. Madden's *Lives* concentrated on the ideals, deeds and characters of the United Irishmen themselves, and this took a deal of the attention away from the actual rebellion itself, in which few of them had played any active part. These biographies inspired New Irelanders and sympathizers like Ingram to glorify the United Irishmen in songs and ballads. However, other forces were also at work. By 1870, when the first version of Father Patrick Kavanagh's *Popular history of the insurrection of 1798* was produced, the rebellion was transformed once again into a glorious uprising by the (Catholic) people of Wexford, led by their leaders, the Catholic clergy, against the intolerable provocation of the government and its agents and allies. The role of the United Irishmen was downplayed, in order to promote new clerical heroes and the equation of Catholicism with Irishness. The result of this was to bring back the fear element, except this time it was Catholic fears about the extermination of themselves and their religion. In this version, the Wexford element of the rebellion was inspired by the reluctant Father John Murphy of Boolavogue, who, initially having counselled his parishioners to turn in their weapons and obey the law, 'eventually deemed it better to die like men with arms in their hands, than wait to be butchered like dogs in the ditches'.[13]

The most spectacular and enduring images of the 1798 rebellion, however, and the clearest example of the transmission of fear-inducing information, remain a series of engravings created more than four decades after the fact by an illustrator who had never even been to Ireland. George Cruikshank produced the illustrations for William Hamilton Maxwell's *History of the Irish rebellion in 1798* (1845). These plates – illustrating such events as the attack on the barracks at Prosperous Co. Kildare, the massacre at Scullabogue, the pikings on Wexford Bridge and other murders, as well as chaotic scenes at the camp at Vinegar Hill and in houses captured by the rebels – depicted the insurgents as having simian features and carrying religious paraphernalia. Their victims and opponents were all handsome and dashing, and the effect was that of a grotesque and horrific yet strangely comic nightmare. Undoubtedly this was intended to be the effect, with the apparently comic antics of the half-human rebels helping to inspire an even greater degree of horror upon the realization that real human beings are being killed. The message of the engravings, at least, was clear: the rebels were sub-human sectarian savages who massacred clearly English-looking, Protestant, victims. The constant reproduction of these plates in subsequent histories helped to reinforce this inter-

13 Revd Patrick F. Kavanagh, *A popular history of the insurrection of 1798: derived from every available record and reliable tradition,* centenary (2nd) ed. ([1870]: Cork, 1898), p. 95.

Two of the most famous of Cruikshank's 1798 illustrations: 'The massacre at Scullabogue' (top) and 'The massacre of Protestant prisoners on the bridge at Wexford' (below). Their power as transmitters of associative fear can be seen in the caption accompanying them when reprinted in *The Strand* magazine later in the century. 'Scenes from the Irish rebellion of 1798; or, What the Irish Loyalists have to fight against if Mr Gladstone triumphs'. Illustrations courtesy of the National Library of Ireland.

pretation. Even when other publications included the illustrations to demonstrate how the rebellion was misrepresented, the images presented an interpretation of the rebellion that the accompanying text, no matter how critical of them, could not easily dispel. Of the eighteen "action" plates, eight show rebels in the act of killing, and three more show them in the act of plundering. Of the remaining seven, two depict battle scenes, two show the capture of rebel leaders, and three illustrate heroic scenes of defence by loyalists. Although plenty of dead rebels are shown, only one plate presents a rebel actually being killed, and even then the rebel is being shot. Rebel killings invariably involved piking their victims to death, and the motif of several rebels plunging their pikes into the same victim is repeated in seven of the eight plates in which rebels are shown in the act of killing. The simian features of the Irish rebels had earlier been seen in the cartoons of Gilray, and would be repeated in *Punch* cartoons of the later nineteenth century, thus establishing an associative link – associative fear, if you like – with the activities of O'Connell's mass-membership organizations, the New Irelanders, the Land Leaguers and the Fenians.

The effect of these plates, and of the conservative historical narratives, would lead one to the conclusion that the 1798 rebellion was an unrelenting attack on the Protestant population of Ireland by a sectarian mob, with innocent civilians – particularly women and children – the prime targets, and that loyalists bore the brunt of the casualties. However, the statistics we do have suggest that women and children were rarely casualties, and Protestant women and children even less likely to be so. It must be remembered that the overwhelming majority of deaths – at least 80 per cent by a rough reckoning – occurred among the rebels and the Catholic population in general.[14] Thomas Pakenham, in *The year of liberty* (1969, rev. ed. 1997) – still the most comprehensive, if not universally accepted, general history of the rebellion – has drawn attention to the great imbalance in terms of documentary evidence about the rebellion. While there are over 10,000 sources available from the government, military and loyalist side, there are less than 100 contemporary sources from the rebel perspective. What this means is that there are huge silences not just about rebel motivations and experiences but also about the experiences of the vast majority of silent victims of government and loyalist activity. The system set in place for the compensation of people whose property was destroyed by rebels during the rebellion, and the system of affidavits used to investigate rebel atrocities, means that we have a detailed picture of the experiences of loyalists during the rebellion, but little or no sense of what happened on the other side. As Pakenham observed, we must rely on 'second-hand (and sometimes second-rate) material'.[15] Scullabogue and Wexford Bridge are not represen-

14 Louis Cullen, 'Rebellion mortality in Wexford in 1798', *Journal of the Wexford Historical Society*, 17 (1998–9), 7–29; P. McCarthy, 'Rebel casualties in 1798: an unresolved question', *Irish Sword*, 21:85 (Summer, 1999), 346–7. 15 Thomas Pakenham, *The year of liberty: the great Irish rebellion of 1798*, rev. ed. ([1969]:

tative of the experiences of Protestants and loyalists in general during 1798, but they did occur, and have become tropes for a wider fear held by Protestants, loyalists and conservatives about their fate in a changing Ireland. In a wider context, they also became tropes for a fear of the Catholic Irish peasantry that needed to be addressed by Irish apologists in the nineteenth century.

***

The 1798 rebellion was the single most popular historical topic in Irish fiction of the nineteenth century. Its unresolved and contentious nature made it a metaphor for the unresolved and contentious nature of Irish history itself, and the rebellion was used in various ways by all shades of political opinion. The attraction of 1798 as a trope for a conservative Protestant fear of change was its strong narrative qualities and those well-publicized massacres which, however unrepresentative of the general experience of 1798, provided irrefutable evidence of the dangers Protestants had faced in the past, and had no reason to think would not face again. The Act of Union in 1801 is generally seen as providing the impulse for the development of the "national tale", a form of novel that endeavoured to explain Ireland and the Irish to a largely English readership; but it was not so much the act of union, but the perceived horrors of the 1798 rebellion, that immediately captured the imagination, and provided the subtext for the national tale. Although the major Irish novelists of the time – with the exception of Maria Edgeworth – did not deal with the rebellion directly, its shadowy presence can be seen in two of the most important and popular Irish novels of the first decade of the nineteenth century, *The wild Irish girl* (1806) by Sydney Owenson (later Lady Morgan), and Charles Maturin's *The Milesian chief* (1812). The reluctance of the major writers to engage directly with the rebellion has led critics to the conclusion that there was a general reluctance to write fiction about it, but this is far from true. In fact, the first full-length novel based on the events of 1798, *The Rebel*, was published in 1799, before any actual history of the rebellion itself was published. Not surprisingly, it showed all the hallmarks of the anti-Jacobin novels that had been particularly popular in the 1790s, and which actually reached a production peak in the 1797–1800 period.[16] Along with Charles Lucas's *The infernal Quixote* (1801) and the anonymous *The soldier of Pennaflor* (1810), *The Rebel* established an intermittent tradition of anti-Jacobin writing about 1798 that had echoes in novels like the anonymous *Land of the Kelt* (1860) right up to Adela Orpen's *Corrageen in '98*, published in 1898, the centenary year of the rebellion.

The anti-Jacobin novel relied for much of its effect on creating a sense of fear in the reader by demonstrating how easy it was for revolution and rebellion to

London, 1997), p. 14. **16** M.O. Grenby, *The anti-Jacobin novel: British conservatism and the French revolution* (Cambridge, 2001), p. 7.

occur if dangerous revolutionary principles were allowed to spread unchecked, and infect already impressionable or corrupted minds. It was important that the actual reasons for rebellion remained either inexplicable or selfish, thus increasing the fear factor for the presumably confused reader. Like other anti-Jacobin novels, *The Rebel* concentrated mainly on the sensational and provocative, playing on the widespread fear after the French Revolution of imminent revolution and social upheaval, suspicion of the role and aim of democratic politics and a concomitant suspicion of the lower classes. Anti-Jacobin writers in Britain and Ireland found in the events of 1798 a perfect analogue for the excesses of the French Revolution, and a confirmation of the essentially evil nature of social revolution and demo-cratic thought. The shock of the 1798 rebellion proved that these fears were real, and the excesses of the rebels, coupled with the undoubtedly sectarian character of some of them, confirmed that only evil could come of revolution and the dem-ocratic "disease". In *The Rebel*, there are no specific political reasons given for the rebellion; it appears to be the product of an ungrateful and jealous lower class, encouraged by the Catholic clergy and an unscrupulous, opportunistic, immoral and atheistic leadership. The rebels simply appear to want to replace those in power with themselves. "Emancipation" as a concept is ridiculed either as a term that the ordinary rebels cannot understand, or else understood as "emancipation" from labour. The rebellion is portrayed as sectarian, and the rebels as scarcely human: in one scene, in an echo of Scullabogue, the rebels are described as tossing a child on the end of their pikes, 'as you would a ball'.[17] This novel thus uses some of the more sensational views of the rebellion to create an atmosphere of fear rather than one of rational analysis, which is hardly surprising in itself, but the most chilling and fearful element for the reader of the time is the sense that this rebellion is unfinished and may re-erupt at any time. As one character observes:

> The wise and mild measures of lord C[ornwallis] have operated on the minds of the rebels in appearance, and they still continue to take the oaths of allegiance, and deliver up their arms; but what confidence can be put in a people, who would, if in their power, have overturned the government, and crushed their king? […] I yet fear many incendiaries are lurking in their traitorous haunts, watching the moment, when they again may blow the least spark of disaffection, into a blaze! […] The country at present appears tolerably quiet, but the leaves wear a russet hue, and I dread the approaching winter. [18]

The reader is left with a strong sense of foreboding about the future. In 1799 when this was published, there was no sense that the rebellion was a resolved issue.

---

17 'A Lady', *The Rebel: a tale of the times* ([1799]: Dublin, 1801), p. 45.   18 Ibid., pp 108–9.

The shock of the 1798 rebellion meant that a form of the anti-Jacobin novel persisted in Irish writing long after fears of a revolution in England had eased. *The soldier of Pennaflor* (1810) also denies that there were valid reasons for rebellion, despite an articulate outburst concerning the misrule of Ireland by one gentlewoman in the novel. When we finally come face to face with a rebel leader, however, he is deprived of the power of speech, and only his physical threat is described. This 'demon like figure', when compared to his opponents, was 'taller, and infinitely stronger [...] his black harsh malignant countenance bespoke the passions that nerved his athletic frame, while his hollow eyes peering in flames through their red circlets, glared the spirit of the cause they guided, anarchy, murder and devastation'.[19] Not giving the face of rebellion a voice removes any possibility of justification or explanation, and makes its occurrence seem all the more inexplicable.

A less obvious way that fear of another 1798 was manipulated is seen in Mrs Kelly's *The matron of Erin* (1816). The writer is either Catholic or sympathetic to Catholicism, and uses the fear of another rebellion to argue for Catholic Emancipation as a bulwark against a reoccurrence. This would be a dangerous game if the Catholics in the novel did not so clearly share the values of "respectable" Protestant Ireland. The wealthy Catholic family at the centre of the novel is seen to practice a form of Christianity and hold political views that would be totally acceptable to any conservative Protestant reader. *The matron of Erin* ultimately promotes the view that the incorporation of such people fully into the ruling class is the best protection against further rebellion.

Throughout the 1820s and beyond, the rebellion remained *the* great trope for the general conservative fear of political and social change. This is not surprising as the 1820s was the highpoint of sectarian tension in Ireland, when a conjunction of Protestant proselytism, a proliferation of Bible societies – parodied by Thomas Moore in *Captain Rock* (1824) – and the provision of schools promoting the Protestant ethos among the Catholic poor, forced the normally cautious Catholic clergy to become more assertive in their parishes.[20] The declaration of a 'second Reformation' by the Protestant archbishop of Dublin, William Magee, the continued agrarian disturbances and the mass organization of the Catholic lower classes by Daniel O'Connell in a concerted campaign for Catholic Emancipation, concentrated Protestant minds. There was also a level of anticipation created by the arrival of the fateful date of 25 December 1824: the date central to the 'Pastorini Prophesies', which were based on a book written by an English Catholic bishop in 1771. For many Catholics the date heralded the imminent destruction of Protestantism, and many Protestants interpreted this to mean that they would be mas-

19 'A Lady', *The soldier of Pennaflor: or, A season in Ireland. A tale of the eighteenth century*, 5 vols (Cork, 1810), iii, pp 155–6.   **20** Thomas Bartlett, *The fall and rise of the Irish nation: the Catholic question, 1690–1830* (Dublin, 1992), p. 332.

sacred. These prophesies were reputedly widely believed by the Catholic peasantry, and created a specific crisis moment for Protestants. Thus, anxiety and fear was the lot of many Irish Protestants in the 1820s. It is not surprising, therefore, that there was little in the spirit of detached and rational historical analysis of 1798 at this time. While there had been a few novels that had adopted the historical approach inspired by Walter Scott's *Waverley* (1814) – such as John Gamble's *Charlton* (1823) and James McHenry's *The insurgent chief* (1824) – these had focused on the less problematic Ulster element of the rebellion, which could be portrayed as the high-point of militant Presbyterian radicalism and part of a safely resolved past. It was not until the publication of Michael Banim's *The Croppy* in 1828 that any fictional account of the rebellion in Wexford was attempted.

One of the most remarkable ironies, however, of this period is that the writer of the history that had contained Cruikshank's illustrations – William Hamilton Maxwell – was also the author of a novel which portrayed the rebellion as an imaginative enactment along the lines of the American Revolution; the kind of rebellion Ireland might have had if the Volunteer movement of the 1780s had ever fired a shot in anger. *O'Hara: or, 1798* (1825) was written almost twenty years before his history and is the work of a frustrated Irish patriot of the eighteenth-century variety. By the mid-1840s, when his history of the rebellion was published, Maxwell is more conservative and, perhaps, embittered and frightened by what he saw as the perversion of patriotic principles by Daniel O'Connell and his Catholic hordes and the more aggressive nationalism of Young Ireland.[21] Although *O'Hara* does not substitute an idealized rebellion for the actual one, it is the first novel to adopt a celebratory approach, and to represent the rebellion as both the revolution that that Volunteers never engaged in and a matter of honour, revenge and personal loyalty. Unwittingly, Maxwell's gung-ho attitude to things martial had hinted at an approach that later novelists would use to address Ingram's fear of misrepresentation.

The romanticization of 1798 had obvious consequences for the rebellion's power as a conservative fear trope. This romanticization had its origins not just in the publication of United Irish memoirs and Madden's *Lives of the United Irishmen*, but also in the passing of the Catholic Emancipation act in 1829. Emancipation retrospectively validated one of the expressed purposes of the rebellion from a United Irish perspective, and therefore retrospectively rehabilitated its leaders. From the 1850s on there was a series of novels which attempted to portray the United Irish leadership as heroic and idealistic. *The rebels of Glenfawn* (1852), for example, has the carefully planned rebellion prematurely beginning in March 1798, and consisting of one large-scale military engagement near the fictional town of

---

21 See Maxwell's pamphlet, *The Irish movements: their rise, progress and certain termination; with a few broad hints to patriots and pikemen* (London, 1848).

Glenfawn in Co. Cork. The work of traitors and informers means that the American-style revolution is strangled in its infancy, so that the "real" rebellion that breaks out in May is seen to be leaderless and unconnected with the original conception. William Bernard MacCabe's *Agnes Arnold* (1860) adopts a different strategy, and draws a comparison with the American revolution by testing the actions of the government against the British constitution and suggesting that once the crown fails to protect a subject's life, liberty or property, 'then the ties of allegiance are broken, rebellion becomes a virtue, and insurrection a duty.'[22] This is the logic used to defend the actions of Father Murphy of Boolavogue, and this is the first novel in which he appears as a character. Once again, however, the idea that the rebellion that occurred was not the one that was planned is stressed, and the actual rebellion is seen to be the result of a deliberate policy by the government to provoke a premature insurrection, thus depriving the United Irish of what they really intended: 'a revolution, and not a rebellion', in the words of one character.[23] Rosa Mulholland's sanitized version of the rebellion in *Hester's history* (1869), blames an abrogation of responsibility by the ruling class, claiming that if the people had been led by those whom they had a right to expect would lead them – that is, their social betters – the rebellion would have been a truly national one that maintained a representative element within it. Charles Graham Halpine's *The patriot brothers* (1869) retells the story of John and Henry Sheares and is based largely on Madden's account in his *Lives*. John Sheares is portrayed as a man whose sense of honour will not allow him to withdraw from the proposed rebellion even though he knows that it will not be the idealistic rebellion envisaged by the United Irishmen. These novels, in stressing the idealism of the United Irish leadership and the role of the government and its agents in bringing about the actual rebellion, played a key role in preparing the way for the overtly nationalist novels that were to follow in the 1870s, and that would stress not Protestant, but rebel fears.

One other important area where the question of political fear was addressed was in Presbyterian novels about the events of 1798. Novels like Marion Clarke's *Strong as death* (1875), Mary Damant's *Peggy Thornhill* (1887) and Wesley Guard Lyttle's *Betsy Gray* (1888), all promoted the idea that while there may have been good reasons for a rebellion in 1798, those reasons no longer exist, thus negating its role as a transmitter of political fear. In general, unionist writers tended to retreat from the grand narrative approach and instead stress personal experience. In Eleanor de Butt's novel, *Great-grandmother's days* (1883), for example, the heroine's fearful experience of rebellion changes her from an ardent Irish patriot into a committed monarchist and unionist. The relatively conciliatory nature of unionist 1798 novels in the second half of the century suggests that the power of 1798 as a trope for conservative Protestant fear had diminished.

---

22 William Bernard MacCabe, *Agnes Arnold*, 3 vols (London, 1860), iii, p. 108.   23 Ibid., i, p. 157.

There remained, however, the open sore of Scullabogue, and the irrefutable evidence that, as even a reluctant Kavanagh wrote in his *Popular history*, 'there were men amongst the insurgents as cruel and cowardly as amongst their enemies'. Although he goes on to say 'for one black deed such as the one now referred to, we can cite hundreds perpetrated by the partisans of English rule, not in the madness of passion, but with cold-blooded deliberation', it remained a difficult topic for nationalist writers and a trump card for conservatives.[24] One nationalist novel of 1798, James Murphy's *The forge of Clohogue* (1885), brazenly blames the massacre at Scullabogue on retreating soldiers, thus transforming it into yet another example of state atrocity and oppression. Such a tactic highlights one of the difficulties of portraying the totality of Irish history as a relatively simple and recurring morality tale: sometimes that history needs to be tailored to suit. In John Hill's *Ninety-eight* (1897), Scullabogue is contextualized as a terrible but understandable reaction to outrages committed by government forces, in particular the burning of an alleged rebel hospital in New Ross. One of the main characters in the novel loses his true love in the burning hospital, which is 'not by accident, but wilfully and wantonly, set on fire' by the yeomanry, who 'stood by laughing'. After that, the rebels took 'blood for blood without remorse'.[25] The existence of this hospital and its deliberate burning is still a matter of dispute among historians, with some accepting its existence as a matter of fact, and others seeing it as an attempt to have a rebel equivalent of Scullabogue.[26] Significantly, perhaps, it is only mentioned in passing by Kavanagh, and then only in connection with Scullabogue.[27]

The last reference to Scullabogue as a fear trope in the novels considered here is in Adela Orpen's *Corrageen in '98*. *Corrageen* is a return to the anti-Jacobin sentiments of the earliest 1798 novels, in that it sees any interference with the established order of things as opening a Pandora's box of terrors. The revolutionary sympathies of the two main characters in the novel, Lady Laura Rossiter and Horace Brandon, are seen to be products of romanticism and arrogance, and the reality of rebellion is terrifyingly brought home to Laura when she narrowly escapes being burnt to death in the barn at Scullabogue. Her young son is presumed to have perished in the barn until he is returned to her at the end of the novel. Horace Brandon, who had been a leader of the rebels until he had lost control of their activities, thinks both of them have perished and blows his brains out. Scullabogue thus once again becomes both the point of agnorisis for deluded liberals and the ultimate moment of fear and terror for Protestant conservatives.

***

24 Kavanagh, *Popular history*, p. 154. 25 'Patrick C. Faly' [John Hill], *Ninety-eight* (London, 1897), pp 302–3. 26 See Tom Dunne, *Rebellions: memoir, memory and 1798* (Dublin, 2004), pp 131; 227–30. 27 Kavanagh, *Popular history*, p. 155.

As the nineteenth century progressed, the 1798 rebellion gradually lost its general shock value and its primary fear-inducing effect. It remained, however, a strong trope of political fear for Protestant conservatives, something aided by a wider perception of the distinction between the ideal rebellion proposed by the United Irishmen and the actuality. The rebellion's transformation into a heroic and noble national struggle gave strength and succour to the developing forms of nationalism and constitutional agitation, but the primary fear trope of the rebellion itself – the Scullabogue massacre – remained an uncomfortable blot on the reputation of the United Irishmen and the Irish Catholic peasant. "Scullabogue" remains the ultimate "atrocity" moment of 1798, partly because the relative paucity of documents from anything other than official sources means that it is difficult to establish a "parity of atrocity", with details of government outrages being vague and difficult to establish with certainty. In addition, as the century progressed, nationalists were more interested in the idealistic elements of the rebellion, and promoting the cult of the leaders of '98, either in the persons of the United Irish leadership who remained relatively unsullied by the actuality of the rebellion, or the heroic priest-leaders, like John Murphy of Boolavogue, who were seen as being forced into action. In contrast, 1798 for conservative Protestants remained a trope for their potential destruction, and its association with 1641 was established at an early stage in conservative narratives. The power of Scullabogue remains: the wording of the recently-erected memorial to the event does not state that the victims were almost all Protestants; nor does it say who or what group carried out the act. It does however assert that, 'The remorse of the United Irish at this outrage, a tragic departure from their ideals, is shared by the people of Ireland'. This wording gives some indication of the difficulty that nationalist Ireland has in facing up to this particular atrocity. In attempting to exorcize one particular fear it has to confront another, namely Ingram's fear that the rebellion will be seen as a source of shame rather than pride. It seems that fear, of one sort or another, remains central to the way we remember 1798.

Die gelbe gefahr, le péril jaune, the yellow peril: the geopolitics of a fear

DAVID GLOVER

Fear, wrote Freud, *c.*1925, is an emotion that 'is unmistakably associated with *expectation*; it is fear *of* something.'[1] If Freud is correct, then what was it that Westerners feared when they invoked the threat of "the yellow peril" at the turn of the nineteenth century (and beyond)? One might be forgiven for thinking that the answer is obvious: it must signify China, though today this hackneyed phrase can be applied to almost anything. However, a brief history of this colourful label suggests that its meaning was always far less clear-cut, more closely hedged about with complications, than we might initially have thought. Long before Britain's Channel 4 News used it as the headline for a news item on the risks facing world production of bananas in May 2006, "the yellow peril" was already a surprisingly slippery notion. Outrageously lurid even when masquerading as learned discourse, the polemical thrust of anti-Chinese sentiment reflected intra-national as much as international troubles. It is the aim of this essay to bring the local and the global aspects of this popular fear together.

Where better to begin a discussion of fear than with a murder mystery, a mode of fiction whose entire *raison d'être* rests upon the creation of fear and putting fears to rest? Consider an example that appeared just four years before Freud's near canonical work *Inhibitions, symptoms and anxiety* appeared in print. In 1922 the writer G.K. Chesterton brought out a collection of previously published short stories under the new (and subsequently much-borrowed) title *The man who knew too much.* The book makes for strange reading, despite the ostensible cosiness of the genre to which it belongs, with its house parties, 'long riverside gar-

---

1 See the new translation, entitled 'Inhibition, symptom and fear', in Sigmund Freud, *Beyond the pleasure principle and other writings*, ed. Mark Edmundson, trans. John Reddick (London, 2003), p. 233. Reddick's revised English version of Freud translates 'angst' as 'fear', rather than following James Strachey's use of 'anxiety' in the *Standard edition*, and thereby disrupts the conventional psychoanalytic distinction between 'fear' and 'anxiety'.

dens' and equally long trail of dead bodies.[2] Each chapter can be read as a self-contained detective story, but cumulatively they add up to considerably more than the sum of their parts – which is to say that *in toto* they produce a greater sense of opacity and disturbance than the solution to any individual narrative can put to rest.

The book's detective is a Hamlet-like figure named Horne Fisher. He is exquisitely well-connected – the stories provide an imaginary Cook's tour through England's ruling class – but his over-abundance of knowledge about his family, friends and associates is precisely what makes it impossible for him to act and thus set the world to rights. Reluctantly and with considerable prevarication, Fisher eventually becomes an agent of enlightenment. His role is not so much to solve crimes – although it is important that he delivers the answers to us – as it is to tell the reader exactly what it is he knows. By the time the penultimate pages have been reached, the reader is left in no doubt that the country is going to rack and ruin and that it is disastrously ill-prepared for an imminent invasion from the East whose inescapable momentum is dramatically revealed in the book's finale. Much of the blame for this sorry state of affairs lies with England's political class which has, as Fisher reveals, turned hopelessly corrupt. In the concluding story Fisher does act decisively at last. But when he does so, he has to kill his own uncle in a duel in order to prevent this wayward relative from betraying England's defence plans to the invading army. Most poignantly of all, Fisher is himself killed almost as soon as the battle to save England has begun, after having just released the signal calling his compatriots to arms. Lying in the shadows 'as stiff as the stick' of one of his own rockets, 'the man who knew too much' now knows precisely 'what is worth knowing'.[3]

But who are these invaders? We don't really know. Allusions to them are often vague or enigmatic. At one point there is a passing hint that the enemy might be Sweden, but it soon becomes clear that this is not where the root of the problem truly lies. The real enemy is never properly named and remains uncannily elusive, with veiled references to a 'new power which had arisen in Siberia, backed by Japan and other powerful allies' that is never quite identified. If Chesterton's loose description deliberately leaves his readers guessing, the pretext for an invasion by this 'new power' does bring the threat closer to home, for it takes the form of 'complaints of the ill-treatment of harmless foreigners, chiefly Asiatics, who happened to be employed in the new scientific works constructed on the coast.' A few pages later, Fisher puts the point more graphically: the so-called 'outrages on Orientals' have allegedly arisen because of the introduction of 'Chinese labour into this country with the deliberate intention of reducing workmen and peasants to

---

2 G.K. Chesterton, *The man who knew too much* (London, 1922; repr. New York, 1986), p. 120.   3 Ibid., p. 190.

starvation.'[4] England is, it seems, in the grip of a version of "the yellow peril", though Chesterton is too fastidious a craftsman to employ such a clumsy and slightly shop-worn phrase. Nevertheless, his book does contain the basic ingredients of this potent fantasy: the undercutting of ordinary English living standards by a less civilized race, which is in turn little more than a screen for naked aggression. However, there is a curiously belated quality about Chesterton's collection. For in conjuring up this old adversary, Chesterton implicitly appears to be appealing to the past, pushing his narrative back in time towards the Edwardian interregnum, as though the roots of Britain's crisis could be definitively located in the gilded age before the Great War. It is perhaps no accident that the book's international crisis is depicted as a war among capitalists, rather than an epic struggle between capitalism and communism.

Fear of the East is, of course, an old story. Thomas De Quincey, for example, could not write about China without dwelling upon 'Chinese treachery', the 'vindictive cruelty' of a people always ready to 'spring forward with a tiger bound'. Even when casting doubt upon 'those hyperbolical numbers' that exaggerated the real size of China's population, a phantasmatic terror of the 'monstrous aggregations of human beings' that thronged 'the suburbs of [its] mighty cities' continued to haunt his waking moments no less than his opium-sodden dreams.[5] "Yellow peril" is not, however, De Quincey's coinage. It comes into general circulation significantly later and is, as my title emphasizes, a pan-European currency. The earliest citation of the phrase in English given by the *OED* is from the *Daily News* in July 1900 which refers to the '"yellow peril" in its most serious form.'[6] But historically, the epithet belongs to the mid-1890s. German newspapers began using a version of the phrase towards the end of the war between China and Japan over Korea in April 1895 and it was subsequently associated with and popularized by Kaiser Wilhelm II.[7] In September of that year the Kaiser sealed a military alliance with Russia by sending Tsar Nicholas a specially commissioned drawing with the caption 'Peoples of Europe, protect your most sacred possessions' in which China was depicted allegorically as the "Yellow Peril."[8] The following year references to "le péril jaune" began to appear in French commercial periodicals, giving a new and vivid name to those nervous projections that had been warning of the destabilizing effect of China's growing economic power since at least the 1880s.[9] In Britain the phrase was familiar enough for the Orientalist and Japanophile Arthur

4 Ibid., pp 168, 172. 5 'Canton expedition and conventions', *Blackwood's Edinburgh Magazine*, 50 (November 1841), pp 682, 688. This article appeared anonymously, but is attributed to De Quincey by John Barrell, *The infection of Thomas De Quincey: a psychopathology of Imperialism* (New Haven, 1991), p. 6. 6 *Compact edition of the Oxford English dictionary*, 3 vols (Oxford, 1987), ii, p. 3855. 7 E. Malcolm Carroll, *Germany and the great powers, 1866–1914: a study in public opinion and foreign policy* (Hamden, 1966), p. 333. 8 *The Kaiser's letters to the Tsar*, ed. N.F. Grant (London, 1920), pp 17–22. 9 See John Laffey's 1976 pioneering essay 'Racism and imperialism: French views of the "yellow peril": 1894–1914' reprinted in his *Imperialism and ideology: an historical perspective* (Montréal, 2000).

Diósy to use it as the title for a chapter on the likely role of China in the modern world in his conspectus of *The new Far East* in 1898, an essay that earnestly debunked the Kaiser's 'allegorical drawing' as rank imperialist scaremongering.[10] In the space of just two years, "the yellow peril" had secured a sufficiently strong hold on the European imagination to stand in need of firm rebuttal.

But a drawing is not easily refuted, despite Diósy's patient deconstruction of the inconsistencies in its imagery. His earnest attempt to draw up a political and economic balance sheet of China's likely future sought to replace the battle of representations by reasoned argument. But confronted by a work as ferocious and bloody-minded as M.P. Shiel's hugely popular potboiler *The yellow danger* (1898) – far worse in Diósy's eyes than the Kaiser's wildest fancies – his carefully cultivated air of sobriety deserted him and, unable to bring himself to mention its author by name, he poured scorn on this '"bluggy" novel', dismissing it as 'a farrago of absurdities'.[11] Shiel, a writer who has wrongly, if understandably, been credited as the originator of the term "yellow peril", deserved everything he got.[12] The plot of his 1898 novel is every bit as crude, or one might more aptly say as functional, as an avowedly geopolitical melodrama needs to be. It presents the antagonisms between the world's great powers in such stark, apocalyptic terms as to provide a perfect fictional counterpart to the most paranoid view of Britain's national interest. Indeed, according to one source, a passage from *The yellow danger* was once quoted by Lord Roberts in a parliamentary debate on the nation's defence budget.[13] Shiel's founding assumption in the novel is that race war is inevitable and ineradicable, a zero-sum contest that will be fought to the bitter end: 'the yellow man is doomed – *if* the white man is not; in your heart you think it.'[14] The speaker is Dr Yen How, bringing to heel the Emperor's 'head of affairs in Pekin', a sign that he is a rising star in Chinese politics. As we will see, Dr Yen How is very much the prototype of the Oriental mastermind, the formidable super-villain who was to stalk the pages of numerous thrillers, plays and film scripts.[15]

The political background to *The yellow danger* highlights how much a novel of its time it was, packed with historical references that mimic the tensions of the period, tensions that are ultimately displaced on to a deeper conflict between "the yellow" and "the white." Here is Shiel's brief summary of the first phase of the conflict:

10 Arthur Diósy, *The new Far East* (London, 1898), pp 327–30.   11 Ibid., p. 327.   12 Sandra Kemp, David Trotter and Charlotte Mitchell, *Edwardian fiction: an Oxford companion* (Oxford, 1997), p. 360.   13 See C.J. Keep, 'M.P. Shiel', *Dictionary of literary biography* 153, ed. G.M. Johnson (Detroit, 1995), p. 272.   14 M.P. Shiel, *The yellow danger* (London, 1898), p. 16 (emphasis added).   15 The most successful of the evil Chinese geniuses, Dr Fu-Manchu, first appeared in Sax Rohmer's novel *The mystery of Fu-Manchu* (1913) and in numerous sequels (including stage and film adaptations) until the late 1950s. Among many others, Edgar Wallace's *The yellow snake* (1926) and Agatha Christie's Hercules Poirot mystery *The big four* (1927) also featured Oriental super-villains, as did Ian Fleming's *Dr No* (1958) whose eponymous Chinese-German mastermind was, like Fu-Manchu, bent on world domination. This novel formed the basis of the first of the James Bond films in 1962.

The principal cause of fear had been what had looked uncommonly like a conspiracy of the three great Continental Powers to oust England from predominance in the East. First there was the seizure of Kiao-Chau, the bombastic farewells of the German Royal brothers; then immediately, the aggressive attitude of Russia at Port Arthur; then immediately, the rumour France had seized Hainan, was sending an expedition to Yun-nan, and had ships in Hoi-How harbour.[16]

This inter-imperial rivalry is however quickly dissipated and a new pattern forms. For the hatred felt between the French, the Germans and the Russians is what Shiel's narrator calls 'the hatred of brothers, always ready to combine against the outsider.'[17] Although Shiel chooses not to dwell upon this dogma, its implications reverberate chaotically throughout the text. Like the story of the murderous band of brothers in Freud's *Totem and taboo* (1913), the hasty, enthymemic, yet somehow knowing explanation given in *The yellow danger* seems to posit a fragile social solidarity originating in a primordial moment of intra-familial breakdown that must be denied and deflected. Except that here, sibling rivalry is quenched through war against an 'outsider'. There is no 'violent, jealous father who keeps all the females to himself and drives his sons away as they grow up' – although one could read Freud's words as a possible psycho-analytic description of imperial dominance – and nor is there a point in the novel when the father is 'killed and devoured' – though there are scenes of cannibalism.[18] On one level, the hostility that 'England' attracts is curiously unmotivated, as though the intensity of fraternal antagonism desperately seeks an object, *any* object if it is to be made bearable. And it may be England's aloofness, her (invariably 'her') stubborn independence, that singles her out to play this unique role. 'Alone and friendless', her destiny is to 'tread the wine press of modern history, solitary in her majesty', 'prepared' to find 'the rest of Europe' taking up arms against her, an outsider virtually by choice, as well as by social and political circumstance.[19]

At the same time, the conspiracy *against* England is over-determined. Fostering pan-European conflict is the opening move in Dr Yen How's plan to disarm and fatally weaken 'the white races' of the West by fomenting division among its nations, initially by turning them against the English (since the English are judged by Yen How to be 'the worst'). Then, after 'their mutual slaughter', when the European 'treasuries [are] exhausted', the combined forces of China and Japan can lay waste to their natural enemies. *The yellow danger* is thus a tale of multiple outsiders; or, rather, of the re-alignment of outsider statuses through the intervention of racial categories. The logic of racial difference is what neutralizes 'the

16 Ibid., p. 2. 17 Ibid. 18 See 'Totem and taboo. Some correspondences between the psychical lives of savages and neurotics', in Sigmund Freud, *On murder, mourning and melancholia*, ed. Maud Ellmann, trans. Shaun Whiteside (London, 2005), p. 141. 19 Shiel, *Yellow danger*, p. 2.

hatred of brothers', yet it does so in such a way as to secure England's position as *primus inter pares* within the West. In its capacity as saviour of those nations whose vision is clouded by archaic emotions, England is charged with carrying the "white man's burden", providing a model of "stately progress". But this burden also includes holding up an ideal that others are condemned to copy, to emulate without hope of success. Japan imagines itself to be 'the Britain of the East'; instead, its fate is to join 'a League of the yellow races' dedicated to the extermination of its white adversaries, a project that will inevitably fail.[20]

The main source of the racial categories that animate *The yellow danger* are to be found in Arthur de Gobineau's notorious treatise *The inequality of human races* (1853–5) with its hierarchical division between the 'three great and clearly marked types, the black, the yellow, and the white', whose physiological distinctions can be identified 'with absolute certainty'.[21] He was certainly not the first racial theorist to advance this kind of typology: the biologist Georges Cuvier had advanced the same crude differentiation earlier in the century.[22] However, as Robert Young has noted, Gobineau's work is as much a philosophical history of the rise and fall of civilizations as it is a philosophy of racial difference, since the two are inextricably connected, with race supplying the motor of historical change.[23] As in most other nineteenth-century racial typologies the decisive advantage lies with the white race, from whom '*all* civilizations derive'. The 'energetic intelligence' of 'the white races', their determination in the face of obstacles, the importance they attach to honour, their 'extraordinary instinct for order' and their 'greater physical power' contrast sharply with the attributes displayed by their less favoured competitors. To take one particularly loaded formulation, Gobineau insists that the white races 'have a remarkable, and even extreme, love of liberty, and are openly hostile to the formalism under which the Chinese are glad to vegetate, as well as to the strict despotism which is the only way of governing the negro.' Whites have a higher level of self-consciousness and their 'reflective energy' gives them their civilizing edge. Similarly, their 'feeling for utility' is 'far wider and higher, more courageous and ideal, than the yellow races', and 'they are more sparing of life.' The corollaries of this natural nobility sometimes point in opposite directions to those that Gobineau presumably had in mind, suggesting the instrumental or Machiavellian rather than the humane or the sensitive. So, when the white races are cruel, they – unlike the other races – 'are *conscious* of their cruelty', a dubious virtue at best.[24]

---

20 Ibid., pp 16–17, 2, 11, 14. 21 Arthur de Gobineau, *The inequality of human races*, trans. Adrian Collins (New York, 1967), p. 305. 22 Georges Cuvier's tripartite racial classification can be found in his most famous work *Le Règne animal distribue d'après son organisation pour servir de base à l'histoire naturelle des animaux et d'introduction à l'anatomie comparée*, 4 vols (Paris, 1817). 23 Robert J.C. Young, *Colonial desire: hybridity in theory, culture and race* (London, 1995), pp 99–100. 24 Gobineau, *Inequality*, pp 210 (emphasis added), 207.

It is impossible to know whether Shiel had read Gobineau but, given his linguistic gifts and his wide knowledge of Continental literature, it is quite likely that he had, or at least that he had absorbed a version of this racial theory secondhand. However this may be, *The yellow danger* is in many respects, though not in all, a very Gobineauesque book. Like *The inequality of human races*, Shiel's novel makes racial hybridity the chief factor offsetting the stagnation that results from a world divided into discrete racial blocs, if not always with happy results. In this sense, Yen How – unlike the later Dr Fu-Manchu – is a bad hybrid, a textbook Gobineau villain. Indeed, his true racial status is his most guilty secret. Despite the fact that, as with many kindred Gothic figures, he is 'of noble feudal descent', he is 'the son of a Japanese father by a Chinese woman', combining two 'antagonistic races in one man.' It should be said at once that Shiel is blissfully inconsistent on the question of racial conflict between China and Japan. Yen How's dual inheritance – a so-called 'admixture of blood' that is elsewhere described as 'his double personality' – is hardly visible and he is able to pass between the two cultures with ease, while at the same time he is well aware that if his mixed parentage were to be discovered he would immediately be excluded from public office. But at other points in the book, the biological incommensurability between Chinese and Japanese is submerged into a single undifferentiated 'yellow wave'. The revelation of Yen How's miscegenated origins is not the only moment in the novel where racial inmixing supervenes in the brute contest between the races. When the book's English naval hero, John Hardy, travels through northern China *en route* to join his ship in Nagasaki, he finds that its inhabitants – in contrast to their compatriots in the south – are 'a hard, ferocious, and treacherous race […] their bony toughness being derived from the Tartar blood with which their tribes were infused.' On the same lines, the Russians are judged 'the most English of the Continentals, or tended to be, when once their races became homogeneous'; nevertheless, their racial identity contains 'a certain Orientalism – a vermilion line in the gray of their character'.[25]

In these and other passages we can glimpse Shiel's ambivalence around the question of racial purity, an ambivalence which echoes that of Gobineau for whom 'peoples degenerate only in consequence of the various admixtures of blood which they undergo'.[26] The good of racial hybridity is never, so to speak, unalloyed and always carries the danger of slippage or spillage, of getting the 'admixture' disastrously wrong. How English are the Russians? And to what extent does that vivid streak of Eastern promise enliven the more stolid aspects of their nature? Shiel, like Gobineau before him, is unclear. His novel seeks to safeguard the structure of race from ossification, while at the same time insisting that *plus ça change, plus ça meme chose*. It is in articulating the narcissism of minor dif-

25 Shiel, *Yellow danger*, pp 4, 11–12, 256, 117, 101. **26** Gobineau, *Inequality*, p. 211.

ferences, positioning itself against its fraternal rivals, that racialized desire makes its voice heard most stridently. Assessing the condition of Europe, John Hardy draws up a general inventory of the 'over-civilized' and the 'raw'. The French are 'very nice people' (particularly their women), but 'they are *old*, they are no good any more, they have not got any youth and go left in them.' They resemble '*patté* [sic] *de foie gras*, nice but tainted'; whereas the Germans suffer from the shallowness that comes of being 'a young nation' and the Russians are too 'new' to be 'a nation at all.' None of them has what it takes to be 'the chosen race', '*the peculiar people.*'[27] In Shiel's world, as opposed to Donald Rumsfeld's, the choice between old and new Europe is no choice at all.

By linking Shiel to Gobineau I do not mean to efface the important divergences between them – in Shiel's novel 'the yellow races' are far more pugnacious than the torpid mediocrities of Gobineau's imagination, their 'will-power' being 'obstinate' rather than 'violent'.[28] Nor were these two the only variants of this powerful ideological stance. Charles H. Pearson's futuristic *National life and character* (provocatively subtitled '*A forecast*') utilized the tripartite colour line to bring a grim colonial perspective into modern politics. Pearson was a former Oxford don and professor of modern history at King's College, London who in 1871 emigrated to Australia to devote himself to a healthy outdoor life of sheep-farming, but who subsequently drifted into provincial government. *National life and character* seems to have been written after his unexpected return to England in 1892 due to ill-health and was published the following year. An enormous success, it went through two editions and several printings in the early 1890s before being reprinted once more in 1913. Pearson's pessimistic extrapolations belong among the bleak, but highly influential contemporary diagnoses that were becoming increasingly popular in the *fin de siècle*, works epitomized by Max Nordau's *magnum opus*, *Degeneration*, whose first (German) edition also appeared in 1893. Despite the familiarity of many of its themes – worries about the growth of socialism and the effects of urban living, coupled with a fear of the imagined consequences of democracy – what distinguishes *National life and character* is its indebtedness to Pearson's experience and concerns as a colonial politician and administrator. His view of the world is that of the Pacific margins, rather than the metropolitan centre; or, perhaps more precisely, the metropolitan centre seen from the standpoint of the Pacific margins. At times the result is a kind of Australasian Max Nordau, paralleling several of *Degeneration*'s more morbid fixations: that, for example, in an increasingly 'sensuous, genial, and fibreless society' in which 'Puritan family life' was on the wane, the differences between men and women were gradually being erased; or that the great achievements in the arts – 'the epic, the drama, the pastoral, and the satire' – were now redundant.[29] Yet when Pearson

27 Shiel, *Yellow danger*, pp 102–3.   **28** Ibid., p. 206.   **29** C.H. Pearson, *National life and character: a forecast*

turns his attention to the world stage, these affinities begin to fade. For there one finds the impending drama of the races playing itself out along similar lines to those that Gobineau had earlier predicted, but with significant variations.

Pearson's opening chapter deals with what he calls 'The Unchangeable Limits of the Higher Races.' His main aim here is to challenge the widely held belief that, in an imperial age, 'the higher races [...] are everywhere triumphing over the lower.' Set against the sheer scale of territory and population in Africa or the Far East, Pearson argues, it is impossible that the Australian scenario in which a 'weak', 'evanescent' racial minority were easily overwhelmed by white colonists would be duplicated elsewhere. The telling counterfactual history that Pearson interposes at this point conjures up the spectre that haunts the book as a whole. 'Had Chinamen or Japanese descended upon New Zealand instead of the Maories,' he writes, 'those islands would long ago have been covered with a population of several millions, such as no modern European power would have attempted to displace.' For all the manifest advantages enjoyed by the white races, they are insufficiently robust when faced with harsh climates and too civilized in their imperial mission to prevent the eventual supremacy of their lesser rivals. Indeed, many of the advances that the Europeans have pioneered such as improvements in medicine and sanitation can only have the paradoxical effect of increasing the populations of inferior peoples, augmenting their numbers at what Pearson dubs an 'Oriental rate of progression'. In this Malthusian nightmare, population growth drives an expansionist dynamic that will in time reverse the general direction of colonial conquest. So Pearson predicts that:

> [t]he day will come, and perhaps is not far distant, when the European observer will look round to see the globe girdled with a continuous zone of the black and yellow races, no longer too weak for aggression or under tutelage, but independent [...] in government, monopolising the trade of their own regions, and circumscribing the industry of the European.[30]

When that day does finally dawn, the seas of Europe will have become a haven for the ships of non-European fleets.

As a prediction, Pearson's prognosis is close to the scenario imagined in Shiel's *The yellow danger*, but the latter differs from Pearson in important respects too. Shiel's novel is of course very much preoccupied with preserving Britain's naval supremacy – in the earlier chapters John Hardy makes his reputation by leading the defeat of the French, Russian and German navies in a re-creation of the battle of Trafalgar (complete with diagrams of naval tactics), a battle which is then pursued in Chinese waters. The "yellow peril" is not however primarily sea-born:

(London, 1893; repr. 1913), pp 274–5. **30** Ibid., pp 32, 34, 35, 79, 89.

when the Chinese start to build cruisers their ambition is described as a 'pantomime' and their ships 'promenading the boulevards of the seas' are explicitly
feminized as a parade of the latest in '*chic*'. The threat to Europe from the East is
essentially land-based, a supposition that is predicated upon the allegedly unstop-
pable weight of Chinese numbers. It makes no sense for England to try to van-
quish Yen How's forces by beating them on the ground. Instead, a perverse form
of naval warfare takes place in which the barges of the invading army are first captured and then towed into a maelstrom. A hundred-and-fifty Chinese soldiers are
spared this fate only to be injected with the plague bacillus and landed at seventy-
five European ports from Amsterdam to Odessa where they fatally infect their
waiting comrades, killing 'within three weeks [...] a hundred and fifty millions'.[31]

While hardly lacking in technological wizardry – the future predicted in the
novel is one in which air travel will, as Shiel puts it, 'annihilate' space – the racialized threat envisaged in *The yellow danger* focuses upon armed conflict, whereas
in Pearson (and arguably in Chesterton's stories too) Chinese labour is at least as
great a danger. In *National life and character* it is not always easy to separate the
military from the economic and by the close of Chesterton's *The man who knew
too much* we have also come to see that the two are inextricably intertwined. Once
China has become 'an aggressive military power', says Pearson, we can picture her
'sending out her armies in millions to cross the Himalayas [...] or occupying the
islands and the northern parts of Australia, by pouring in immigrants protected
by fleets.' Such a 'fear of Chinese immigration' is, he notes, quite unintelligible to
'Englishmen at home'. Were they to be 'allowed to come in freely' they could
force white colonial workers to the brink of starvation or compel them 'to submit
to harder work or a much lower standard of wages.'[32] And in giving voice to these
fears, Pearson allows us to see how it was that the regulation of migrant Chinese
labour came to provide both the pretext and the template for modern immigration control from the United States to Australasia to South Africa. When the bill
that became Australia's Immigration Restriction Act was undergoing its second
reading in 1901 – an act primarily directed against Chinese migrants – the Prime
Minister Edmund Barton drew heavily upon Pearson's writings to lend
respectability to his alarmist rhetoric.[33] And together, one might say that *National
life and character* and *The yellow danger* helped spread the fear of Chinese superiority to the doors of 'Englishmen at home' – for certainly by 1904, when Shiel
was embarking on his second, markedly more conciliatory "yellow peril" novel
The yellow wave (1905), the role of Chinese workers in South Africa was starting
to become a heated issue in British politics, reaching a climax in the 1906 general
election. Ironically, few at home appreciated that the growth of a global labour

---

31 Ibid., pp 130, 343.   32 Pearson, *National character*, pp 140, 17, 132.   33 A. Markus, *Fear and hatred: puri-
fying Australia and California, 1850–1901* (Sydney, 1979), p. xi.

market, and especially China's central position in the international movement of working people, were partly a product of the British presence in Chinese coastal zones like Hong Kong and the overseas recruitment of indigenous workers that British colonists encouraged.

We usually think of "fear" as something primitive or elemental, a force that breaks through the comfortable surface of everyday civility, as an uncontrollable intensity of raw emotion or what Sartre once described as an 'internal hemorrhage in the world', paralysing us and making it impossible to act.[34] What makes John Hardy the hero of *The yellow danger* is that, even when subjected to Chinese water torture and worse, he entirely lacks 'the instinct of Fear' – written with a capital "F". Against this simple fearlessness, the dread that Dr Yen How's inspires is far from superficial. While the unwholesomeness of his appearance is the outer sign of an inner depravity and thus the absolute opposite of the brave Hardy, the threat that is epitomized by Yen How's suspect racial origins and revealed by 'the specially dirty shade in the yellow tan of his skin' is intensified by his having insinuated himself into the world that he is pledged to destroy. With his medical degree from the University of Heidelberg and his clinical experience gained in San Francisco, his dangerousness derives from his closeness to 'Western civilisation', his familiarity with its 'minutiae'. For '[i]f ever man was cosmopolitan, that man was Dr Yen How [...] here was a man who simply breathed Western modernity, and who yet was an Eastern of the Easterns.'[35] In an abundantly horrific text, *The yellow danger*'s most disturbing effects stem from the sense that Western modernity is being subverted from within and made hideous.

Shiel's Dr Yen How found a worthy successor some fifteen years later in the extraordinarily successful figure of Dr Fu-Manchu, a man who is a recipient of the 'degrees of three European universities' and whose 'knowledge of medicine exceeds that of any doctor in the Western world.' It is Dr Yen How who is the true original of Fu- Manchu – and not the chance sighting of 'a tall and very dignified Chinaman' emerging from the 'sordid mystery' and 'frequent fogs' of Limehouse, as his creator Sax Rohmer (Arthur Henry Ward) told eager listeners to the BBC's Empire Station in the early 1930s. Like Yen How, Fu-Manchu stands ready to 'sweep aside the white races [...] and win domination for his own', but in Sax Rohmer's fiction – and certainly in the sequence of stories that made up *The mystery of Dr Fu-Manchu* in 1913 – the narrative line has turned inwards.[36] This first Fu-Manchu novel consists of what are in essence a series of locked-room mysteries, highly theatrical conjuring tricks from the 'giant intellect' of a grand illusionist, reflecting Rohmer's early connections with popular drama and the music hall

34 Jean-Paul Sartre, *Being and nothingness*, trans. H. Barnes (London, 1957), p. 295. 35 Shiel, *Yellow danger*, pp 75, 4, 10. 36 Sax Rohmer, 'Meet Dr Fu-Manchu' in *Meet the detective*, intro. Cecil Madden (London, 1935), pp 34–7.

– indeed, the very fact that Fu-Manchu is famously said to have a 'brow like Shakespeare' sounds too like a clue to be ignored.[37]

In another telling reference, Fu-Manchu's implacable foe, the intrepid Nayland Smith, warns that 'China to-day is not the China of '98' (and therefore no longer the China of Dr Yen How) because the plan for world power has gone underground and China is now 'a huge secret machine'. Dr Fu-Manchu is a clandestine figure, rarely seen, a 'phantom Yellow Peril' that 'materializes under the very eyes of the Western world'. Secrecy has the effect of blurring the sharply drawn battle lines mapped out in *The yellow danger* and London's East End becomes a beachhead for 'the establishment of a potential Yellow Empire', a parodic sub-imperial space occupied by '[a]liens of every shade of colour [...] emerging from burrow-like alleys.' When Dr Petrie, Nayland Smith's *aide-de-camp*, describes the two men's journey 'from the bright world of the West into the dubious underworld of the East', he is speaking of London, but a London containing or embodying the traces of a global struggle, a place whose cosmopolitanism is a hazard and not a source of strength.[38]

From the turn of the century onwards, the "cosmopolitan" was precisely the figure who lacked a sense of national belonging, the one without a proper sense of loyalty or solidarity, and who was hated and feared because of this very inconstancy. The East End was viewed from without as the acme of cosmopolitanism in a double sense, for it was also the home of England's Jewish population, to whom the word "cosmopolitan" was frequently applied as a coded term of opprobrium, a synonym for what was irremediably alien. Jews were 'a danger to the [Russian] Empire' in Pearson's *National life and character*, dangerous because, like the Chinese, they were 'too numerous, and it may be feared, too detested to be absorbed into the general population' and, suitably transposed, such sentiments were part of the stock-in-trade of East End racism.[39] One should not therefore be surprised to learn that it is the Jew who is ultimately behind the importation of Chinese labour in Chesterton's *The man who knew too much*: 'coolie capitalism' as Jewish conspiracy, or what the *Times* in 1920, referring to *The protocols of the learned elders of Zion*, called 'The Jewish Peril'.[40]

The man who knew too much pictures the outsider as cosmopolitan, a person who is able to dissemble, to pass as a true-born Englishman, yet whose real allegiances lie elsewhere: just as Drs Yen How and Fu-Manchu are able to use their impeccable occidental knowledge against the West. We are used to thinking of fears as discrete, each with its own particular object of dread. But fears also draw their energies from other fears, and one fear can provide a model that can be redeployed elsewhere, as when King Vajiravudh, a leading light in early twentieth-cen-

---

37 Sax Rohmer, *The mystery of Dr Fu-Manchu* (1913; repr. London, 1967), p. 16.   38 Ibid., pp 47–8, 132, 139–40.   39 Pearson, *National character*, pp 84–5.   40 See R. Finzi, *Anti-Semitism: from its European roots to the Holocaust*, trans. M. Jackson (Moreton-in-Marsh, 1999), p. 61.

tury Thai nationalism drew upon the anti-Semitism he had witnessed as a student in London and dubbed the Chinese 'the Jews of the Orient', calling them a people 'without morals, without conscience, without mercy, without pity [...] where money is concerned.'[41] It has become fashionable of late to think of popular fears as, by their very nature, uncontainable, diffuse, and volatile.[42] "The yellow peril" was, by contrast, highly structured yet immensely pliable; a model racism for an increasingly turbulent imperial world, an insidious vision of a different, less hospitable modernity.

41 K. Tejapira, 'Imagined uncommunity: The *Lookjin* middle class and Thai official nationalism', in D. Chirot and A. Reid (eds), *Essential outsiders: Chinese and Jews in the modern transformation of southeast Asia and central Europe* (Seattle, 1997), p. 77.   42 Cf. Z. Bauman, *Liquid fears* (Cambridge, 2006).

'Advertising to victory': American ad culture and propaganda in the wake of World War I

ELIZABETH McCARTHY

Recounting the early history of advertising, Greg Myers identifies a crucial shift which he describes in the following terms: from the 1890s to the early twentieth century advertisers told consumers to 'Buy OUR SOAP,' by the 1920s, however, advertisers were telling the consumer to 'Buy a better life by buying OUR SOAP.'[1] The circumstances occasioning this fundamental change in advertising's terms of reference – a change from product promotion to consumer satisfaction – involve a variety of socio-cultural and technological developments, the most notable being the Great War (1914–18) and its aftermath.

Few would argue that an incisive exploration of American advertising's early stages should consider the effects of the First World War on American culture. As the US's first institutionally coordinated program of national propaganda, the war was also the first to explicitly co-opt the techniques of commercial advertising. Immediately following America's entry into the war Woodrow Wilson (1856–1924) set up the Committee on Public Information (CPI), a propaganda and censorship agency. Under the ministrations of George Creel (1876–1953) the CPI's mission was to influence public opinion towards supporting America's involvement in the war. Charged with the task of "selling the War to America", this is quite literally what Creel and the CPI did. In fact, the most immediate evidence of the Committees' debt to the advertising trade can be gleaned from the title of Creel's 1920 memoir, *How we advertised America: the first telling of the amazing story of the Committee on Public Information that carried the gospel of Americanism to every corner of the globe.*[2] In his frank and uncompromisingly positive take on the Committees' mission, Creel describes 'the fight for the *minds* of men, for the "conquest of their convictions",' and goes on to explain how:

---

1 Greg Myers, *Words in ads* (London, 1994), p. 26.   2 George Creel, *How we advertised America: the first telling of the amazing story of the Committee on Public Information that carried the gospel of Americanism to every corner of the globe* (New York, 1920).

> In all things from first to last, without halt or change, it was a plain pub-
> licity proposition, a vast enterprise in salesmanship, the world's greatest
> adventure in advertising.[3]

Indeed, the Committees' task *was* immense, for not only had it to convince the
American public that the war "over there" in Europe was of direct consequence to
them, it also had to induce public co-operation and commitment on an unprece-
dented scale. However, it did not face this task alone. The CPI's Advertising Division included some of America's most talented advertising agents and artists. Still
establishing itself as a credible profession, advertising welcomed the opportunity to
prove itself a valuable and proficient force of modernity. This is precisely what
advertisers involved in the war effort felt they had achieved. As ad-man, William
D'Arcy, remarks in his 1918 publication *The achievements of advertising in a year*,
'the past year's work' has shown advertising to be 'a forearm and standard-bearer of
war for human rights.' The outcome is 'a proud page in advertising's history.'[4] The
J. Walter Thompson Advertising Agency described this collaboration with the
American government as 'an opportunity not only to render a valuable patriotic
service [...] but also to reveal to a wide circle of influential men [...] the real character of advertising and the important function which it performs.'[5] In fact,
through its participation in the CPI, advertising had, above all else, promoted itself.

Unparalleled in its scale and forcefulness, the CPI's campaign to rouse support
for the War utilized every means available in promulgating its message. A mass
media operation was undertaken; newspapers and magazines, books, speeches,
films, sermons, posters, radio programmes, handbills and billboard ads inundated
the American public. As Creel writes, 'There was no part of the Great War
machinery that we did not touch, no medium of appeal that we did not employ.
The printed word, the spoken word, the motion picture, the telegraph, the cable,
the wireless, the poster, the sign-board – all these were used in our campaign to
make our own people and all other peoples understand the causes that compelled
America to take arms.'[6] This pervasive and unrelenting promotion of war effectively 'enveloped American citizens at every venue in their personal lives', much
like commercial advertising does in our own time.[7]

Today, the convergence of advertising and political propaganda is an aspect of
mass media communication all too often taken for granted. However, during this
period the government employment of ad men was revolutionary, not to mention

---

3 Creel, *How we advertised America* quoted in Garth S. Jowett & Victoria O'Donnell, *Propaganda and persuasion* (California, 2006), p. 162.   4 William D'Arcy, *The achievements of advertising in a year* (1918) quoted
in J. Michael Sproule, *Propaganda and democracy: the American experience of media and mass persuasion*
(Cambridge, 1997), p. 17.   5 Quoted in Roland Marchand, *Advertising the American dream: making way
for modernity, 1920–1940* (London, 1985), p. 7.   6 Creel, *How we advertised America*, p. 5.   7 Sproule, *Propaganda and democracy*, p. 10.

controversial, especially as the goal of this collaboration was to get Americans to go to war. Of course, it is perfectly legitimate to reason that advertising is itself propaganda. Indeed, if one accepts modern definitions of propaganda, such as the one put forth by Jowett and O'Donnell, then they are on a most fundamental level the same:

> Propaganda is the deliberate, systematic attempt to shape perceptions, manipulate cognitions, and direct behaviour to achieve a response that furthers the desired intent of the propagandist.[8]

This supposition that advertising and propaganda are interchangeable terms is borne out by Creel's book title, *How we advertised America*; a title which he undoubtedly chose, at least in part, as a means of avoiding the negative connotations associated with the word "propaganda", 'We did not call it propaganda, for that word, in German hands, had come to be associated with deceit and corruption. Our effort was educational and informative throughout, for we had such confidence in our case as to feel that no other argument was needed than the simple, straightforward presentation of facts'.[9]

Not surprisingly perhaps, the true potential of commercial advertising as political propaganda was recognized most clearly by advertisers themselves. Heady with the possibilities of this newfound power, advertising trade journals of the period were awash with self-glorification and visions of world domination. The examples are many, the following comment by J. Walter Thompson is among the more pugnacious, arguing that wartime advertising has shown that 'it is possible to sway the minds of whole populations, change their habits of life, and create belief, practically universal, in any policy or idea.'[10] Many political commentators, for their part, not only acknowledged the possibility of such powers of persuasion, they saw them as a fundamental element of modern war. In his seminal 1927 publication, *Propaganda techniques in the World War*, the political scientist and communications theorist, Harold Lasswell (1902–78) makes this connection in the most forthright terms, 'There is no question but that government management of opinions is an inescapable corollary of large scale modern war'.[11]

These "advertisements for war" undertook various campaigns to sell war bonds, enlist army and navy recruits, enhance worker morale and promote the conservation of food and resources. On the home front, there was virtually no aspect of everyday living which could not be, in some way, tied into the war effort, from knitting socks to maintaining your health. In what must have been a rather unnatural position for advertisers, many magazine and poster campaigns

8 Jowett & O'Donnell, *Propaganda and persuasion*, p. 6.   9 Creel, *How we advertised America*, p. 5.   10 Quoted in Marchand, *Advertising the American dream*, p. 7.   11 Howard Lasswell, *Propaganda techniques in the World War* (New York, 1938), p. 15.

extolled the virtues of frugality, declaring 'Save a loaf a week – Help win the war' and 'Food is Ammunition – Don't waste it'.[12] Whatever the specific message and no matter how innocuous or homely the subject, these campaigns took every opportunity to associate civilian activity with warfare: food is ammunition, 'Rivets are Bayonets', and the Victory gardener's insecticide a Hun-killing poison. One of the most successful and insistent of these campaigns was the push to buy war bonds with the assurance that their purchase would quite simply 'Halt the Hun!'[13] Along with compelling their audience to enlist, save food, stay healthy and buy war bonds, many of these propaganda campaigns, not surprisingly, also aimed at provoking a widespread fear and hated of the Germans. A major source of anti-German propaganda was atrocity stories involving the German armies' occupation of Belgium. These largely unfounded tales of German massacres, which were predominantly the product of British propaganda (not least of which was the Bryce Report [May 1915]), became the basis for an almost inexhaustible diatribe on the virulent evil and inhumanity of the Germans. The stories told of various outrages included German soldiers gouging out the eyes of civilians, cutting off the hands of teenage boys, raping and sexually mutilating women, giving children hand grenades to play with, bayoneting babies and crucifying captured soldiers. It was also claimed that they operated a corpse factory where they distilled glycerin from the bodies of the dead.[14] Predictably, such tales were keenly represented in visual form, in both still and moving images.[15]

As has often proved the case in matters of war propaganda, soldiers engaged in direct battle were among the first to discount these atrocity stories about the enemy. For combatants like Robert Graves (1895–1985), serving on the Western Front, 'Propaganda reports of atrocities were, it was agreed, ridiculous [...] We no longer believed the highly-coloured accounts of German atrocities in Belgium.'[16] Graves' phrase 'highly-coloured' is an apt one. In conjunction with their Advertising Division, the CPI's propaganda campaign drew on this repository of startling imagery in an effort to rouse the American public into a full-blooded support of US entry into the War in 1917. Among the most memorable and effective examples of this anti-German propaganda were images of skeletons in blood-sodden German uniforms clutching at the globe or turning cities to rubble, and giant apes in spiked helmets ravaging women and running riot on American soil.

12 'Save a loaf a week – Help win the war', artist unknown (New York, 1917); 'Food is Ammunition –Don't waste it ', artist John E. Sheridan (New York, 1918).   13 'Halt the Hun! Buy U.S. Government bonds, third liberty loan', artist Henry Raleigh (Chicago, 1918).   14 See Francis O. Wilcox, 'The use of atrocity stories in war', *American Political Science Review*, 34:6 (Dec. 1940), 1167–78; A. Ponsonby, *Falsehood in war-time* (New York, 1928).   15 The CPI liaised with movie studios, among the more major results of these collaborations were D.W. Griffith's *Hearts of the world* (1918) and Carl Laemmle's *The Kaiser, the beast of Berlin* (1918).   16 Robert Graves, *Goodbye to all that* (c.1957; London, 1998), p. 190.

Crucially, despite the varying nature of their appeals – from 'Buy war bonds' to 'Enlist!' – the intensity of the violence represented in these propaganda posters remains consistent. This unrelenting and unequivocal demand to face the German's brutality placed individual consumer choices, regarding food and war bond purchases, on a par with direct involvement in battle. As I shall argue later, this technique of disproportionate comparisons proved to be an important facet of the hard-sell tactics employed by American advertising in the post-war years. Indeed, as the vast majority of the CPI's propaganda campaign was directed at America's civilian non-combatant population, it is curious to note the high level of references there are to actual battle; references which often inculcate the viewer directly in the fighting. A popular means of achieving this was through the use of images depicting an American solider looking out at the viewer, his hand stretched forward, pleading for more ammunition; the entreaty underneath 'Bonds Buy Bullets'. While these depictions of direct warfare may most obviously be read as attempts to impress upon their audience the urgency and magnitude of the situation at the battlefront, they do of course contain implicit threats, just as the unspoken assumption behind the imperative 'Halt the Hun!' is "The Hun are Coming!"[17]

Some of the most intimidating of these images, however, do not depict the *enemy*, rather they focus on American figures – the solider, Uncle Sam and the Statue of Liberty. Images of power and authority directing their accusing glare at the viewer, demanding a specific response. Censorious and recriminating, the threat couched within these images is of a very different nature to those of the bloody and ape-like Hun. The fear and dread they endeavour to provoke is not of direct violence but the condemnation of those from whom one wishes to gain acceptance and validation. One such image depicts a grim-faced American solider with bayonet at the ready, standing over the body of a dead German, while in mid-charge towards the viewer. The message written over the bayonet, 'Come on!' and then at the bottom of the poster, 'Buy more Liberty Bonds'. Attempting to stir its viewer into a specific mode of action by provoking feelings of shame and guilt, ominous war bond ads like these have much in common with war posters entreating men to enlist. Clearly borrowing from Lord Kitchener's 'Britons [... Kitchener] Wants You!' recruitment banner, innumerable posters portrayed Uncle Sam and the Statute of Liberty pointing out at the viewer with harsh expressions, the word 'YOU' written in large letters, followed by 'Buy a Liberty Bond Lest I Perish'. A variation on this shows Uncle Sam in the classic pose of a reproachful patriarch, fists balled and planted on his hips, as he sternly proclaims 'I am telling you. On June 28th I expect you to enlist in the army of war savers to back up my army of fighters'.[18]

17 'Ammunition! And remember – bonds buy bullets!', artist Vincent Lynel (Philadelphia, 1918).   **18** 'Britons, Wants You!', artist Alfred Leete (London, 1914); 'Come on! Buy more Liberty Bonds', artist Walter Whitehead (Philadelphia, 1918); 'You – Buy a Liberty Bond Lest I Perish', artist C.R. Macauley (Publishing details unknown, 1917); 'I am telling you', artist James Montgomery Flagg (New York, 1918).

C.R. Macauley, 'You – Buy a Liberty Bond Lest I Perish' (1917) (Courtesy Library of
Congress, Prints & Photographs Division, WWI Posters [LC-USZC4-8032] Public Domain).

Laura Brey, 'Enlist – On which side of the window are YOU?' (1917) (Courtesy Library of Congress, Prints & Photographs Division, WWI Posters [LC-USZC4-9659] Public Domain).

The power of the direct address in such images is *not* that it is personal but that it is slippery and indiscriminate; it is difficult to elude its challenge. Often such direct addresses include a question (sometimes rhetorical in nature) but always framed in such as way as to reduce any issue to two distinct and opposing perspectives. Enlistment posters are particularly fond of utilizing this methodology. One, for example, shows a man in civilian dress, standing almost in silhouette as he looks out a window at a troop of soldiers who march by in the bright sunlight, a huge fluttering "stars and stripes" held above their heads. Along with the word 'Enlist', the poster asks the question 'On which side of the window are YOU?'[19] Such posters petitioning men to enlist offer two positions for the war-eligible male; quite clearly, on one side is courage, pride and a sense of self-esteem, while on the other, cowardice, shame and a profound feeling of inadequacy. Closing down all other possibilities, these images may be accurately defined as 'emotionally potent over-simplifications'.[20]

Other examples of this polarized representation of those who had and those who hadn't enlisted included posters which juxtaposed images of a soldier on duty with a man reclining in an arm- or deckchair, smoking a pipe and reading a paper or book, around him are the signs of a leisurely lifestyle, a tennis racket, a golf club and a tall cold drink. Occasionally these posters also included the reclining man's thoughts, appearing in thought-bubbles or clouds of tobacco smoke. These thoughts consisted of nightclub dancers, cocktail parties, baseball games and so on. The message here is clear – if a man is not at the front fighting, he is living the life of a slacker and playboy. Just in case this recriminating scenario is not enough to provoke the war-eligible male into doing the right thing, these contrasting figures of manhood in the face of war are often accompanied by questions like "Which Picture would your Father like to show his friends?" Probably the best known example of a war image which used this type of guilt-driven rhetoric is the British enlistment poster with the text 'Daddy what did YOU do in the Great War?'[21] It shows a homely scene. In a comfortable armchair sits a man, Daddy, on his knee a young girl who holds a book open with her finger on a line of text, quite possibly about the Great War. She has turned to her father, presumably to ask him this question. On the floor in front of them a young boy plays contentedly with toy soldiers. Daddy looks out at the viewer, a serious worried expression on his face. The intimation here is obvious – when the war is over and the time comes will you be able to face your children and account for your actions with a sense of pride? Whatever reasoning lies behind your choice to fight or not fight, it should be demonstrable to a 5-year-old otherwise it is automatically disin-

---

19 'Enlist – On which side of the window are YOU?', artist Laura Brey (Chicago, 1917).   20 Reinhold Niebuhr, *Moral man and immoral society: a study in ethics and politics* (New York, 1932) quoted in Noam Chomsky, *Necessary illusions: thought control in democratic societies* (London, 1989), p. 17.   21 'Daddy, what did YOU do in the Great War?' designed and printed by Johnson & Riddle (London, 1915).

genuous. Outside of these narrow ethical parameters there is nothing but cowardice and doubletalk.

The arguments put forward in these posters attempt to provoke deep feelings of guilt and shame by using indirect appeals to the viewers' sense of self-worth, all the while avoiding any consideration of the validity of involvement in warfare:

> When we feel guilty we typically pay little attention to the cogency of an argument, to the merits of a suggested course of action. Instead, our thoughts and actions are directed to removing the feeling of guilt – to somehow making things right or do the right thing.[22]

Of course, the persuasive tactics utilized in these posters do not end here. Their focus moves beyond self-recrimination to include the reproach of others. As well as the allegorical figures of Liberty and Uncle Sam, the viewer is asked to consider his worth in the eyes of his children, his father, his father's friends, his neighbours, passers-by in the street who note his lack of uniform and so on, in an ever-widening circle of judgement. This mode of persuasion focuses on what others *might* say or think *if* one does not enlist – its threat lies in the unforeseen, the frightening and boundless "what-if?" of the future. Broadening their terms of reference from a personal sense of guilt to a seemingly endless chain of accusation, these dramatic tableaux aim to persuade by a process termed 'the fear appeal', which, working much in the same way as the incitement of guilt, seeks to 'redirect attention away form the merits of a particular proposal and toward steps that can be taken to reduce the fear.'[23] Invoking a fear of social malediction as well as a sense of personal shame, such images have a far greater potential to motivate. As Bertrand Russell (1872–1970) observed in his 1917 commentary on the war, *Why men fight*, 'The impulse to avoid the hostility of public opinion is one of the strongest in human nature'.[24]

Unmistakably, such appeals play on the manhood and masculinity of their intended audience; the war-eligible male. The fact that they do this by focusing on what others think is, in itself, predictable if one assumes that concepts such as masculinity are socially constructed. However, with the introduction of conscription in the early stages of America's entry into the war, the main focus of the CPI's propaganda operation soon moved away from enlistment to domestic and economic matters. Without doubt the most forceful and insistent theme in this poster campaign was the buying of war bonds. Not surprisingly, the ad men involved in pushing this particular aspect of the CPI's war effort rose to the challenge most enthusiastically. As one commentator notes:

22 Anthony Pratkanis & Elliot Aronson, *Age of propaganda: the everyday use and abuse of persuasion* (New York, 1991), p. 229.   23 Aaron Delwiche, 'Common techniques: special appeals', *Propaganda critic* 29 Sept. 2002. www.propagandacritic.com/articles/ct.sa.fear.html, accessed 25 Apr. 2006.   24 Bertrand Russell, *Why men fight: a method of abolishing the international duel* (New York, 1917), p. 21.

The war bond campaign was a unique fusion of nationalism and consumerism. Seeking to stir the conscience of Americans, it invoked both their financial and moral stake in the war. The sale of war bonds provided a way in which patriotic attitudes and the spirit of sacrifice could be expressed, and became the primary way those on the home-front contributed to the national defense and war effort.[25]

In other words, supporting America by purchasing war bonds was an economically, as well as an ethically, sound proposition: it aided the fight for justice, curbed wartime spending and helped boost the investor's psychological and financial sense of wellbeing. Although framed in a guileless rhetoric of idealism, the CPI's proposition that it made good business sense to get behind the war was not met without severe skepticism in some quarters. A notable instance of such skepticism is Bertrand Russell's 1922 article 'American idealism excoriated'.[26] However, in the battle for magazine space, the CPI's Division of Advertising won out easily over any other socio-economic commentators. Underneath war bond adverts acknowledgements like the following from *Cosmopolitan* (May 1918) testified to the coalition between the CPI's propaganda campaign and big business, 'This space contributed to the winning of the war by the Goodyear Tire and Rubber Co. Through the Division of Advertising. Government Committee on Public Information. Advertising to Victory.'[27] With the generous *contribution* of such prime magazine space the CPI had ample opportunity to outline the numerous benefits of purchasing war bonds. Magazine and newspaper advertisements, like this *Cosmopolitan* ad, urged Americans to 'Be practical. Look squarely at the facts. We will either invest our money with Uncle Sam now, at good interest rates, to help him win this war, or we give it up later to pay Germany's war cost – and as much more as Germany chooses to collect. Invest in U.S. Gov't Bonds. Third Liberty Loan.'[28] If this argument alone did not convince the wary investor then the accompanying illustration would. It gives two possible scenarios; the first shows a businessman seated at his desk, in conversation with Uncle Sam, who stands in an authoritative business-like pose, his hat removed and placed on the desk. The posture of both figures suggests a frank and open dialogue. The second illustration is the same scene, only now Uncle Sam has been replaced by a German solider, wearing a pitted helmet and cape, he stands with his hand thrust towards the, now cowering, businessman who fumbles in his wallet. But this is not all that has changed; the view outside the window has altered too. The

25 'Advertising and Marketing War Loans and Bonds', *Ad access: John W. Harlman centre for sales*, Duke University 1999. scriptorium.lib.duke.edu/adaccess/warbonds.html#search, accessed 14 Mar. 2006. **26** Bertrand Russell, 'American idealism excoriated', *Literary Digest* Mar. 1922. **27** 'Third Liberty Loan', *Cosmopolitan* for May 1918, *Tri-Counties genealogy & history* by Joyce M. Tice, 8 Nov. 2003. www.rootsweb.com/~srgp/jmtindex.htm, accessed 26 Feb. 2006. **28** Ibid.

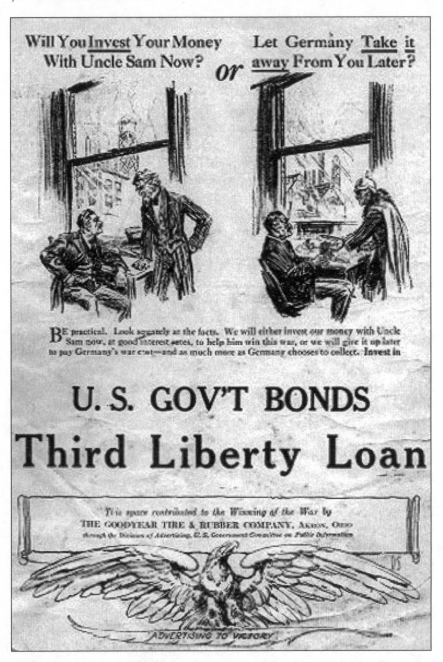

'Third Liberty Loan', *Cosmopolitan* May 1918 (Courtesy of *Tri-Counties genealogy & history*, Joyce M. Tice, 8 Nov. 2003. www.rootsweb.com/~srgp/jmtindex.htm).

modern cityscape in the first image has, under German rule, been replaced by a scene of nineteenth-century industrialism, with the smoking stacks of factories taking the place of office blocks; thereby linking personal financial loss with a national economic regression. Such ads promoted the purchase of war bonds as a morally (i.e. patriotically) commendable and financially astute act, while also highlighting the loss of personal liberty and money that would inevitably follow a failed war effort.

With their emphasis on the power of purchasing, the war bond campaign promoted the belief that individual security, liberty and happiness could be bought. Conflating the figure of the good citizen and the good consumer, buying acted as manifest proof of the individual's complete confidence in America and its way of life. As tangible evidence of this good citizenship, certificates proving that a family had contributed to the Liberty Bond drive were given out to be displayed in the windows of people's homes and places of work. There is perhaps no stronger image of this fusion between patriotism and financial outlay than Gerrit A. Beneker's 1918 Victory Liberty Loan poster which depicts an all-American farmer wearing a pair of dungarees with several Victory war bond badges pinned on the chest. With a rosy-cheeked smile he proclaims 'Sure! We'll Finish the Job', as he reaches deep down into his pocket.[29]

After the fall in business activity and prices in 1921 and the even greater crisis on Wall Street in 1929 this notion of financial investment as an "act of faith" quite comfortably found its way into to the world of commercial advertising. As a 1930's Packard Motor Company anti-hoarding ad declared, 'To buy today is a patriotic duty.'[30] In this instance the display of a new model car becomes the sign of good citizenship.

Although the war had ended, the pervasive selling of America to the American public continued. A sizable part of this endeavour ground its terms in subtle (and sometimes not so subtle) intimation and, predictably, its most proficient exponent was the advertising business. Known in the trade as "scare copy"; advertisements for a diverse range of products 'sought to jolt the potential consumer into a new consciousness by enacting dramatic episodes of social failures and accusing judgements.'[31] Many ads did this by adopting the rhetoric of the CPI's propaganda campaign, threatening their audience with the stigma of bad citizenship and its resultant social shame and ostracism. Assuming the weighty moral tone and social imperatives attached to enlistment and the purchasing of war bonds, post-war advertising – and Depression-era advertising in particular – placed these imperatives onto the most everyday and seemingly insignificant of situations. Presenting their role as a valuable public service, advertisers emphasized the ethical implica-

29 'Sure! We'll Finish the Job: Victory Liberty Loan', artist Gerrit A. Beneker (Chicago, 1918). **30** Quoted in Marchand, *Advertising the American dream*, p. 324. **31** Marchand, *Advertising the American dream*, p. 14.

tions of consumer choice just as propaganda had in the war years, when all manner of private affairs were the matter of public concern. The underlying assumption behind such tactics was the belief (genuine or otherwise) that the public did not know what was best for them. This evaluation of the public was very much in concurrence with that of contemporary propaganda theorists. Journalist and advisor to Woodrow Wilson during the war, Walter Lippmann (1889–1974), who, under the influence of Plato, infamously described the public as a 'bewildered herd'[32], succinctly captured this view when he proclaimed that 'The common interests elude public opinion entirely.'[33] The following observation made in 1927 by John Benson, the President of the American Association of Advertising Agencies sums up a similar attitude:

> To tell the naked truth might make no appeal. It may be necessary to fool people for their own good. Doctors and even preachers know that and practice it. Average intelligence is surprisingly low. It is much more effectively guided by its subconscious impulses and instincts than by its reason.[34]

This imperative to appeal to the consumer's 'subconscious impulses', rather than to his or her intellect, makes the advertiser's penchant for "scare copy" quite logical. Combined with the 'surprisingly low' intelligence of the general public, the economic decline after the war created a new set of challenges for the advertiser. This would of course be intensified at the end of the decade in the wake of the Wall Street Crash. The Depression was another war; an insidious battle which must be fought through the spending power of the individual. Indeed, ad men themselves often referred to their own struggle to increase sales as a war; a war to be waged against a wary and tight-fisted public. Following this line of reasoning, advertisers enlisted every means available to win over that old enemy, frugality, and crush what they referred to as the "buyers' strike". In his 1933 study, 'Changing opinions about business prosperity: a consensus of magazine opinion in the U.S. 1929–32', sociologist Hart Hornell noted the prevailing sense among 'various magazines', 'that the Depression has been fundamentally a psychological problem'.[35] Cleary the advertising industries method of attack had to be psychological warfare. Pervasive and relentless, post-war advertising launched a propaganda campaign every bit as powerful and urgent as the CPI's had been during the war years.

<hr>

32 Walter Lippmann, *The phantom public* (New York, 1925), p. 155.   **33** Walter Lippmann, *Public opinion* (c.1922; New York, 1965), p. 195.   **34** Quoted in Marchand, *Advertising the American dream*, p.85. It is curious to note Benson's glaring omission of politicians from this list of social bastions who must 'fool people for their own good.'   **35** Hart Hornell, 'Changing opinions about business prosperity: a consensus of magazine opinion in the U.S. 1929–32', *American Journal of Sociology* 38 (1933), 665–87.

Intensifying everyday problems and concocting some new ones, post-war advertising increasingly relied on the tactics of the "fear appeal"; focusing its audience's attention on the innumerable pitfalls of life, it offered expert and sympathetic advice on how to avoid them. Of course, once this advice was given, there could be no excuse for not following it. After all, as a 1923 Pepsodent advertisement proclaimed, 'No excuse now for dingy film on teeth.'[36] While the areas of work, home and family featured heavily in this "scare copy" campaign, advertisements for personal grooming and intimate hygiene were among its most popular themes.

In the wake of the Great War advertisements had brought an array of new troubling hygiene issues to the attention of an unsuspecting public. According to these ads, jobs were lost, romances shattered, marriages ruined and social standing utterly destroyed by the curse of complaints such as B.O., halitosis and offensive feminine odours, while other minor physical imperfections like dandruff, stubble, scruffy nails and sloppy clothes became the cause of complete social disgrace and personal failure. New products appeared and old products, such as Listerine, reinvented themselves.[37] The reasons for this newfound obsession with apparently trivial and very private subjects in advertising are manifold, and find their origin in the trials of modern urban living. Among the more chilling expressions of the anxiety surrounding urban existence was a 1923 Lever Brothers advertisement for Lifebuoy Health Soap. It shows a throng of people on a street; men and women of different classes and different ages; some women hold babies, others toy dogs; some men sweat and take off their jackets or mop their foreheads with a handkerchief. Above this claustrophobic image are the words 'Crowds Breed Contagion'. The editorial that follows informs us that 'Human beings were meant to live in the open, guarded by the prophylactics of sunshine and pure air. There is always a danger of contagion in crowds – in factories, elevators, streetcars, theatres. [...] Things which many people touch are always dangerous – car straps, public telephones, door knobs, books, soiled money, stair rails.' Lifebuoy ads were particularly keen on stressing the dangers of modern life and how their Health Soap could protect against all manner of 'Every-day dirt danger'. Another one of their advertisements in the *Philadelphia Ledger* of April 1923 warned 'If you handle money, use Lifebuoy regularly. A soiled dollar bill under a microscope is an evil sight [...] *everyone* is exposed to the menace of dirty money'.[38]

---

36 'No excuse now for dingy film on teeth', *People's Popular Monthly*, 1923. *Ad access: John W. Harlman centre for sales*, Duke University 1999, scriptorium.lib.duke.edu/adaccess/warbonds.html#search, accessed 14 Mar. 2006.   37 These product turnarounds included the Lambert Pharmaceutical Co.'s conversion of floor disinfectant into a mouth wash and vaginal douche. See Vincent Vinikas, *Soft soap, hard sell: American hygiene in an age of advertisement* (Ames, IA, 1992).   38 'Crowds Breed Contagion', *Saturday Evening Post*, 1923; 'Every-day dirt danger – Every-day Protection', *Ladies' Home Journal*, 1926; 'If you handle money, use Lifebuoy regularly', *Philadelphia Ledger*, 1923. *Ad access: John W. Harlman centre for sales*, Duke University 1999. scriptorium.lib.duke.edu/adaccess/warbonds.html#search, accessed 14 Mar. 2006.

In the context of a fast-paced, impersonal and increasingly complex lifestyle, where danger lurked everywhere and no-one could be sure they were safe, these ads not only offered scientifically expert up-to-date advice, they often acted as both confidants and arbiters.[39] While your friends and family were either too busy or too incompetent to inform or advise you of your personal short-comings, advertisers were not. They could be frank, even hurtful in order to help you. The fact that they offered advice on subjects that most people found too embarrassing to discuss with anyone face-to-face meant they were less likely to be dismissed out-right as there was no real alternative or authoritative discourse. After all, where else could a young woman turn for '[t]he safe solution of women's greatest hygiene problem'? (Kotex Sanitary Napkins). Many ads kept the potential consumer informed of new problems: 'Do you know that women disfigure their complexions with misguided kindness?' (Ivory Soap). All promised to give invaluable counsel: 'I wish all girls knew how important this is' (Kotex Sanitary Napkins). Other advertisements posed troubling questions in an attempt to fuel their audience's underlying insecurities. In the early 1920s, for example, Palmolive beauty soap launched an all-out attack on female self-confidence, with questions like, 'Will others he meets outrival you in natural charm?' and 'Would your husband marry you again?'[40] The male consumer was not overlooked amidst this deluge of personal guidance. Williams' Shaving Cream warned 'Critical eyes are sizing you up right now – Let your face reflect confidence – not worry! It's the "look" of you by which you are judged most often', while Lifebuoy lamented 'He might have won her – if it hadn't been for B.O.'[41] Broken engagements, spousal infidelity, indeed any failure at social interaction could thus be traced to inadequate cleanliness or poor grooming.

This logic further reveals why "scare copy" was so frequently employed in the promotion of personal hygiene products. In its incommunicably vague yet intimate way, personal hygiene – or, more accurately, unease about personal hygiene – acted as catchall for any and every insecurity and concern a modern urban dweller might harbour. Foremost among these insecurities was the apparent arbitrariness and impersonal nature of many everyday interactions. With the ever-increasing pace and scale of modern living came the pressure to make a good first impression. As Roland Marchand suggests, the advertising industry was sensitive

39 See Myers, *Words in ads* & Marchand, *Advertising the American dream*. As Marchland points out, the rise of the tabloid press and its use of confessional style and exposé narratives was also influential in the increase of this intimate and revealing type of copy.   **40** 'The Safe Solution of Women's Greatest Hygienic Problem', *Saturday Evening Post*, 1927; 'Do you know that women disfigure their complexions with misguided kindness?' *New York News*, 1926; 'I wish all girls knew how important this is' *New York Sun*, 1929; 'Will others he meets outrival you in natural charm?', *Motion Picture*, 1926; 'Would your husband marry you again?', *Harper's Bazaar*, 1921. Ad access: *John W. Harlman centre for sales*, Duke University 1999. scriptorium.lib.duke.edu/adaccess/warbonds.html#search, accessed 14 Mar. 2006.   **41** 'Critical eyes are sizing you up right now', *Saturday Evening Post*, 1932; 'He might have won her – if it hadn't been for B.O.' *New York News*, 1931.

to the trials of modernity, and the fear and stress it so often provoked. Its 'parable of the First Impression', where everything was lost or gained within the first few seconds of a social encounter, was just one way of '[c]apitalising on an increasing public uncertainty that true ability and character would always win out in the scramble for success.'[42] Indeed, despite the quite obvious devastating impact of the Depression – which by 1932 had left one out of every four Americans unemployed[43] – advertisers assured their public that it was nothing other than their unkempt appearance which stopped them finding a job. Offering a palliative to the bitter hurt of impersonal judgements and the experience of inexplicable failure, advertisers explained the causes of these problems and offered a solution, all at an affordable price.

One aspect of the Depression that the ad business *did* acknowledge was the supposition that life was a highly competitive economic struggle for survival. America may have helped "Halt the Hun" but it now faced the more spectral threat of the most severe economic crisis of modern times. By 1935, official government advertising had responded to this national emergency with WPA's (Works Progress Administration – part of F.D. Roosevelt's New Deal) massive public information programme, designed to publicize health and safety programmes; cultural programmes; educational programmes and community activities. These peacetime propaganda campaigns to make healthier and happier Americans left no area of private or public living unexamined, from slum clearance and food preparation to personal hygiene and sexual activity. With rather vague connotations, numerous WPA posters promoted the concept of the individual worker and the family as an economic and biological unit whose maintenance secured national interests.

However, prior to the WPA's public information programme, commercial advertising was already advancing a connection between personal and domestic wellbeing and broader national recovery strategies. It represented the grim realities of the Depression as a challenge to be met by making the correct consumer choices, no matter how insignificant or mundane these choices appeared to be. Furthermore, using the "public advice"/propaganda model of earlier government campaigns, advertising guaranteed that it could help the consumer to make the right choices and thus 'render a valuable patriotic service', once again proving itself to be 'a forearm and standard-bearer of war for human rights.'[44] At the forefront of this battle for human rights were conglomerates like the Association of American Soap and Glycerine Producers who united to form the Cleanliness Institute in order to instruct the public on the importance of using plenty of soap.[45]

---

42 Marchand, *Advertising the American dream*, p. 210.   43 Statistics sourced at *American cultural history, 1930 – 1939*, Bettye Sutton, *Kingwood College Library* June 30, 2005. kclibrary.nhmccd.edu/decade30.html, accessed 12 Feb. 2007.   44 Thompson quoted in Marchand, *Advertising the American dream*, p. 7; D'Arcy, *The achievements of advertising in a year* (1918) quoted in Sproule, *Propaganda and democracy*, p. 17.   45 See

Just as the multifarious propaganda techniques of the Great War had inculcated individual consumer choices (regarding financial investment, the conservation of food and the maintenance of good health) into its plan to win the war,
advertisers designated their products as key to the daily battle of living, especially
in Depression-era America. With such high rates of unemployment and the
income of the average American family reduced by 40 per cent, any promise of
an advantage, no matter how small, was welcome.[46] In light of these acute circumstances, the advertising industry's use of "scare copy" during this period – with its
disproportionate comparisons and wild claims – becomes more explicable. Perhaps bad breath may cost a secretary her job or maybe the right deodorant will
help a salesman close that deal.

It is in this context that various "health" products were also advertised. With
so many people and so few jobs, ill health and ensuing sick leave were deemed
an unmitigated calamity, not only for the employer and employee but also for
the economic wellbeing of the national economy. Such absenteeism was also
inexcusable when all that was needed to ward off sickness was a specific breakfast
cereal or iron tonic.[47] In these scenarios of the competitive struggle for survival
children were not forgotten. A child's skinny appearance and lack of good grades
at school could be traced to a parent's negligence in providing the right vitamin-
enriched malt drink.[48] These ads marvelled at the parent who could allow such a
state of affairs to continue. 'Whose fault when children are so frail?' asked one
ad, the answer was obvious, especially when it was 'so easy now to put on weight'
with Cocomalt.[49] These advertisements, like the ones promoting personal
hygiene products, encouraged their audience to see themselves through other
people's eyes; to be acutely aware of how one would be judged by others – be
they loved ones, acquaintances or strangers. This was a sales tactic that relied, and
built, upon the consumer's susceptibility to fears of social humiliation. While
sympathizing with the victim of pitiless harsh social judgements, the advertiser
nonetheless acknowledges their justice and validity. Emphasising public censure
over personal desires, these ads employed a combination of the fear appeal –
'redirect[ing] attention away form the merits of a particular proposal and toward
steps that can be taken to reduce the fear'- and the guilt factor – '[w]hen we feel
guilty we typically pay little attention to the cogency of an argument, to the
merits of a suggested course of action'.[50]

Vinikas, *Soft soap, hard sell: American hygiene in an age of advertisement.* **46** *American cultural history, 1930
– 1939.* kclibrary.nhmccd.edu/decade30.html, accessed 12 Feb. 2007.   **47** While car manufacturers were
discovering the marketing ploy of built-in obsolescence, promoters of health and hygiene products realized
that the human body itself could be represented as constantly on the brink of obsolescence and thus in regular need of tuning and repair.   **48** See Marchand, *Advertising the American dream,* pp 296–9.   **49** 'Whose
fault when children are so frail?', *Ladies' Home Journal,* 1931.   **50** Delwiche, 'Common techniques: special
appeals', *Propaganda critic* 29 Sept. 2002. www.propagandacritic.com/articles/ct.sa.fear.html, accessed 25
Apr. 2006; Pratkanis & Aronson, *Age of propaganda* p. 229.

With an almost identical rhetoric to the accusatory and shaming appeals of the war era, ad copy placed the individual within an ever-widening circle of judgement, which could only be escaped by following a directed course of action. Of course, while the CPI's suggested course of action was enlistment and financial investment in war bonds, the advertiser's was the purchase and use of such life-saving products as shaving cream, soap and mouth-wash. The tremendous impact of these advertisements lies in their ability to address all manner of fears, and to offer easily indefinable reasons for failure as well as a positive and, most important of all, an easy course of action to remedy the situation.

In a study of propaganda techniques from 1991, Pratkanis and Aronson argue that, 'All other things being equal, the more frightened a person is by a communication the more likely he or she is to take positive preventive action.'[51] Yet, any imperative to act in the face of fear is more likely to succeed if an effective and reasonable solution is offered: in the proffering of their assorted products, this is precisely what advertising companies themselves did. However, if the advertising world of this era did offer a valuable public service, it was in their capacity to express and give a name to indefinable fears; vague feelings of personal and social inadequacy. It remains highly debatable whether they in fact contributed to their intensification.

51 Pratkanis & Aronson, *Age of propaganda*, p. 210.

'Chaos. Bloody fucking chaos.'
GB84 and counter-insurgency

DEAGLÁN Ó DONGHAILE

As Declan Kiberd suggested in the 1980s, Ireland occupied a special place in the British imperial imagination. In his essay 'Anglo-Irish attitudes', Kiberd maintained that little had changed in over eight hundred years of colonial occupation because the colonial mentality that viewed the Irish as experimental guinea-pigs had not been erased: 'The laboratory-theory is alive and well, and beginning to trouble the English left-wing.'[1] This view of events in the north of Ireland was endorsed by British socialists who, during the same decade, viewed the conflict in Ireland as 'an extremely relevant question' for those concerned with British domestic politics, and even spoke of the Irish troubles as a 'time-bomb' ready to explode in the face of British democracy.[2] In 1984 Tariq Ali pointed to the possibility of counter-insurgency practice, with its legacy of corruption and anti-democratic leanings, making its way back to the imperial centre, and Ken Livingstone concurred: 'Our army and police have undoubtedly been "politicized".' Livingstone pointed to the militarization of British society which, as he saw it, had become characterized by an increasingly paranoid state given to the 'use of arms, more modernized riot-control, more public surveillance.'[3] With these views in mind, it is worth considering David Peace's novel of recent history, *GB84* (2004),[4] in which the hard-fought coalminers' strike of 1984–5 is viewed in the light of this reversed colonial practice, as a reflection on the manner in which 'metropolitan power [...] has invariably become more corrupted by the [imperial] experience.'[5] Through the fictional hindsight of this novel the class warfare that erupted between striking miners and the British Conservative government takes on the dimensions of an undeclared 'civil war'.[6] But a central concern of the novel, which underlines Peace's vision of Britain as a state that is at war with itself, is his con-

1 Declan Kiberd, 'Anglo-Irish attitudes', *Ireland's field day* (London, 1985), p. 103. 2 Ali Tariq & Ken Livingstone, *Who's afraid of Margaret Thatcher? Tariq Ali in conversation with Ken Livingstone* (London, 1984), p. 9. 3 Ibid., p. 61. 4 David Peace, *GB84* (London, 2004). 5 Ibid., p. 60. 6 Ibid., p. 202.

sistent acknowledgement that the methods by which the new 'civil war'[7] is being fought were perfected in Ireland during the 1970s. By making constant references to colonial counter-insurgency practice, Peace suggests that Britain's latest, internal war will be conducted by the state with irregular but distinctly political methods. As the government eavesdropper, Malcolm Morris, hears a target announce on one of his surveillance tapes, 'We are going down the royal road in this country that Northern Ireland went down in 1969'.[8]

British counter-insurgency practice was developed in the decades following World War II, when, as the British General and Chief of the General Staff in 1970, Sir Michael Carver put it, the British army found itself fighting an 'unfamiliar type of warfare' against 'terrorists'.[9] The British responded to this kind of unorthodox combat with an 'official army doctrine' which was outlined by Brigadier Frank Kitson in his famous counter-insurgency manual, *Low intensity operations*, first published in 1971. While Kitson had first-hand experience of this kind of fighting, to which 'the intimate integration of intelligence and operations' is vital, he argued in the later 1991 edition of the book that the unique experience of the British army in Ireland during the 1970s suggested that low intensity operations could be developed further for domestic use. 'It could be argued', he wrote, 'that the circumstances of the campaign in Northern Ireland point to the need for counter-insurgency to be carried out in a more defensive way' and that its lessons would be learned not just by soldiers, but also 'by those other groups of people, such as politicians, civil servants, and policemen, whose understanding of the problems is as important as that of the soldiers themselves'.[10]

Kitson cited thirty-two instances of the British army 'countering subversion or insurgency' in the period between 1945 and 1970. The most notorious of these conflicts occurred in Kenya (which was turned into an open-air concentration camp, processing hundreds of thousands of men and women),[11] Malaya and Cyprus. Kitson served in each of these theatres of action, and as the historian Caroline Elkins has pointed out, counter-insurgency policies targeting entire populations in each conflict were developed from practices perfected in earlier conflicts. Thus 'hearts and minds precedents' such as mass internment were set in Malaya, transplanted into Kenya.[12] As David Peace acknowledges in *GB84*, these oppressive practices were refined even further in Ireland during the 1970s, where, as Kitson admitted, useful lessons were learned about the possibility of putting counter-insurgency measures into effect in England. *GB84* may be a novel about the 1984 miners' strike but its discussion of this conflict suggests that there were specifically colonial ramifications for the domestic class struggle that erupted in Britain during the mid-1980s.

7 Ibid., p. 202. 8 Ibid., p. 140. 9 Michael Carver, 1970 foreword, in Frank Kitson, *Low intensity operations* (London, 1991), xv. 10 Ibid., xv. 11 See Caroline Elkins, *Britain's gulag: the brutal end of Empire in Kenya* (London, 2005). 12 Ibid. p. 101.

Frank Kitson and Low intensity operations

In *GB84* the Tory government and the conservative press treat the miners' strike as if it was a seditious war against the state, with newspapers defining the strike as a subversive attack on the state: 'There was a war on, declared *The Times*.'[13] Peace draws heavily on the counter-insurgency theories of Frank Kitson, who outlined a revolutionary strategy for combating subversion both in colonial and domestic scenarios in his 1971 book, *Low intensity operations*, a manual designed to instruct soldiers in 'the importance of handling the population.'[14] Kitson's book was influential in the field of counter-insurgency, first appearing in 1971 and then going through a further three reprints within four years. It was reissued in January 1991 on the eve of an expected, but ultimately unrealized, invasion of Iraq. A brigadier in the British army, Kitson outlined a series of finely-tuned methods by which left-wing and anti-colonial movements could be contained. Modelled on his experiences of counter-insurgency in Oman, Malaya and Ireland – but with particular emphasis on his colonial expertise in Kenya[15] – *Low intensity operations* presents an outline for action by the military against civilian populations (Kitson also points to Nazi counter-subversion activity, which was carried out in occupied European countries during the Second World War, as a model for his techniques). Most significantly, the book argues for the co-option of civil administration and for the adoption of policing duties by the British army in times of emergency. As Kitson pointed out, this framework, involving 'various political, economic and psychological aspects of a government's programme' was not exclusively reserved for dealing with anti-colonial revolt, but could also be applied 'during a prolonged period of strikes and civil disturbance' and to this end he proposed a 'whole national programme of civil military action'.[16] As Kitson reminded his readers, the book was originally published when 'the British army was struggling to adapt ideas gained in the colonies to the circumstances prevailing in part of the United Kingdom, i.e. Northern Ireland'.[17]

Clearly, these methods were not designed exclusively for colonial applications since they also could be adapted for quelling domestic dissent as subversion could include 'the use of political and economic pressure' such as 'strikes' and 'protest marches'.[18] Kitson was himself in command of 39th Brigade in Belfast in 1972 when one of his battalions, the First Battalion of the Parachute Regiment, was transferred to Derry. There, on 30 January, his troops opened fire on an anti-internment demonstration, killing fourteen civilians taking part in 'the illegal march' (in *Low intensity operations* even non-violent protest is described as a form of subversive warfare).[19]

---

13 Peace, *GB84*, p. 177. 14 Kitson, *Low intensity operations*, p. 143. 15 See Kitson, *Low intensity operations* pp 122–6. 16 Ibid., pp 93, 97. 17 Ibid., preface, xiii, x. 18 Ibid., p. 3. 19 Frank Kitson, Statement CK1

Pointing to Mao Tse Tung's famous dictum that the revolutionary can be compared to a fish, and the civilian population to the water in which the fish must swim, Kitson proposed a strategy for 'polluting the water'. In order to do so, military operations must be 'tied in with wider administrative measures' in order to allow the government to 'gain control of the population' by means of an interlocking system of actions, political, economic, psychological and military'. These interdependent measures, he argued, could be based on 'the Committee System', modelled on the County Security Committees that were established in the six northern Irish counties after the defeat of the Royal Ulster Constabulary and the auxiliary 'Special Constabulary', the B-Specials in the Battle of the Bogside in Derry in August 1969 by a mass uprising in the city.[20] This system allowed for the military to advise the police on an area-by-area basis and could 'co-opt members representing other interests', although Kitson does not define which interests these might be. On a local level this system allows for the overlapping of 'police, administrative and military boundaries' creating, in effect, a militarized state run by a 'supreme body' of 'machinery at the top':

> This supreme body should consist of the head of the government together with the individuals controlling the most important departments of state, such as Finance, Home Affairs and Defence. It must be advised by the representatives of other relevant agencies such as those dealing with intelligence and propaganda.[21]

In this way the military will assume an explicitly political role, instructing on 'civil as well as military methods' and, given the nature of the army's secretive command machinery, Kitson predicted that there would be little protest: 'There is no danger of political repercussions to this course of action, because consultation can be carried out in strictest secrecy.'[22] The British Left cited the return of Sir Kenneth Newman to England from his role as Chief Constable of the RUC as an indication of the politicization and militarization of domestic policing.[23] Designed to prepare the British army for situations of subversion and insurgency in which 'all parts of the government machinery combine together in pursuit of the objective', such a strategy even allowed the army to 'direct the activities' of the police.[24]

While Frank Kitson's theories on counter-insurgency have been acknowledged as fundamental for colonial occupation, less attention has been paid to the application of his model to domestic scenarios. Kitson himself acknowledged that the British army's experience in Ireland would be central to counter-insurgency theory

to the Bloody Sunday inquiry, 18 Feb. 2000, pp 1–2. Kitson's statements to the inquiry can be accessed at www.bloody-sunday-inquiry.org.uk/index2.asp?p=6, accessed 20 Feb. 2007; Kitson, *Low intensity operations*, p. 91. **20** Kitson, *Low intensity operations*, pp 49, 5, 63. **21** Ibid., pp 55–7. **22** Ibid., p. 68. **23** Livingstone, *Who's afraid of Margaret Thatcher?*, p. 89. **24** Kitson, *Low intensity operations*, pp 7, 166.

and he suggested that the lessons learned there might have to be applied in Britain: 'one commitment will inevitably remain which is the obligation for maintaining law and order within the United Kingdom. Recent events in Northern Ireland serve as a timely reminder that this can not be taken for granted.' Pointing out that 'the regular army was first raised in the seventeenth century' for '"Suppression of the Irish"', Kitson viewed 'the present emergency' as a possible model for dealing with 'other potential trouble spots within the United Kingdom.'[25] While it might bother the British, 'with their traditions of stability to imagine disorders arising beyond the powers of the police to handle', he suggested that this might be inevitable, despite the 'unrivalled affluence' of the 1970s:

> If a genuine and serious grievance arose, such as might result from a significant drop in the standard of living, all those who now dissipate their protest over a wide variety of causes might concentrate their efforts and produce a situation which was beyond the power of the police to handle. Should this happen the army would be required to restore the position rapidly. Fumbling at this juncture might have grave consequences even to the extent of undermining confidence in the whole system of government.[26]

In this modern time of emergency the army, Kitson argued, should also serve a policing role. *Low intensity operations* describes how 'Psychological Operations', or 'PSYOPS', is central to this function of the modern army. Kitson described how this specialized field of counter-insurgency should be carried out by highly trained units adapted to detect opposition, disseminate propaganda and neutralize opposition; their role above all, he maintained, is to have an impact on 'the minds of the people'. Therefore as part of 'the process of counter organization', PSYOPS allows a government to 'build up its control of the population' and acquire 'tight control over the people'. Central to PSYOPS is the employment of unofficial squads, or 'pseudo-gangs', against political opponents of the state. This 'Special Operation' technique was perfected by the Nazis in occupied Europe, where it provided a most elaborate means of countering subversion by sowing fear among partisans (Kitson cites Nazi efforts against entire populations as being illustrative of large-scale counter-insurgency). Kitson built upon this strategy, viewing the activation of these gangs in British colonial territories as part of a wider policy involving the use of Psychological Operations. For Kitson, psychological warfare is essential as it provides soldiers with the means to 'influence the thoughts and actions of other men'; this was deemed necessary in 1970 when his book first appeared because, as Kitson saw it, this moment in history was characterized by 'the changing attitude of people towards authority' (he cites the spread of literacy

25 Ibid., p. 24.   26 Ibid., p. 25.

and the rise of mass communications as being responsible for this decline in political deference).[27]

Counter-insurgency and fiction

The idea that postmodern Britain is enduring serious and prolonged colonial recoil runs throughout David Peace's fiction, particularly his earlier cycle of historical crime novels, the *Red riding quartet*. In each of these *noir* pieces – *Nineteen seventy four* (1999), *Nineteen seventy seven* (2000), *Nineteen eighty* (2001) and *Nineteen eighty three* (2002) – Britain is haunted by spectres from the British military who have crossed over to England from the Irish troubles. These are the returned soldiers and special operatives who have been blooded in Ulster and are ready to carry out further atrocities in England. In the opening novel of the quartet, *Nineteen seventy four*, Peace introduces a particularly politicized version of *crime noir*, offering a hellish vision of modern Britain in which colonial counter-insurgency practice has come home to roost. Here, Yorkshire's corrupt police force is supported by unofficial paramilitary muscle, the "death squads" who operate against the background of the IRA's 1974 Christmas bombing campaign. Eddie Dunford, a reporter investigating the disappearances of several children, is warned about the deadly underside of Britain's secret political culture by his colleague, Barry Gannon: 'You think that shit is just for the Yellow Man or the Indian? There are death squads in every city, every country [...] they train them in Northern Ireland. Give them a taste, then bring them back home hungry.'[28] Later in the novel, Gannon's conspiracy theory is confirmed by his own unexplained death in a car crash

When Dunford meets the Yorkshire crime boss, Derek Box, while investigating the disappearances, the godfather repeats Gannon's bleak description of Britain being at war with itself: 'This country's at war, Mr Dunford, the government and the unions, the Left and the Right, the rich and the poor. Then you got your Paddys, your wogs, your niggers, the puffs and perverts, even the bloody women; they're all out for what they can get.'[29] A pornographer and blackmailer, Box described how he was apprenticed on 'Her Majesty's business [...] fighting the fucking Mau Maus' in Kenya. He tells the reporter that little has changed since the Kenyan crisis: 'It was war, Mr Dunford, just like now.'[30] As Peace suggests later in *GB84*, the colonial unease that saturates his Quartet also characterizes official consciousness: '*It was the State of Britain, 1974. It was a State of Emergency.*'[31] Along with *GB84*, the rest of the *Red riding quartet* shows that this

27 Ibid., pp 78, 80, 100–1, 188, 15. 28 David Peace, *Nineteen seventy four* (London, 1999), p. 59. 29 Ibid., p. 186. 30 Ibid., p. 211. 31 Peace, *GB84*, p. 409.

domestic 'Emergency' is a permanent one. When Dunford finally discovers that Box has been running a child pornography ring along with the local Detective Chief Superintendent, Maurice Jobson, whose goal is to run 'controlled vice' in the north-east of England, he kills the criminal in a shoot-out and injures two policemen who have been protecting him. The attack is covered up by Jobson's force and an official police statement describes the killing as the work of 'armed Irish Republican terrorists'.[32]

Peace's quartet is infested by images of the war in Ireland, 'pictures of Ulster' saturating the television news.[33] In his second novel, *Nineteen seventy seven*, the paramilitary death squads that are at large in Leeds are described as 'The Special Police' and, as a caller to a radio chat show complains, they are enjoying a free-for-all on the streets of Leeds, where 'There's no bloody law for them, that's trouble.'[34] Peace's critique of the emerging police state continues in *Nineteen eighty*, in which the indiscriminate use of surveillance technologies such as the police super-computer is publicized as part of an effort to reassure the public during the investigation into the Yorkshire Ripper who, it is suspected, has served in the military in Ireland. For Peter Hunter, Assistant Commissioner of the Greater Manchester Police, the rise of the surveillant state, along with the political crisis that forms the backdrop to the Ripper investigation, amounts to an endless dialectic of conflict: 'Death and paranoia – Murder and lies, lies and Murder – A total war.'[35]

Peace's next novel, *Nineteen eighty three*, anticipates the class conflict of *GB84*. In this, the concluding piece in the quartet, the north of England is saturated by Tory propaganda and, as Peace's dubious hero, the solicitor Big John Piggott complains, all that can be heard on the radio are chants of 'Thatcher, Thatcher, Thatcher'. Meanwhile, the Irish troubles continue apace, with the IRA plotting assassinations and carrying out bombings, the Prime Minister even being letter-bombed by Irish republicans. The overarching presence of Irish republican activity is described alongside a sense that class conflict is about to impact upon Britain. A sense of looming chaos pervades this novel, with reports of the right-wing League of St George having infiltrated the Tory party and 'Everyone talking Northern bloody Ireland.'[36] Presenting a world of dissimulation and the ongoing emergence of a police state, the novels of the *Red riding quartet* should be considered as a companion project to *GB84*. These fictions construct an image of oncoming, irreversible political disaster emerging out of the vortex of the war in Ireland and waiting for the opportunity to impose itself upon England. The class conflict that erupts in *GB84* occurs after the crescendo of horror outlined in the quartet. And as Peace reminds his readers, much of this horror has a colonial origin.

32 David Peace, *Nineteen eighty three* (London, 2002), pp 54, 227.   33 David Peace, *Nineteen seventy seven* (London, 2000), p. 100.   34 Ibid., pp 47, 250.   35 David Peace, *Nineteen eighty* (London, 2001), pp 81, 256. 36 Peace, *Nineteen eighty three*, pp 128, 145, 185, 161, 177.

Peace's fictional northern England has much in common with the colonial laboratory that is Northern Ireland. This secret history is brought to the fore of *GB84*, in which England is militarized and armed police 'stand on every corner'.[37] In *GB84* striking miners are fought by the state on every level, from pressure applied by the prospect of having their homes repossessed, to the employment of riot police, to the activation of unofficial squads of paramilitary strike breakers. The miners in Peace's novel are not like the destitute workers in Émile Zola's *Germinal* (1885), who are 'dying of starvation' in the Montsou coalmines, under a 'horizon of poverty hemming them in like a tomb.'[38] Benefactors of the affluence described by Kitson and enjoyed by British society during the 1970s, Peace's miners are used to a high standard of living, to having holidays, and to improving their privately owned homes. Many of them have signed up to capitalism, owing much through 'Debts [...] Hire Purchase. Mortgage.' One of Peace's narrators, the striking miner, Martin Daly, reflects on the possibility of this material loss after having an argument with his wife over the hopelessness of the struggle: 'I go out into back garden. I stand in rain where conservatory was going to be.'[39] The miners' dependency on these luxuries is used by the government and police to exert pressure on the strike, allowing the Tory establishment to use the miners' own sense of their place within the class system – as a privileged elite at the higher end of the working class – as a weapon against them.

But as well as being fought on a material level, the class conflict is also a physical 'war', into which unofficial counter-insurgency units are inserted by the army and police. Peace focuses on one of these groups, led by David Johnson, 'The Mechanic', an ex-soldier and former mercenary who, following stints in Ulster and Rhodesia specializes in armed robbery. Given to extreme violence, Johnson is recruited for 'his talents'. A protégé of Kitson – he is described as 'One of Frank's Boys in Ulster' – he is recruited because he is one of a select few 'who have seen slaughter. Felt fear. Tasted terror.' Retrained for domestic deployment by men with 'Warminster and Sandhurst accents', he is left in charge of a gang of thieves and rapists discharged from the Army of the Rhine. Trained and 'Hard wired', fed drugs and emerging onto England 'Black from hell', these squads are prepared by the authorities for a series of ruthless confrontations with the unsuspecting strikers. Unlike the cold-blooded mercenaries who have killed before in Ireland and Rhodesia, the miners are 'soft', even innocent, and unprepared for conflict. Encouraged by the police and let loose with his men in an unrestricted, ultra-violent free-for-all, Johnson is allowed to 'disappear' into the chaos to disrupt pickets by ambushing them in pubs, on their way home from meetings and at protests. The presence of 'special squads' is announced by the Home Secretary[40] and para-

---

37 Peace, *GB84*, p. 119.   38 Émile Zola, *Germinal*, trans. Leonard Tancock (London, 1954), p. 183.   39 Peace, *GB84*, pp 182, 50, 60.   40 Ibid., pp 113, 15, 262, 79, 92, 113, 97.

noid discussion among the miners reveals that Kitson's Psychological Operations have taken hold in England:

> Talk is all of gangs and squads – Hit squads. Super squads. Scab squads. Intercept-or squads – Lads getting hidings from gangs of off-duty coppers – Squaddie gangs [...] Taken anyone in town centre after dark – Beaten fuck out of them. Nicked them.[41]

Johnson's unit has been recruited to enact the final, most violent stages of Operation Vengeance, a policy that has been 'Imported from Ulster' but 'Updated for Yorkshire'.[42] While these squads are almost invisible in Peace's earlier novels, theirs is a central presence in *GB84*. The operation is a domestic manifestation of Frank Kitson's strategy of using PSYOPS against a domestic civilian population.

Due in part to Britain's guilty presence in Ireland, political terror forms part of the fabric of modern British life in *GB84*. Having caused havoc on northern Irish streets, Johnson's units are allowed to run rampage across the northern English landscape. Enraged, the fictional striker, Martin Daly describes the atmosphere of civil war that erupts with police charges on pickets at Orgreave and Cortonwood: 'Hidings on both sides – Snatch squads taking as many prisoners as they can – Taking them hard – By their hair. By their throats. By their balls – Chaos. Bloody fucking chaos'. Charges are made by mounted police, 'Six at a time. Visors down. Batons swinging – Kill you if they could – And they could. They fucking could':

> Split heads. Cracked ribs. Broken limbs. Bloody – Mates nicked. Beaten. Lost. Everyone fucking angry. Fucking furious. Things bastards have done to them. Completely unprovoked. Lads you've never met before telling you to get back down there. Give them what they're fucking asking for. Fucking hiding they've got coming – To pick up bricks. Fence poles. Milk bottles.[43]

The Tory fantasy of unrestricted class warfare pleases Margaret Thatcher's advisor, Stephen Sweet, who tells an exclusive audience at his suite in Claridge's Hotel that this domestic war is unlike any recent colonial struggle: 'at the time of the Falklands conflict, we had to fight an enemy without [...] but the enemy within, much more difficult to fight, is just as dangerous to liberty.' A character based on the multi-millionaire property developer and advisor to the National Coal Board, David Hart, Sweet funds and advises working miners from the hotel, advises Thatcher and attends meetings of the 'Total War Cabinet'. The civil war being fought by Sweet's

41 Ibid., p. 82.   42 Ibid., p. 129.   43 Ibid., pp 100, 110.

auxiliaries, the 'true-blue secret cells' of strike breakers, softens the miners for the climactic police attack on pickets at Orgreave. This decisive and spectacular display of state violence, in which mounted police, dogs and foot units were used, which became known as 'The Battle of Orgreave', occurred on 18 June 1984 when masses of police described by left-wing commentators as resembling 'a conquering army',[44] defeated pickets. In *GB84*, Daly looks on as the police are met by militants, 'lads wanting to get on with it. Lads on about making petrol bombs' and because the police are armed the confrontation assumes potentially deadly proportions: 'Police had got guns, they said. Back of them vans. Be tear gas out next, they said. Rubber bullets. Paras – *Bloody Monday*, that's what this is. Bloody Monday.'[45] The struggle between the coalminers and the state is also fought out against the immediate back-drop of the war in Ireland, which spills into Britain with the threat of demonstrators being gunned down, the actual detonation of the Brighton Bomb during the Tory party conference on 12 October 1984 and against the longer perspective of Frank Kitson's counter-insurgency theory.

Operation Vengeance

While Johnson and his men terrorize the pickets, the war also continues more discreetly. Operation Vengeance is an all-encompassing repressive measure initiated to protect Thatcher's state at any cost. Its means of surveillance are unlimited: intelligence is gleaned using voice-activated phone taps, DHSS and Inland Revenue details and personal bank accounts. As the electronic eavesdropper for the government, Malcolm Morris, acknowledges to himself, this activity is dedicated to 'the collection of words' and to the very appropriation of language by the state, an entire overlapping network of repressive means. After being trained at the Joint Services Intelligence Centre in Ashford, Kent, 'for the collection of words',[46] Morris is sent to the British army HQ at Lisburn where, during the Ulster Worker's Council strike of May 1974, he invents a new sonic eavesdropping system:

> The telephone intercept system known as Pusher (Programmable Ultra and Super-High-Frequency Reception) was failing to provide the necessary information as key figures rightly assumed their phones were being tapped and so spoke only in codes in the privacy of their own guarded homes. Malcolm Gordon Morris, government fairy, the original Tinkerbell, then just thirty, bounced microwaves off the windows of their offices and their homes to monitor the vibrations of the glass in order to reproduce and record the conversations taking place within.[47]

44 Alex Callinicos & Mike Simons, *The great strike: the miners' strike of 1984–5 and it lessons* (London, 1985), p. 170. **45** Peace, *GB84*, pp 169–70, 220, 153, 143. **46** Ibid., pp 128, 127. **47** Ibid., p.179.

Morris resumes this work in England, where he turns his attention to more domestic targets:

> *The names and the places, the tapes and the reels recording it all – Every single resonance and reverberation of every single sound in every single room on every single floor of every single building the Union used –*
> St. James's House. The University. The Royal Victoria. Hallam Towers –
>
> > *To be numbered, dated and copied. Transcribed and collated. Analysed, interpreted and debated –*
> > *In pitch. In tone. In note –*
> > *This beautiful, ugly noise. This heathen cathedral of sound –*
> > *Renovated and repainted for Yorkshire, but conceived and borne of Ulster.*[48]

As one of the miners warns his colleagues, these processes of total surveillance can invade one's very consciousness: 'These are dangerous times [...] Be careful what you say. Be careful what you think.' Another senses the parallel with government activity in Ireland when he starts to receive silent telephone calls at night: 'That's what they do with IRA in Northern Ireland. To keep tabs on them. If they don't see a face about for a bit, they know something's up. Big job coming.' When the miners realize that during the Orgreave clash the police lines have been reinforced by reserves from the British army they see the operation as forming a sequel counter-insurgency in Ulster, providing 'Light relief after Northern Ireland'.[49]

The comparison is not lost on the Right. The Tory MP Eldon Griffiths calls for the imposition of martial law and demands that the police be allowed to fire plastic bullets at pickets, while Dennis Thatcher shouts 'we should intern the lot of them [...] Intern the bloody miners!' The rantings of the Thatcherites remind Sweet's chauffeur and former special forces operative, Neil Fontaine, of the internment camp at Long Kesh, near Lisburn in County Antrim where thousands were held without charge or trial, from 1971–5, under armed military guard. The Tories' demands for mass incarceration call back images of 'Rows and rows of Nissen huts. Rolls and rolls of barbed wire'. The imagery of occupation is not lost on the miners either, as Martin Daly watches the police sealing Thurcroft Colliery: 'I see them. Hundreds of them. Hundreds of bastards – Fucking army of occupation, that's what they are'.[50]

In the overlap of colonial counter-insurgency practice with domestic political conflict, Malcolm Morris finds himself being worn down and his grasp of reality slipping away as his involvement in the class struggle causes the meanings of sounds and voices on his surveillance tapes to disintegrate: 'Everything blurred.

48 Ibid., pp 178–9.   49 Ibid., pp 182, 176, 158.   50 Ibid., pp 248–9, 256.

Everything merged. Distorted and faded.' As normal British domestic reality is undermined and replaced by an atmosphere more akin to a colonial emergency, it seems to him as if the Red Hand, the symbol of Ulster, has Britain in its hold. The Red Hand is the 'fist that held and gripped'; as both Ali and Livingstone asserted in 1985, Ulster exerts a powerful and relentless hold on the British imagination. That hold is so powerful for Peace that it has 'squeezed and crushed' both British democracy and civil rights. Colonial counter-insurgency has come home to roost in *GB84* through the actions of the state and its agents who defeat the miners comprehensively with their Kitsonesque strategies of psychological terror and surveillance. As Martin Daly points out, the state defeats the miners through the application of sheer brutality, leaving them shattered as a political force: 'Lifted. Threatened. Beaten. Hospitalized. Broke in every fucking sense.'[51]

Peace is relentless in pointing to the origins of this strategy. As if to underline this, Morris remembers his time spent carrying out surveillance in Ireland with a list:

> In Lisburn, Ulster –
> *From there everything whispered. Everything echoed. Everything moaned.*
> *These voices from these shadows, these silences and spaces, these truths and*
> *lies* [...] *A deafening deafening wall of horrible, horrible sounds –*
> *MI5, MI6, Special Branch. The RUC. The army and the SAS –*
> *Until everything became one long, long scream –*
> *One long, long scream of places and names, terror and trachery –*
> Derry. The Bogside. Belfast. The Lower Falls. The Shankill Road. Chichester-Clark. Faulkner. Stormont. McGurk's Bar. Bloody Sunday. Widgery. Bloody Friday. Direct Rule. Operation Motorman. Sunningdale. The Ulster Workers' Council. Dublin. Monaghan. Guidford. Birmingham. The Miami Showband. Tullyvallen Orange Hall. Whitecross. Kingsmills. Mrs Marie Drumm. Captain Robert Nairac. The Ulster Unionist Action Council. La Mon Hotel. The Irish National Liberation Army –
> *Directed or undirected, formal or casual, acknowledged or not –*
> *Sources and agencies; agents and informants; information and disinforma-*
> *tion –*
> *Codes changed. Numbers changed. Names changed. Places changed –*
> *Tapes changed, but the job stayed the same –*
> Home or away. Near or far. England or Rhodesia. Yorkshire or Ulster
> –
> *The job stayed the same.*[52]

51 Ibid., pp 416, 110.   52 Ibid., pp 416–17.

The list is a barrage of atrocities, injustices, places, organizations and political players – all rolled into one mass under the omniscient eye of the British state which, in *GB84*, turns its attentions towards a dissident domestic population that becomes aware of the implications of these horrors. As Frank Kitson argued in *Low intensity operations*, 'it is in men's minds that wars of subversion have to be fought and decided.' In *GB84* the state has adopted and applied Frank Kitson's exhaustive apparatus of repression, to the extent that Martin Daly and the rest of the miners can no longer distinguish between Yorkshire and Derry: 'Like something you saw on news from Northern Ireland. From Bogside – Never thought I'd live to see anything like it here. Not here in England. Not in South Yorkshire.'[53] Emerging out of the conspiratorial Britain described in the *Red riding quartet*, *GB84* presents an official plot for widespread oppression that drew on the experience of British counter-insurgency in the north-east of Ireland. The methods and tactics used by the state have been perfected on the streets of Derry and Belfast. In *Nineteen eighty three*, the final novel of Peace's *Red riding quartet*, the solicitor John Pigott reflects on how 'the lies survived, those accepted little lies we called history […] They survived us all.'[54] Considered collectively, Peace's novels amount to an attempt to salvage truth from the wreckage of history. British history, but particularly English history, is read as a nightmare from which Peace's characters will never awake.

53 Ibid., pp 31, 322.   54 Peace, *Nineteen eighty three*, p. 38.

'Is this art or assault?' The politics of fear and the ethics of representing 9/11

JOHN-PAUL COLGAN

We ask every American to use the 'Heroes of 2001' stamp on every letter and package they send. Because by doing this, we are sending a message to our friends and a stark reminder to our enemies: We are Americans. We do not shirk our duty. We do not flee from danger. And we do not forget our heroes.[1] (Statement made by John E. Potter, US Postmaster General, at the dedication ceremony for a 9/11 commemorative stamp in June 2002)

In September 2002 – around the time of the first anniversary of the terrorist attacks on the World Trade Center – a bronze sculpture entitled *Tumbling Woman* was unveiled at New York's Rockefeller Center where it was scheduled to remain on display for a two-week period. This piece, by the American artist Eric Fischl, depicted a human shape contorted by motion and apparently falling headlong; its clasped legs perpendicular to its inverted torso. It was accompanied by a short poem that read, in part: 'We watched / disbelieving and helpless / on that savage day / People we love / began falling / helpless and in disbelief.' A few days later, an article entitled 'Shameful art attack' appeared in the *New York Post* (18 Sept. 2002). Written by columnist Andrea Peyser, this piece – the very title of which appears to imply some sort of equivalence between Fischl's sculpture and the events to which it was intended as a response – began by asking, 'Is this art? Or assault?' Peyser goes on to describe *Tumbling Woman* as a 'violently disturbing sculpture' and accuses Fischl of exploiting the tragedy for his own ends and of showing a callous disregard for the feelings of victims' families. The accompanying poem is cursorily dismissed as 'moronic'. Bemoaning the prominent position of the sculpture on the Rockefeller Center's busy lower concourse, Peyser also claimed that, 'The worst part about the piece is that you can't miss it. Even if you

1 'New fundraising stamp honoring heroes of 9/11 issued today in New York City', *Philatelic News* 7 June 2002. www.usps.com/news/2002/philatelic/sr02%5F029.htm, accessed 24 Mar. 2006.

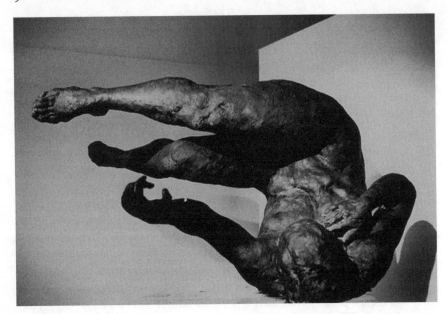

Eric Fischl, *Tumbling Woman* (2002). Photograph copyright Ralph Gibson.

try.'[2] Soon, however, it became possible to avoid the piece without even trying as – following a number of complaints, many of them directly influenced by Peyser's article – *Tumbling Woman* was first hidden from view behind a screen and then permanently removed from display eight days after it was first unveiled.

A statement released by Fischl in response to the removal of his work explained that, 'The sculpture was not meant to hurt anybody. It was a sincere expression of deepest sympathy for the vulnerability of the human condition.'[3] Rockefeller Center landlord Jerry Speyer, himself a renowned collector of contemporary art, defended the decision to display the sculpture in the following terms: 'For centuries, the horrors of war have been sculpted by artists so that people would never forget. That was the intent of this sculpture, and that has been overlooked and misinterpreted.'[4] Writing in the *New York Daily News*, art critic Nick Monteleone also sought to position Fischl's work within a wider artistic tradition. He argued that, 'Artists have, throughout time, shocked and disturbed us into recognizing the world's horrors. Fischl has simply served the traditional function of the artist as social commentator and historical interpreter, but we have asked that

2 Andrea Peyser, 'Shameful art attack', *New York Post*, 18 Sept. 2002. newsmine.org/archive/9–11/tumbling-woman-art.txt, accessed 20 Mar. 2006.   **3** 'Sept. 11 sculpture covered up', *CBS News Website*, 19 Sept. 2002. www.cbsnews.com/stories/2002/09/19/national/main522528.shtml, accessed 15 Mar. 2006.   **4** Quoted in '9/11 bronze brouhaha' by David Ebony, *Art in America*, Nov. 2002. www.findarticles.com/p/articles/mi_m1248/is_11_90/ai_94079478, accessed 15 Mar. 2006.

his voice be turned down.' Monteleone's defence of Fischl concludes by demanding, 'Would we ask Goya to lighten the reds of his Spanish battlefields?'[5]

The controversy that greeted Fischl's *Tumbling Woman* is intensely instructive in that around it seem to crystallize many of the most pertinent issues surrounding the attempts made so far at representing the September 11 terrorist attacks, the response to these attempts and the ways in which both are impacted upon by what we might call "the politics of fear". These issues include whether or not it is appropriate for artists to tackle an event of such personal and national trauma, especially so close both temporally and geographically to the event itself; how and why it was decided that certain images of the attacks were almost immediately deemed inappropriate while other images were granted legitimacy and shown repeatedly; to what extent any imaginative leeway can be granted to an artist attempting such a representation; and, finally, whether, rather than being taboo, it is in fact the duty of the artist to address the September 11 attacks in ways that depart from those that continue to dominate the political and media response.

This essay will explore a number of these issues with reference to some of the already considerable body of work that has accumulated in response to what, for the sake of brevity and standardization, will be referred to as the "9/11" terrorist attacks. Given the sheer volume of this material, the use of sources is, by necessity, selective. Nevertheless, rather than simply focussing on just one or two post-9/11 texts, it is the intention of this essay to make use of a range of particularly illustrative examples in order to provide an introduction to, and overview of, some of the trends, issues and problems that have arisen thus far in attempts to represent and respond to 9/11.

If we take the *Tumbling Woman* controversy as the starting point, the most obvious of these issues surrounding the representation of 9/11 is directly related to ideas of artistic interdiction and censorship. In light of the tone of Andrea Peyser's article and the eventual removal of Fischl's sculpture, the incident raises the possibility that there has existed a prohibition on certain types of representation of 9/11. At the very least, the controversy demonstrates the fact that it quickly became appropriate to talk in terms of an "ethics" of 9/11 representation, however ill-defined those ethics may have been. In her collection of post-9/11 essays, *Precarious life* (2004), Judith Butler argues that, 'The public sphere is constituted in part by what cannot be said and what cannot be shown' and that these limits 'circumscribe the domain in which political speech operates.'[6] However, as the fate of the Fischl sculpture demonstrates, these limits have to some extent also circumscribed the artistic domain in post-9/11 America. Slavoj Žižek has referred to the immediate aftermath of 9/11 as '[a] unique time between the traumatic event and

5 Nick Monteleone, *New York Daily News*, Sept. 2002. www.thememoryhole.org/911/911-art.htm, accessed 15 Mar. 2006.   6 Judith Butler, *Precarious life: the power of mourning and violence* (London, 2004), p. xvii.

its symbolic aftermath' comparable to 'those brief moments after we have been cut, before the full extent of the pain strikes us.'[7] We can see from the fate of *Tumbling Woman* that among the most immediate responses during this period was an almost instinctive or reflex prohibition, an instant sense that certain images were inappropriate as a means of testimony or memorialization and that a still-traumatized public should be protected from these images. Certainly, it is interesting to note that much of the discussion relating to the appropriate function of art post-9/11 has been framed in terms of good taste, a standard that Susan Sontag argues is 'always [...] repressive' when used in conjunction with discussions of what can and cannot be shown of a public event.[8]

In fact, almost five years after the attacks, many of these issues were recapitulated with the appearance of Paul Greengrass' *United 93* and Oliver Stone's *World Trade Center* in cinemas in spring and summer 2006. Early screenings of the trailer for *United 93* were reportedly interrupted by shouts of 'Too soon!' from angry audience members – with one cinema in Manhattan pulling the trailer from its screens following several complaints – while advance publicity for the film was careful to emphasize the fact that it had been made with the full cooperation of victims' families.[9] Perhaps more interestingly, the decision by Stone and his producer Michael Shamberg to screen *World Trade Center* to survivors of the attacks from the New York Police and Fire Departments three weeks ahead of its official release led to a public debate on whether such overtly emotive and dramatized representations have a role to play in the process of recovery from trauma. According to Shamberg, 'Emotionally, it is important that these men and women have the opportunity to see the film first.' However, this opinion was forthrightly countered by the union representing Port Authority workers who warned its members that watching *World Trade Center* could actually result in post-traumatic stress disorder.[10]

Indeed, as Butler points out, such was the weight of national trauma unleashed by 9/11 that it immediately became contentious not only to represent the event itself but also to attempt any reconstruction of what could be termed its 'prehistory'. She writes: 'There is no relevant prehistory to the events of September 11, since to begin to tell the story a different way, to ask how things came to this, is already to complicate the question of agency which [...] leads to a fear of moral equivocation.'[11] What we appear to be left with, then, in establishing the

7 Slavoj Žižek, *Welcome to the desert of the real: five essays on September 11 and related dates* (London, 2002), pp 44–5. 8 Susan Sontag, *Regarding the pain of others* (London, 2003), p. 61. 9 Sean Smith and Jac Chebatoris, 'A dark day revisited', MSNBC website, 10 Apr. 2006. www.msnbc.msn.com/id/12112802/site/newsweek/, accessed 22 July 2006; John Patterson, 'Telling it straight', *Guardian*, 21 Apr. 2006. arts.guardian.co.uk/filmandmusic/story/0,,1757354,00.html, accessed 22 July 2006. 10 'Ground zero heroes to see 9/11 film', CBS News website, 17 July 2006. www.cbsnews.com/stories/2006/07/17/entertainment/main1811388.shtml, accessed 22 July 2006. 11 Butler, *Precarious life*, p. 6.

parameters of an ethics of 9/11 representation, is a sense that 9/11 was immediately grasped by many as belonging to what Hayden White – writing about the issue of Holocaust representation – has referred to as 'a special class of events, such that [...] [it] must be viewed as manifestly one story, as being emplottable in only one way and as signifying only one kind of meaning'.[12]

Returning briefly to the *Tumbling Woman* controversy provides further insight into why this sense of restricted representational options emerged so quickly after 9/11. Reflecting on his decision to respond to 9/11 with a depiction of one of its victims, Fischl noted, 'I realized that I'm not the kind of artist who can make a heroic piece. I don't understand heroes [...] I understand victims. I respond to vulnerability.'[13] The issue of an ethics of 9/11 representation is, of course, made all the more complicated by the fact that the attacks themselves were specifically designed by their perpetrators to demonstrate America's inescapable vulnerability and to provoke a response informed by dramatically heightened levels of fear. A statement from Osama bin Laden broadcast on *Al-Jazeera* in October 2001 begins by invoking the image of an America, 'hit by God in one of its softest spots' and consequently rendered 'full of fear from its north to its south, from its west to its east'.[14] In fact, despite concluding with the hawkish reminder that 'America has stood down enemies before, and we will do so this time', President George W. Bush's address to the nation on the evening of 9/11 also betrays a sense of sudden exposure in its opening reference to victims 'in airplanes, or in their offices; secretaries, businessmen and women, military and federal workers; moms and dads, friends and neighbours.'[15] This deliberately all-encompassing inventory has the effect of simultaneously conjuring both national unity and intense vulnerability.

The implication of Fischl's reading of *Tumbling Woman* is that it was his failure to offer a heroic or redemptive representation of 9/11 – and his decision to focus instead on issues of vulnerability – that provoked so much anger. Interestingly, despite the fact that notions of victimhood and heroism rapidly became conflated in the narrative of 9/11 (a conflation made explicit by a US State Department website that features biographies and photographs of those that died under the title 'September 11: victims and heroes'),[16] there was an almost immediate resistance to or unease about granting this heroic status to the people who

12 Hayden White, 'Historical emplotment and the problem of truth', *The history and narrative Reader*, ed. Geoffrey Roberts (London, 2001), p. 375. 13 Eric Fischl interview with Robert Fishko. www.artdealers.org/ events/forumoot.html, accessed 15 Mar. 2006. 14 Osama bin Laden, statement broadcast on *Al-Jazeera* television, 7 Oct. 2001. Translated from the Arabic by USAToday.com. www.september11news.com/Osama Speeches.htm, accessed 3 Dec. 2006. 15 George W Bush, statement from the President in his address to the nation, *White House Website* 11 Sept. 2001. www.whitehouse.gov/news/ releases/2001/09/20010911–16.html, accessed 3 Dec. 2006. 16 'September 11: victims and heroes,' US department of state international information programs. usinfo.state.gov/albums/911/, accessed 28 Aug. 2006.

jumped or fell from the Trade Center towers – the people to whom Fischl's sculpture was intended as a tribute.

The television documentary 'The falling man' – broadcast as part of the *Dispatches* series on Channel 4 (16 Mar. 2006) – highlighted this unease by describing the efforts made by American journalist Tom Junod to remove what he perceived as the stigma that had become attached to these victims of the attacks. Junod states that, 'From the beginning, the spectacle of doomed people jumping from the upper floors of the World Trade Center resisted redemption.' He continues, 'In the most photographed and videotaped day in the history of the world, the images of people jumping were the only images that became, by consensus, taboo – the only images from which Americans were proud to avert their eyes.' However, Junod also argues that these harrowing images 'are our most intimate connection to the horror of that day.'[17] As a result of what is referred to in the documentary as 'a remarkable, spontaneous act of self-censorship,' news sources in America refused to print or broadcast images that were quickly branded as distasteful, exploitative and voyeuristic.[18] In their place, a consensus emerged as to the type of images that were to dominate the aftermath of the attacks.

The most famous of these is, of course, the image chosen for the 9/11 commemorative stamp 'Heroes of 2001' released by the US Postal Service in June 2002: Thomas Franklin's photograph of three New York firefighters raising the stars and stripes at what became known as "ground zero". The composition and context of this image carries with it deliberate echoes of Joe Rosenthal's Pulitzer Prize-winning photograph of US Marines raising the American flag on Iwo Jima in February 1945 – an image that has achieved a literally monumental significance in the American popular imagination – and the two images were frequently displayed side-by-side in the days following the attacks. As well as enhancing and adding extra legitimacy to the message of resilience and heroic action that emerges from the ground zero photograph, the juxtaposition of the Franklin and Rosenthal photographs also plays upon the parallels that were being made between 9/11 and Pearl Harbour, as well as being resolutely on-message in terms of the newly-launched "War on Terror". Interestingly, early plans by the New York Fire Department to commission a statue based on Franklin's photograph – once again mirroring the US Marine Corp monument based on Rosenthal's photograph in Rosslyn, Virginia – were disrupted by another aspect of the ethics of 9/11 representation and were eventually cancelled following failure to reach agreement over whether this piece should reflect the racial diversity of the NYFD in portraying a black, a white and an Hispanic firefighter or whether it should, as in the original photograph, depict all three firefighters as white.[19]

17 Tom Junod, 'The falling man', *Esquire*, 140:3 (Sept. 2003).   18 '9/11: the falling man.' *Dispatches*. Dir. Henry Singer. Narrated by Steven Mackintosh. Based on an article by Tom Junod. Channel 4, 16 Mar. 2006.   19 Kevin Flynn, 'Firefighters block a plan for statue in Brooklyn', *New York Times*, 18 Jan. 2002.

The other key narrative of heroic action to emerge from 9/11 centres on the fate of United Airlines Flight 93 and, in particular, passenger Todd Beamer's reported shout of 'Let's roll!' just prior to the plane crashing in Shanksville, rural Pennsylvania. This quickly became adopted in both military and civilian circles as a post-9/11 rallying-cry with Beamer's actions cast by many as the first strike in the War on Terror. US Air Force Technical Sergeant Tim Dougherty refers to 'Let's roll!' as 'America's two-word marching order in the fight against terrorism' and a new Air Force crest proclaiming 'Spirit of 9/11: Let's Roll!' was unveiled in December 2001 and displayed on various aircraft active in Afghanistan and, later, Iraq.[20] In fact, the considerable and inventive lengths to which some in America felt it necessary to go to in order to salvage images of redemption and renewal from the pain of 9/11 can be seen by a book, entitled *Faces of hope*, which was published to coincide with the first anniversary of 9/11. This book features photographs of American babies born on 11 September 2001, many shot against a backdrop of the stars and stripes or with other patriotic accoutrements. Christina Naman, the book's compiler, asserted that, 'I feel that babies born on [9/11] have already done something great with their lives'.[21]

What, then, is the fate or function of the artist in a context in which these types of images of heroism or redemption are considered by many – presumably including Andrea Peyser at the *New York Post* – to be the most appropriate responses to 9/11 and in which the spectre of public opprobrium or even prohibition threatens those who deviate significantly from this category of response? The artist like Art Spiegelman who, in his newspaper comic series *In the shadow of no towers* (2004), asks, 'Why did those provincial American flags have to spout out of the embers of Ground Zero?' and reveals himself to be 'haunted [...] by the images [...] of people tumbling to the streets below' and, like a post-9/11 Ancient Mariner, 'doomed to [...] compulsively retell the calamities of September 11 to anyone who'll still listen.'[22] What, also, is the role of the writer like the French novelist Frédéric Beigbeder who, in the course of his novel *Windows on the world* (2004), observes that, 'If I'd hoped to tell charming stories, I picked the wrong subject.'[23] Or like Nick McDonell whose novel *The third brother* (2005) features a lengthy passage in which the protagonist imagines himself as one of the people forced to jump from the Trade Center towers because he believes that 'the greatest horror of that day belongs to those who jumped, who knew early that there was no hope.'[24] Or like Pat Barker who uses Goya's comment about his *Disasters of war* series – 'One

www.nytimes.com/2002/01/18/nyregion/18STAT.html?ex=1170651600&en=54c4cf75403d83b8&ei=5070, accessed 29 July 2006.   **20** Tim Dougherty, 'Let's Roll!' *Air Force Print News*, 21 Dec. 2001. www. herkynoseart.com/letsroll.html, accessed 28 Aug. 2006.   **21** Karen MacPherson, 'Mother counters 9/11 tragedy with "Faces of hope"', *Pittsburgh Post-Gazette*, 11 Sept. 2002, www.post-gazette.com/books/20020911hope0911fnp3.asp, accessed 20 Mar. 2006.   **22** Art Spiegelman, *In the shadow of no towers* (London, 2004), Numbers 7, 6 & 2.   **23** Frédéric Beigbeder, *Windows on the world*, trans. Frank Wynne (2004; London, 2005) p. 207.   **24** Nick McDonell, *The third brother* (2005; London, 2006), pp 207–8.

cannot look at this. I saw it. This is the truth' – as the epigraph for her post-9/11 novel *Double vision* (2003).[25] Or, most relevant to the Fischl controversy, the novelist Jonathan Safran Foer, whose inclusion of a series of photographs of a falling body in his post-9/11 novel *Extremely loud and incredibly close* (2005) angered one reviewer enough for him to suggest that relatives of victims of the attacks would be justified in seeking out Foer and beating him up. According to Andrew Crumey, what is most objectionable about Foer's use of these images resides in the unbridgeable gulf between, on the one hand, the reality of 9/11 and the all-too-real death of the figure in the photograph and, on the other, the fictional world and imaginary concerns of Foer's novel and its protagonist Oskar, a nine-year-old boy coming to terms with the, for Crumey, all-too-unreal death of his father in the World Trade Centre on 9/11.[26]

In fact, when surveying what has been written to date about representations of, and reactions to, 9/11, one fundamental point that dominates much of this material is the issue of whether or not fiction is an adequate or suitable medium for tackling an event of such magnitude; whether, to put it in slightly different terms, fiction is up to the task of depicting and responding to 9/11 or whether, by its very nature, the very fictiveness of fiction violates the emerging ethics of 9/11 representation. In a *New York Times* interview in 2005, V.S. Naipaul dismisses the practice of writing fiction as increasingly irrelevant to contemporary concerns when set alongside the opportunities to confront the global political situation post-9/11 in nonfiction writing; writing that, according to Naipaul, allows one to 'explore the world […] that one didn't fully know.' He says of fiction that, 'You sit and weave a little narrative. And it's O.K., but it's of no account.'[27] As with Crumey's dismissal of *Extremely loud and incredibly close*, the implication of Naipaul's argument is that fiction is fundamentally ill-equipped for dealing with an event of the magnitude of 9/11. In an article accompanying the Naipaul interview – arrestingly entitled 'Truth is stronger than fiction' – Rachel Donadio links the growing market for nonfiction to a public hunger for information, even education, after 9/11. She concludes the article by stating confidently that, 'no novels have yet engaged with the post-September 11 era in any meaningful way'.[28]

Interestingly, Ian McEwan echoes this view of fiction's post-9/11 inconsequentiality in an interview coinciding with the publication of his most recent novel, *Saturday* (2005). He stated that for a period after 9/11 he found it 'wearisome' to read about 'invented characters', finding that instead: 'I wanted to be told about the world. I wanted to be informed. I felt that we had gone through great changes

---

25 Pat Barker, *Double vision* (London, 2003), epigraph.   26 Andrew Crumey, 'Twin towers travesty', review of *Extremely Loud and Incredibly Close* by Jonathan Safran Foer, *Scotland on Sunday*, 15 May 2005. living.scotsman.com/books.cfm?id=526132005, accessed 20 Mar. 2006.   27 V.S. Naipaul, 'The irascible prophet: V.S. Naipaul at home', interview with Rachel Donadio, *New York Times Book Review*, 7 Aug. 2005. 28 Rachel Donadio, 'Truth is stronger than fiction', *New York Times Book Review*, 7 Aug. 2005.

and now was the time to just go back to school.'[29] In fact, McEwan imbues *Saturday*'s protagonist Henry Perowne with just this high-minded aversion to artistic invention. He resists his daughter's attempts to educate him in the literary classics – thinking, 'The times are strange enough. Why make things up?' – and is so anxious not to miss the latest global developments on the day of the worldwide anti-war protests of February 2003 that he even finds himself switching on a news bulletin instead of listening to a CD as he makes dinner; a choice that, he reflects, he would never have made a few years ago.[30]

According to Jean Baudrillard, reality outstripped fiction on 9/11 precisely because it absorbed fiction's energy and won the contest over which could be more unimaginable.[31] This view is, of course, substantiated by the endlessly repeated, but nonetheless germane, comparison between the attacks as spectacle and the spectacular attacks that constitute the enduring images from Hollywood disaster movies. That a significant number of people thought that they were watching a disaster movie – or at the very least thought about disaster movies – when they first saw images of the attack on the World Trade Center is, in this context, highly instructive. As Martin Amis noted a week after the attacks, 'It is already trite – but stringently necessary – to emphasize that such a *mise en scène* would have embarrassed a studio executive's storyboard or a thriller-writer's notebook.'[3] However, if, as Slavoj Žižek claims, 9/11 stands in relation to these Hollywood films as snuff pornography stands in relation to the theatrical sado-masochism of many pornographic movies – in other words, an unbearably real distortion and intensification of images and tropes that are themselves an exaggeration and a fantasy – then the idea of fictional representation becomes extremely problematic.[3]

Interestingly, the most commercially successful representations of, and responses to, 9/11 have, up to this point, generally been of a nonfiction or documentary nature. *The 9/11 Commission report* – perhaps the apotheosis of post-9/11 texts – has sold well over a million copies in the US since its publication in July 2004. In fact, the *Report* made so much money for its publishers, W.W. Norton, that they were put under pressure to make sizeable donations to 'programmes focussed on emergency preparedness and international relations.'[34] Michael Moore's *Fahrenheit 9/11* (2004) became the highest grossing documentary movie of all time – taking over $100 million in its first six weeks at the US box office.[35]

29 Quoted in Jay McInerney, 'The uses of invention', *Guardian* Review, 17 Sept. 2005. **30** Ian McEwan, *Saturday* (London, 2005), pp 66, 176. **31** Jean Baudrillard, *The spirit of terrorism and requiem for the twin towers*, trans. Chris Turner (London, 2002), p. 28. **32** Martin Amis, 'Fear and loathing', *Guardian*, 18 Sept. 2001. **33** Žižek, *Welcome to the desert of the real*, p. 11. **34** Edward Wyatt, 'Publishers of *9/11 Commission report* donates portion of profits,' *Foundation Center Website*, 25 July 2005. fdncenter.org/pnd/news/story.jhtml?id=11230004, accessed 9 Nov. 2005. **35** John Berger, 'Michael Moore, artist and patriot', *Open democracy website*, 17 Aug. 2004. www.opendemocracy.net/arts-Film/ article_2048.jsp accessed 14 Feb. 2007.

This post-9/11 shift to nonfiction is also reflected in the recent output of Norman Mailer and Gore Vidal, two of the most politically-engaged American novelists of the last half century. Both writers have addressed the attacks and the response of the Bush administration in slim nonfiction volumes close in tone to old-fashioned political pamphlets – Vidal's *Perpetual war for perpetual peace* (2002) and *Dreaming war* (2003) and Mailer's *Why are we at war?* (2003).

This apparent incompatibility between 9/11 and a fictional aesthetic is worth exploring in greater depth. Judith Butler has referred to 9/11 as an 'enormous trauma that undermines narrative capacity.'[36] This sentiment appears to be echoed by Frédéric Beigbeder – who concedes that, 'It's impossible to write about this subject' – and by the staff at satirical newspaper the *Onion* whose "infographic" on the cover of their by-now-legendary post-9/11 edition simply read 'Holy Fucking Shit: Attack on America.'[37] However, by beginning one of his *No towers* comic strips with a caption reading. 'In our last episode, as you might remember, the world ended', Art Spiegelman's playfully destabilizes both the eschatological rhetoric that dominated the post-9/11 period and also the assumption that the form taken by responses to the tragedy was somehow foreclosed along the 'repressive' lines invoked by Susan Sontag.[38] In fact, with its stark image of the silhouetted twin towers against a dark navy background, Spiegelman's cover for the *New Yorker*'s post-9/11 issue evinces a determined resistance to the either instinctive or ideologically-motivated desire to seek immediate comfort in redemptive, heroic and patriotic images, a resistance that he later expands upon in his *No Towers* series and that is shared by many other writers and artists who began to tackle 9/11.

In the course of *Windows on the world* – the chapters of which alternate between an account of a man who is trapped with his two young sons in the restaurant at the top of the World Trade Center on the morning of 9/11 and nonfictional chapters concerned largely with the challenges faced by a writer trying to write about 9/11 – Beigbeder raises the issue of whether an artist should even attempt to represent such a traumatic event. He writes, 'Will I be able to look myself in the eye after publishing this book?'[39] Later, his anxiety about the ethics of representing 9/11 comes to a head when he expresses relief that, while clearing immigration in New York on a research trip for the novel, he is not confronted with the question 'Are you intending to write a novel about September 11?'[40]

Beigbeder is, in other words, not only aware that his novel must try to act as a window on a world that is impossible to describe fully – at one point he writes, 'Even if I go deep, deep into the horror, my book will always remain 1,350 feet below the truth' – but he is also aware that his novel must deal with subject matter that is inherently resistant to happy or redemptive endings.[41] If, as he tells

---

36 Butler, *Precarious life*, p. 7.   **37** Beigbeder, 8; *The Onion*, 26 Sept. 2001.   **38** Spiegelman, *In the shadow of no tower*, Number 1.   **39** Beigbeder, *The Onion*, 26 Sept. 2001, p. 130.   **40** Ibid., p. 163.   **41** Ibid., p. 124.

his readers at the start of the novel, they already know that the story must end with the death of all of the characters – the opening sentence reads: 'You know how it ends: everybody dies' – then much of the rest of *Windows* is taken up with trying to find a role for the novel in this challenging context.[42] For this reason, it is a useful and illuminating point from which to start moving towards some tentative conclusions about the role of art in attempting to represent 9/11.

Towards the end of the novel, after the protagonist and his sons have jumped to their deaths, Beigbeder writes:

> I truly don't know why I wrote this book. Perhaps because I couldn't see the point of speaking of anything else. What else is there to write? The only interesting subjects are those which are taboo. We must write what is forbidden. [...] Nowadays, books must go where television does not. Show the invisible, speak the unspeakable. It may be impossible, but that is its *raison d'être*. Literature is a 'mission impossible'.[43]

Interestingly, Pat Barker's *Double vision* (2003) features a sculptor who, like Eric Fischl, is working on a piece inspired by 9/11. Kate Frobisher – whose war photographer husband is killed in Afghanistan during the post-9/11 invasion – is planning a sequence of figures representing the men who hijacked the planes because, she thinks, 'nobody had been there to photograph what chiefly compelled her imagination.'[44] In other words, in the context of artistic representations of 9/11, Beigbeder's idea of going 'where television does not' is particularly apposite. As Ian McEwan noted in a *Guardian* article published the day after the attacks, 'Always, it seemed, it was what we could not see that was so frightening. [...] We were watching death on an unbelievable scale, but we saw no one die. The nightmare was in the gulf of imagining. The horror was in the distance.'[45] Žižek refers to this gulf between the repeated emphasis on the number of victims and the absence of actual images of death as a 'derealization of the horror' of 9/11 – a gulf that existed, of course, both for practical reasons and due to editorial decisions made by the news networks and other media sources.[46] For Beigbeder, his decision to take on such subject matter is justified by the novel's ability to evade the confines of 9/11 as media spectacle – a spectacle that soon becomes indistinguishable from the range of political responses with which it rapidly forms a mutually-sustaining relationship – and to think its way into otherwise inaccessible parts of the tragedy that justifies.

In his essay 'In the ruins of the future' (2001), Don DeLillo argues that, while 9/11 marked the end of modern America's dreams of technology, progress and

42 Ibid., p. 1.   43 Ibid., p. 301.   44 Barker, *Double vision*, pp 65–6.   45 McEwan, 'Beyond belief', *Guardian*, 12 Sept. 2001.   46 Žižek, *Welcome to the desert of the real*, p. 13.

consumption – itself, as John Gray asserts in his 2003 work *Al Qaeda and what it means to be modern*, a highly problematic pronouncement– there is, perhaps, the opportunity to create another story. 'The narrative ends in the rubble,' he writes, 'and it is left to us to create the counternarrative.'[47] In a context in which the sense of urgent expression felt by writers and artists in relation to 9/11 frequently comes into conflict with a prohibitive sense of what can and cannot be represented, this notion of a post-9/11 counternarrative is compelling. This view is echoed by Jonathan Safran Foer who argues for a specific need for fictional responses to 9/11. He says: 'In America right now [...] rhetoric is grounded in ideas of capital-G Good, capital-E Evil, and it's very clear who is on which side. But in a book you can do just the opposite. You can use all lower case words.'[48]

Conversant as he is with the political uses of spectacle, Slavoj Žižek insists that it is vitally important that attempts are made to address the grief and shock of 9/11. This, of course, runs directly contrary to the views of Andrea Peyser who, in her outrage at *Tumbling Woman*, claimed that visitors to the Rockefeller Center were effectively being dragged back in time and forced to relive the most brutal and shocking moments of 9/11. According to Žižek, '[The] true choice apropos historical traumas is not the one between remembering or forgetting them: traumas we are not ready or able to remember haunt us all the more forcefully. We should therefore accept the paradox that, in order to really forget an event, we must first summon up the strength to remember it properly.'[4] Interestingly, in reflecting on the anger inspired by *Tumbling Woman*, Eric Fischl echoes this view, asserting that he intended his sculpture to act 'as a healing tool'. He notes that, 'One of the ways to heal is to make visible the things that hurt us, so they can be dealt with.'[50]

In spite of Fischl's downbeat conclusion – he states of his sculpture that, 'I thought it would heal, but I was wrong' – Žižek's idea of attempting to remember 9/11 properly seems particularly pertinent to the case of *Tumbling Woman*. In other words, the desire to make use of the opportunity to address 9/11 and its aftermath in terms that differ from those that continue to dominate the political and media response is, for the moment at least, the most useful standard by which to measure artistic representations and responses.

---

47 DeLillo, 'In the ruins of the future', *Harper's* Dec. 2001. Reprinted in *Guardian*, Saturday Review, 22 Dec. 2001.   48 Jonathan Safran Foer, 'Something happened,' interview with Suzie Mackenzie, *Guardian*, Weekend Magazine, 21 May 2005.   49 Žižek, *Welcome to the desert of the real*, p. 22.   50 Fischl interview with Robert Fishko. See note 14.

Hunters and patriots: the fiction of the American neo-Nazi movement

DARRYL JONES

On 19 April 1995, a bomb detonated in a Ryder Rental Truck, containing 5000lbs of ammonium nitrate and nitromethane, destroyed the Alfred P. Murrah Federal Building in downtown Oklahoma City, killing 168 people (including 15 children) and injuring many hundreds more. Within ninety minutes, federal agents had arrested Timothy McVeigh, a decorated Gulf War veteran with known connections to extreme right survivalist movements; he was convicted of the murder of eight federal employees who worked in the building, and executed after several unsuccessful appeals on 11 June 2001. His associate, Terry Nichols, was also arrested as an accomplice (he did not place the bomb himself – that was McVeigh's job – but certainly conspired in planning the operation), and convicted of eight counts of manslaughter; the state of Oklahoma then successfully prosecuted Nichols on 161 counts of first-degree murder. He is currently serving successive life sentences in a Colorado "super-max" prison.

The Oklahoma bombing followed in the wake of two notorious incidents of federal heavy-handedness in dealing with the holders of fringe or dissident beliefs. The first was the siege above Ruby Creek, Idaho, in August 1992, in a place which came to be known as "Ruby Ridge". As part of their investigation against the Aryan Nations Neo-Nazi organization based in nearby Hayden Lake, federal agents attempted to coerce a local survivalist (or 'separatist', to use his own preferred term), Randy Weaver (who had ambiguous affiliations with the Aryan Nations) into acting as an infiltrator by use of a trumped-up weapons charge. The issue came to a head when Weaver missed a court appearance, and a heavily-armed team of federal agents were sent in, killing Weaver's wife (who was holding a baby, Elisheba, at the time) and his young son Sam, and wounding Weaver himself and family friend Kevin Harris. A highly-decorated US Marshal, William Degan, was killed in an exchange of fire with Harris and Sam Weaver (Harris and all the Weavers were invariably heavily armed). There followed an eight-day siege of Weaver's cabin.

Accounts of what happened at Ruby Ridge are, to put it mildly, conflicting, but what is certain is that the FBI's Rules of Engagement permitting the use of deadly force were revised specifically for the Weaver siege, and with tragic consequences. The standard Rules of Engagement, framed and hung on a classroom wall at the FBI Academy in Quantico, Virginia, read as follows:

> Agents are not to use deadly force against any person except as necessary in self-defense or in the defense of another when they have reason to believe they or another are in danger of death or grievous bodily harm. Whenever feasible, verbal warning should be given before deadly force is applied.[1]

Richard Rogers, the head of Quantico's Hostage Rescue Team, drafted new Rules of Engagement as follows:

> If any *adult* is seen with a weapon in the vicinity of where this firefight took place, of the Weaver cabin, then this individual *could be the subject of deadly* force [...] Any child is going to come under standard FBI rules, meaning that if an FBI agent is threatened with death by a child, then clearly that agent could use a weapon to shoot a child.[2]

Over the succeeding days, these new Rules were either further redrafted or misapplied: 'deadly force *could* be used' became 'deadly force *can* be used', which in turn became 'deadly force *can and should* be used'. One FBI agent later admitted that the rules amounted to 'If you see 'em, shoot 'em'.[3]

During the subsequent trial of the Weavers and Kevin Harris, the FBI engaged in what looked to many observers like a cover-up. FBI agents denied knowledge of the new Rules, and shredded incriminating documents. Crucial evidence, including drawings made around the time of the siege by FBI sharpshooter Lon Horiuchi (who shot Vicki Weaver), which seemingly contradicted evidence he had given at the Weaver/Harris trial, was mailed to the defence *fourth class* by the FBI. Federal agencies were heavily criticized, not least by the trial judge, who openly accused the agency of stalling and of obstructing justice in ways which he found 'totally unacceptable'.[4] In hearings in 1995 Horiuchi took the Fifth Amendment, and FBI director Louis J. Freeh acknowledged that 'at Ruby Ridge, the FBI did not perform at the level which the American people expect or deserve from the FBI'.[5] However, Jess Walter, in his study of the Weaver case, criticizes Freeh

---

1 Jess Walter, *Every knee shall bow: the truth and tragedy of Ruby Ridge and the Randy Weaver family* (New York, 1995), p. 190. 2 Ibid., p. 180 (emphasis added). 3 Ibid., pp 183, 187, 190. 4 Ibid., pp 330, 334. 5 Michael Barkun, *Religion and the racist right: the origins of the Christian Identity movement* (Chapel Hill, 1997), p. 276.

for 'doling out minor punishments' to agents under his jurisdiction, who had var-
iously either exceeded their authority or possibly violated the Constitution; for
maintaining, in the face of very persuasive evidence, that 'no FBI agents committed crimes or engaged in any intentional misconduct'; and for stating that, while
the rewritten Rules of Engagement were 'poorly drafted, confusing, and [could]
be read to direct agents to act contrary to the law and FBI policy', nobody at
Ruby Ridge, including Horiuchi, had actually followed these new Rules.[6] Weaver
and his surviving family members were paid over $1 million each in an out-of-
court settlement. Weaver's Ruby Ridge cabin became a shrine for survivalists and
far-right radicals: Timothy McVeigh is known to have visited there a few months
before his attack on the Murrah Building.

The second event preceding the Oklahoma bombing, which achieved much
more prominence than Ruby Ridge, was the fifty-one day siege of the Branch
Davidian headquarters at Mount Carmel near Waco, Texas, which began on 28
February 1993. Believing that the Davidian leader David Koresh had been hoard-
ing weapons for possible seditious purposes, the Bureau of Alcohol, Tobacco and
Firearms raided Mount Carmel. The Davidians had been tipped-off in advance
(and the ATF were aware of this): in the ensuing shoot-out, five Davidians and
four agents were killed. Fifty-one days later, Attorney General Janet Reno inter-
vened in the siege, ordering agents to storm Mount Carmel. For reasons which
are still contested, the siege ended in disaster as the building caught fire (there is
persuasive evidence to suggest that the authorities were responsible for the fire).
76 Davidians, including 17 children under the age of 12, were killed – at least 20
of these (5 children) by gunshots (again, there is persuasive evidence that they
were shot by FBI marksmen).[7] McVeigh and Nichols timed the Oklahoma bombing to coincide with the second anniversary of the Waco massacre.

Together, these two events, Ruby Ridge and Waco, were taken by the radical
right 'as validation of its own worldview'.[8] The journalist Jon Ronson, who inves-
tigated and spent time with Neo-Nazis and their associates in the 1990s, writes:

> for hundreds of thousands of Americans, perhaps even millions, the
> Weaver siege and the burning of David Koresh's church are forever linked,
> proof of a government gone crazy, of a New World Order coming to kill
> whoever does not bow down to them.[9]

6 Walter, *Every knee shall bow*, p. 370. Other commentators, however, disagree: Kenneth S. Stern, in his
brilliant study of the rise of the militia movement, believes that 'Most careful observers of the case, however,
agree with FBI director Louis J. Freeh's conclusion that the killing of Vicki Weaver was accidental.' Stern,
A force upon the plain: The American militia movement and the politics of hate (New York, 1996), p. 40.   **7**
For these (and other) allegations, see William Gazecki's Oscar-nominated documentary, *Waco: the rules of
engagement* (1997). For the definitive account of the Branch Davidians, see Kenneth G.C. Newport, *The
branch Davidians of Waco* (Oxford, 2006).   **8** Barkun, *Religion and the racist right*, p. 278.   **9** Jon Ronson,
Them: adventures with extremists (London, 2001), p. 74.

Gore Vidal, who became McVeigh's unlikely champion and correspondent as he awaited execution, wrote in the same vein:

> Ruby Ridge, Waco, Oklahoma City. Three warning bells from a heartland that most of us who are urban dwellers know little or nothing about [...] One thing shared by the victims at Ruby Ridge and Waco, and Timothy McVeigh, who may have committed mass murder in their name in Oklahoma City, was the conviction that the government of the United States is their implacable enemy and that they can only save themselves by hiding out in the wilderness, or by joining a commune centred on a messianic figure, or, as revenge for the cold-blooded federal murders of two members of the Weaver family at Ruby Ridge, blow up the building that contained the bureau responsible for the murders.[10]

These kinds of concern were given added impetus and force by the rise of the American militia movement in the 1990s – and it is important to remember that, although it has many precursors, the militia movement *is* primarily a 1990s phenomenon. With the end of the Cold War, certain sections of American society began to turn upon their own government the hostile energies formerly focused on Communism. Its rise is directly linked to the Weaver siege – two months after Ruby Ridge, Pete Peters, a neo-Nazi organizer, called a meeting in Estes Park, Colorado which was to lay the foundations for the militia movement – more than 150 far-right leaders from a wide and disparate range of organizations gathered together to formulate a report accusing the federal government of 'genocide'.[11] Described by anti-Nazi activist and writer Kenneth S. Stern as 'the fastest-growing mass movement any of us had seen', the appearance of the militias prompted Stern and his colleagues to produce, on 10 April 1995, their own lengthy report entitled *Militias: a growing danger*.[12] Nine days later, McVeigh's Ryder truck drove up outside the Murrah building.

Although not formally militiamen themselves, McVeigh and Nichols had certainly had active connections with Norman Olson's Northern Michigan Militia, a notoriously well-armed organization whose goal was, in Olson's words, to 'stand against tyranny, globalism, moral relativism, humanism and the New World Order threatening to undermine these here Unites States of America [...] Many thousands are prepared to go to Washington in uniform, carry their guns, prepared to present an ultimatum to the President and to Congress.'[13] The anti-federalism of these militias and separatists is deeply ingrained in the American

---

10 Gore Vidal, *Perpetual war for perpetual peace: how we got to be so hated, causes of conflict in the last empire* (Forest Row, 2002), pp 59–60. 11 Stern, *A force upon the plain*, pp 35–6. 12 Kenneth S. Stern, *Militias: A growing danger* (New York, 1995). See also Stern, *A force upon the plain*, p. 13. 13 Stern, *A force upon the plain*, p. 97.

ideological psyche, one of whose foundational symbols is the cabin in the woods, where a man can be a man, self-defining, away from the emasculating bureaucracy of federal government. Thus of course *Walden* (1854), Henry David Thoreau's masterpiece of Transcendentalist self-reliance, and one of the key documents in American intellectual history, opens with the following statement:

> When I wrote the following pages, or rather the bulk of them, I lived alone, in the woods, a mile from my neighbour, in a house I had built myself, on the shore of Walden Pond, in Concord, Massachussetts, and earned my living by the labor of my hands only.[14]

This is precisely the desire – for solitude, for freedom from political control – which animated Randy Weaver to build his own cabin far from centres of civilization, a desire which Weaver shares with many on the radical right. And not only the radical right – as, similarly acting in the American grain, Theodore Kaczynski, like Thoreau a graduate of Harvard and later a mathematics professor at Berkeley, retreated to his own remote cabin outside Lincoln, Montana, to write, act and live according to his eco-anarchist principles. Kaczynski became known as the Unabomber, and his Manifesto, *Industrial society and its future* (1995), is a terrifyingly articulate statement of the beliefs that led him to embark on a devastating letter-bombing campaign which lasted from 1978 to 1994.[15]

Among McVeigh's books, the FBI found a copy of *The Turner diaries* (1978), a far-right terrorist novel written by Andrew Macdonald, the pseudonym of William Luther Pierce, a major ideologue of the American neo-Nazi movement and the founder of the National Alliance, an organization with links to the American Nazi Party, but propounding a distinctive white supremacist theology, Cosmotheism. Macdonald's follow-up to *The Turner diaries*, the vigilante novel *Hunter* (1989), was found in the library of Terry Nichols, and offered as exhibit 158 in his trial.[16] According to the FBI, *The Turner diaries* provided McVeigh with the 'blueprint' for the Oklahoma bombing.[17] Photocopies of two pages from the novel, detailing a terrorist mortar attack on the White House, were found in McVeigh's car; the novel also contains a lengthy account of the blowing-up of the

14 Henry David Thoreau, '*Walden' and 'Civil disobedience'*, (ed.) Michael Meyer (1854; London, 1983), p. 45. 15 Theodore Kaczynski, *Industrial society and its future* ['The Unabomber manifesto'] published by the *New York Times* and *Washington Post*, Sept. 1995. en.wikisource.org/wiki/Industrial_Society_and_ Its_Future, accessed 21 Mar. 2007. Though hardly a neo-Nazi, Kaczynski certainly also dissociated himself from the radical left, believing that 'Leftism is in the long run inconsistent with wild nature, with human freedom and with the elimination of modern technology [...] Leftism is a totalitarian force.' 16 See the transcript of Nichols's trial: www.courttv.com/archive/casefiles/oklahoma/nichtranscripts/1105am.html, accessed 21 Mar. 2007. 17 Lyle Stuart, 'Introduction', in Andrew Macdonald, *The Turner diaries* (1978; Fort Lee, NJ, 1996), np. Stuart, who died in 2006, was an anarchist publisher whose imprint, Barricade Books, first came to prominence as the publishers of the notorious underground handbook *The anarchist cookbook* in 1970.

FBI headquarters in Washington, D.C., by a truck bomb, an attack which kills 700 people. As Ann Larabee notes, Macdonald's books attained the status of 'literary Satans' (this phrase is taken from the nineteenth-century anarchist Johann Most – other 'literary Satans' would include the Unabomber Manifesto and *The anarchist cookbook*, as well as such contemporary classics as William Gurstelle's *Backyard ballistics* and 'Uncle Fester's *Home workshop explosives*);[18] the very act of reading these books could be construed as *de facto* proof of guilt.[19] This is certainly how Joseph Hartzler, the Prosecutor in the McVeigh trial, chose to emphasize the significance of *The Turner diaries* early in his opening statement:

> McVeigh's dislike for the federal government was revealed while he was still in the Army. Even at that early stage in his life, he expressed an enthusiasm for the book *The Turner diaries*. And you will hear more about that book during this trial [...] Friends, acquaintances and family members of McVeigh will testify that he carried the book with him, gave copies to them, urged them to read this book.
>
> We will show you [the jury] passages from this book, and you'll see how the bombing in the book served as a blueprint for McVeigh and for his planning and execution of the bombing of Oklahoma City.[20]

Further evidence, if it were needed, of the toxic effect *The Turner diaries* could have on its intended readership (that is, those with, or susceptible to, far-right leanings) lies in the fact that McVeigh was certainly not the first reader to act on its inspiration with deadly consequences. In 1983 Robert Mathews founded an anti-Semitic terror group which he called the Order, named after the inner racist circle to which Earl Turner eventually gains entry in Macdonald's novel. After embarking on a campaign of armed bank robberies, on 18 June 1984, the Order killed Jewish radio presenter Alan Berg, who had invited their members on to his Denver show and then mocked them (an event fictionalized in Oliver Stone's 1988 film *Talk radio*). On 27 November 1984, the Order issued an official 'Declaration of War' against the US government.[21]

Reading these novels and researching these subjects can be depressing, infuriating, and occasionally (inadvertently) hilarious. It leads one into a hidden world, a world with its own political ideologies, scientific theories, theologies, histories, myths and heroes. Together, these elements (though they are often wildly incon-

18 William Gurstelle, *Backyard ballistics: build potato cannons, paper match rockets, Cincinnati fire kites, tennis ball mortars, and more dynamite devices* (Atlanta, 2001); 'Uncle Fester' (Steve Preisler), *Home workshop explosives* (Green Bay, 2002). 19 Ann Larabee, 'It's not how to make a bomb that's the problem, but why', *History News Service*, August 4 2005: www.h-net.org/~hns/articles/2005/080405a.html, accessed 21 Mar. 2007. 20 'Opening statement of prosecutor Joseph Hartzler in the trial of Timothy McVeigh', www.law.umkc.edu/faculty/projects/ftrials/mcveigh/prosecutionopen.html, accessed 21 Mar. 2007. 21 Stern, *Militias*, pp 53–6.

sistent and contradictory) form a body of what the political theorist Michael Barkun has called 'rejected knowledge' – that is, 'ideas outside the academy's definition of respectable knowledge'.[22] The canon of 'rejected knowledge' is enormous, and contains, among many other things: most political conspiracy theories; most forms of religious fundamentalism, and the activities and beliefs of fringe religious organizations; creationism; astrology; most kinds of racial theorizing; most forms of UFO and paranormal investigation, and beliefs in spiritualism and the supernatural. This kind of rejection of certain forms of knowledge may well be standard practice in the academy: as Frank Kermode has written, some ideas are so self-evidently *wrong* to the academic specialist that it's not worth taking the time to disprove them.[23] And anyway, such thinking is often immune to the Popperian principle of falsifiability as the first principle of any serious theory.[24] I am aware that much of what I have just said about rejected knowledge and the academy is highly controversial and problematic. For one thing, it implies that we in universities have what might be called a discursive monopoly on knowledge, whose boundaries we police mercilessly. However, there is I think a major disconnection here between the academy and the world beyond its walls, as these kinds of 'rejected knowledge', time and again, prove themselves enormously appealing to huge numbers of people who *do* believe in astrology, UFO abduction, the literal truth of the Bible, creationism and other forms of seemingly arcane, esoteric or bizarre belief. Witness here the runaway success of *The Da Vinci code* (2003), or the even more spectacular success (62 million sales and counting) of Tim LaHaye and Jerry B. Jenkins's *Left behind* series of Evangelical Christian apocalyptic thrillers (1995–2004).

I am arguing that there *is* a continuum here between these seemingly disparate forms of rejected knowledge. At the soft end, as it were, the Christian Right is in danger of monopolizing American political discourse, and is marshalling its energies to roll back the Enlightenment, to reverse modernity. The *Left behind* novels are currently the biggest-selling books in America, which address politically what has become the most powerful constituency in American politics.[25] Thirty-nine per cent of Americans describe themselves as having been 'born again'; one third of registered American voters are white Evangelical Protestants. Evangelicals have now overtaken Catholics to comprise the largest single religious group in America; significantly, in a PBS poll of April 2004, 71 per cent of Evangelicals said they would vote for George W. Bush. These novels constitute mainstream, and perhaps

22 Barkun, *Religion and the racist right*, p. 12. 23 Frank Kermode, *The art of telling: essays on fiction* (Cambridge, 1983). 24 Karl Popper, *The logic of scientific discovery* (1959; London, 1992). 25 For my account of the *Left behind* novels which is very much a companion-piece to this essay, and on which I draw for the information adduced here on the Evangelicals and their voting practices, see Darryl Jones, 'The Liberal Antichrist: *Left Behind* in America', in Kenneth G. C. Newport & Crawford Gribben (eds), *Expecting the end: millenialism in social and historical context* (Waco, TX, 2006).

even majoritarian, American thinking – and their authors are happy to make rhetorical accommodations with the militia movements, seeing them as part of a united front against secular modernity. When the forces of evil, led by the Antichrist Nicolae Carpathia, take over America in a UN-backed *coup* in the second novel in the series, *Tribulation force* (1996), only 'the American militia movement' remains loyal to the President, who tells the heroic Rayford Steele that 'patriotic militia forces in the US were determined to take action before it was too late.'[26] Rayford 'recalled not liking the militias, not understanding them, assuming them criminals. But that had been when the American government was also their enemy. Now they were allies of lame duck United States President Gerald Fitzhugh, and their enemy was Rayford's enemy.'[27]

At the far end, in extreme cases, the official/academic dismissal of some of these forms of 'rejected knowledge' can lead to tragic consequences, as, long ignored, these voices irrupt into the public consciousness in forms of spectacular violence, as was the case with the Oklahoma bombing. Though their beliefs are invariably vile, ignorant, and monstrous, it is important to remember that many on the American far right are life's victims – the dispossessed, the disenfranchised, the poorly educated, those who feel that they have had a rough deal from the Government. Often, they are decorated combat veterans – men like Bo Gritz, the multiply-honoured Special Forces Colonel turned Far-Right Patriot (and 1988 Presidential candidate); or Randy Weaver and Timothy McVeigh themselves – who returned to civilian life only to find themselves social rejects. Jeff Berry, Imperial Wizard of the American Knights of the Ku Klux Klan, is surely onto something, alas, when he claims, 'I appeal to the working man'.[28] Furthermore, as Mike Davis has recently argued, car and truck bombs of the kind imagined by Macdonald and used by McVeigh, have become perhaps *the* major equalizer available to disaffected fringe ideologues, or the aggrieved disenfranchised: 'the most dramatic impact of the car bomb has been precisely its enfranchisement of marginal actors in modern history. Vehicle bombs offer extraordinary socio-political leverage to small, even ad hoc groups without significant constituencies or mass political legitimacy [...] It also flourished in the badlands of extreme inequality, on the edges of poor cities, and even in the embittered recesses of the American heartland.'[29] This is because of their extreme cheapness and the ease with which their major components are acquired, as well as their extraordinary explosive potency. McVeigh's combination of ammonium nitrate (fertilizer) and nitromethane (racing fuel) was developed (one hesitates to use the word "perfected" in this context) by the IRA in the 1970s, and has since become a standard

26 Tim LaHaye & Jerry B. Jenkins, *Tribulation force: the continuing drama of those left behind* (Wheaton, IL, 1996), pp 127, 424.   27 LaHaye & Jenkins, *Nicolae: the rise of Antichrist* (Wheaton, IL, 1997), p. 20.   28 Ronson, *Them*, p. 214.   29 Mike Davis, *Buda's wagon: a brief history of the car bomb* (London, 2007), pp 11, 189.

weapon for the car bomber, a means of literally getting more bang for your buck. McVeigh's explosives, including the truck rental, cost less than $5000.[30]

The Turner diaries works within a familiar genre – it is a future war novel; or, more precisely, a sociological utopian future fiction. The novel takes the form of the journals of Earl Turner, written from 1989 to 1993 (the novel was first published in 1978, though it had been published serially in the National Alliance publication *Attack!* in the period 1975–8), detailing the successful revolution of 'The Organization', a neo-Nazi movement led by a shadowy central committee 'The Order', against 'The System', a modern liberal polity which the novel figures as decadent, corrupt and controlled by Jews:

> We are forging the nucleus of a new society, a whole new civilization [Turner writes], which will rise from the ashes of the old. And it is because our new civilization will be based on an entirely different world view than the present one that it can only replace the other in a revolutionary manner. There is no way a society based on Aryan values and an Aryan outlook can evolve peacefully from a society which has succumbed to Jewish spiritual corruption.[31]

These diaries are presented by the novel as historical documents, collated in a future (a century or so from now) in which the Organization has assumed global control and created its neo-Nazi utopia. The Revolution is precipitated by two events: the 'Cohen Act' of 1988, which prohibits personal ownership of firearms, and an energy crisis brought about by 'the disastrous effect Washington's Israel-dominated foreign policy during the last two decades has had on America's supply of foreign oil.'[32] (There *was* of course an energy crisis in America in the mid-/late-1970s, a crisis which in 1979 gave Stephen King the idea for his own – ideologically ill-judged – novel of apocalyptic social breakdown and the New World Order, *The Stand*.)

After a series of increasingly spectacular terrorist atrocities, the Organization seizes control of Southern California, including the nuclear missiles kept at Vandenberg Air Force Base. The Organization then begins a programme of racial purification through the forced removal of non-whites to other states (where this massive influx will increase already-simmering racial tensions), while those of ambiguous ethnicity (mostly Jews) are sent to extermination camps:

---

30 Ibid., p. 9. As Davis goes on to point out, 'In contrast, the cruise missiles that have become the classic American riposte to overseas terrorist attacks cost nearly $1 million each.'   **31** Andrew Macdonald, *The Turner diaries* (1978; Fort Lee, NJ, 1996), p. 111.   **32** Ibid., p. 26. The Cohen Act is an anti-Semitic foreshadowing of the Brady Handgun Violence Prevention Act ("Brady Bill"), singed into law by Bill Clinton in 1993, which has attracted the ire of many on the American right.

Back at HQ I inquired about a strange column [of deportees]. No one was sure, although the consensus was that they were the Jews and mixed-breeds of too light a hue to be included with the evacuees who were sent east. I remember now something which puzzled me a few days ago: the separation of the very light Blacks – the almost Whites, the octoroons and quadroons, the unclassifiable mongrels from various Asian and southern climes – from the others during the concentration and evacuation operations.

And I think I now understand. The clearly distinguishable non-Whites are the ones we want to increase the racial pressure on others outside California. The presence of more almost-White mongrels would merely confuse the issue – and there is always the danger that they will later 'pass' as White. Better to deal with them now, as soon as we get our hands on them. I have a suspicion their trip into that canyon north of here will be a one-way affair![33]

The Organization cements its regime domestically through 'The Day of the Rope', in which liberals, Jews and other undesirables – 'the politicians, the lawyers, the businessmen, the TV newscasters, the newspaper reporters and editors, the judges, the teachers, the school officials, the "civic leaders", the preachers'[34] – are rounded up and publicly hanged from lamp-posts, their bodies bearing the placards 'I Betrayed My Race', or (in the case of those conducting inter-racial relationships) 'I Defiled My Race'. Turner views these atrocities as a regrettable but necessary prelude to Organization control. The Organization also acts nationally and globally, launching a simultaneous nuclear strike against New York and Israel. The Soviets join in the ensuing nuclear war, in which tens of millions are killed. The Organization emerges victorious from this social collapse which they have engineered, rebuilding society firstly through establishing eugenic enclaves:

Those who were admitted – and that meant only children, women of childbearing age, and able-bodied men willing to fight in the Organization's ranks – were subjected to much more severe racial screening than had been used to separate Whites from non-Whites in California. It was no longer sufficient to be merely White; in order to eat one had to be judged the bearer of especially valuable genes.

In Detroit the practice was first established (and it was later adopted elsewhere) of providing any able-bodied White male who sought admittance to the Organization's enclave with one hot meal and a bayonet or other edged weapon. His forehead was then marked with an indelible dye, and he was turned out and could be readmitted permanently only by

33 Ibid., p. 158.   34 Ibid., p. 162.

bringing back the head of a freshly-killed black or other non-White. This practice assured that precious food would not be wasted on those who would not or could not add to the Organization's fighting strength, but it took a terrible toll on the weaker and more decadent White elements.[35]

There follows 'the mopping-up period, when the last of the non-White bands were hunted down and exterminated, followed by the final purge of undesirable racial elements among the remaining White population.'[36] Then only the Chinese remain as a threat:

> Therefore, the Organization resorted to a combination of chemical, biological and radiological means, on an enormous scale, to deal with the problem. Over a period of four years some 16 million square miles of the earth's surface, from the Ural Mountains to the Pacific and from the Arctic Ocean to the Indian Ocean, were effectively sterilized. Thus was the Great Eastern Waste created.[37]

The novel closes with the Organization 'spread[ing] its wise and benevolent rule over the earth for all time to come.'[38]

Central to *The Turner diaries* and *Hunter*, and to the neo-Nazi worldview in general, is the idea of the International Jewish Conspiracy. According to this theory, the world is secretly governed by a cabal of shadowy Jewish plutocrats and ideologues (300 is the figure often adduced), who guide global foreign and economic policy for their own ends, and use the media (which they also control) to further their agenda, prior to assuming total control at some point in the near future. The extreme version of this thinking asserts that *every* significant international and domestic policy decision is covertly made by the International Jewish Conspiracy. This, certainly, is what Randy and Vicki Weaver believed.[39] Ronson records the following exchange with Pastor Richard Butler, spiritual leader of the Aryan Nations:

> 'Randy Weaver came out here to be away from the multicultural trash that's infected our nation,' explained Pastor Butler. 'Very sad that his wife and son were murdered. The philosophy of the New World Order is to murder children.'
> 'Who is in charge of the New World Order?' I asked him.
> 'The anti-Christ Jew,' he said. 'The same one that murdered Abel.'
> 'All Jews or just some Jews?' I asked him.

35 Ibid., pp 206–7.   36 Ibid., p. 209.   37 Ibid., p. 210.   38 Ibid., p. 211.   39 Ronson, *Them*, p. 50; Walter, *Every knee shall bow*, pp 41–2 and passim; Stern, *Militias*, pp 21–3.

'*All* Jews,' he said. 'It's a blood order. DNA has proved it.'

'But not all bankers and multinationalists are Jews,' I said.

'If you against the white race, you are anti-Christ. And if you are anti-Christ, you are a Jew,' he said. 'Simple as that.'[40]

Jews, Oscar Yeager is told in *Hunter*, are 'certainly not White [...] Virtually all of the media are controlled by Jews, and they call the tune for everyone else in the media. The elimination of our race is at the top of their agenda.'[41] While Yeager begins by murdering inter-racial couples, he soon moves on to high-profile Jews in politics and the media, killing newspaper columnist David Jacobs, and liberal Congressman Stephen Horowitz. Likewise, *all* of the action of *The Turner diaries* is in a sense motivated by one event, the passing of the 'Cohen Act' of 1988, which 'outlawed all private ownership of firearms in the United States', an act which politicizes Earl Turner and many others like him into joining the Organization.[42] Turner's first act as a member of the Organization is the killing of a Jewish shopkeeper, Saul I. Berman; he comes to realize that terrorism is the only option, as 'the Jews have taken over the country fair and square, according to the Constitution'.[43] The cataclysmic nuclear war which closes the novel, precipitating the destruction of the System and the revolution which brings about the Organization's New World Order, is described thus:

> We knew the fat was really in the fire; we were in the middle of a nuclear civil war, and within the next few days the fate of the planet would be decided for all time. Now it was either the Jews or the White race, and everyone knew the game was for keeps.[44]

In neo-Nazi parlance, the US government is frequently referred to as ZOG, which stands for 'Zionist Occupation Government', a term coined by (alleged) former CIA agent Eric Thomson in his 1976 article 'Welcome to ZOG-World'. Thomson is still writing, or was until 2003: his website contains hundreds of his articles, on ZOG, Israel, Darwinism (an 'unwieldy tool of ZOG'), Jewish genetics, 'The Yellow Peril Revisited', 'The Hitler We Loved and Why' and George Orwell (of whom Thomson is a devotee, but for completely the wrong reasons).[45] Being an admirer of Orwell, Thomson also writes fiction, in which he expounds his characteristic worldview of anti-Semitism and Jewish conspiracy theorizing ('ZOG'), combined with Odinism, 'the putative religion of the pre-Christian Nordics', with its 'watchwords' of 'Faith, Folk, Family' and its governing 'Court

40 Ibid., p. 223. 41 Andrew Macdonald, *Hunter* (1989; Hillsboro, WV, 1998), p. 41. 42 Macdonald, *The Turner diaries*, p. 1. 43 Ibid., p. 173. 44 Ibid., pp 181–2. 45 For Thomson's website, 'BLUE/ERIC: Writings of Eric Thomson', see www.faem.com/eric/, accessed 21 Mar. 2007.

of Gothar', to which some of the outer fringes of the Far Right adhere.[46] I want to quote at length here the opening section of Thomson's 'The Awakening – An Odinist Short Story', which I think gives a good sense of the man and his preoccupations, not to mention his prose, which falls somewhat short of Orwell – though it's worth remembering that Thomson's ideas are taken with great seriousness by some very dangerous men:

'But Rabbi, a goy is a goy is a goy!' Israel shook his untidy head, causing his frizzy Afro hairdo to gyrate like tiny coiled springs.

The Elder raised his hand to still the outburst. 'Enough of your chutzpah. I should not have to tell you that our tribe depends for its survival on information. We must be informed always and in advance of the goyims' intentions.'

'Yes,' interjected another member of the hook-nosed company. 'What you tell us of this shiksa's activities is most interesting. You say she is behaving like a missionary, talking of a "Great Awakening"!'

The Elders, being Jews, were in the habit of interrupting others' conversations, and the fat rabbi was no exception. 'Nach! But most important, you say she does not speak of these things with all the students, just the Whites!'

'Most unusual at a university. By such time a goy should be thoroughly bent to our teaching,' mused the first Elder as he scratched his nose.

A chill of windswept snow entered the chamber, causing the candles to flicker upon the seven-stemmed candelabra, for a moment dispelling the rank odor of kosher bodies.

'Shut the door, schmuck. You vant ve should freeze our asses off?' shouted the fat Elder. 'Oh, it's you, Rabbi Kitzel. Excuse me for saying it, but good you don't look.'

The melting snow still dripped from the rabbi's proboscis as he flung a sodden leaflet upon the gold-inlaid kaballistic symbols which decorated the top of the Council Table. 'Good I don't feel. Look at that!' He pointed a claw-like finger at the leaflet.

Responding to the heat of the stuffy room or to the command of some Higher Power, the leaflet unfolded, blossoming like a flower of purity in the midst of the vampiric assembly. Defiantly emblazoned upon the single sheet of white paper were the bold letters forming the slogan 'BUY ARYAN!'[47]

46 Barkun, *Religion and the racist right*, p. 68. My account of the precepts and governance of Odinism is taken from the official Odinist website, 'The Odinic Rite: Odinism for the Modern World', www.odinic-rite.org/index2.html, accessed 21 Mar. 2007. Many Odinists refute any connections with the Far Right: see for example 'Odinism v. Nazism', www.angelfire.com/wy/wyrd/odinvsnazi.html (accessed 21 Mar. 2007) whose author comments that 'the name "Odinism" in [the] USA has been defiled due to the actions of some people who commit terrorism and racism and have become monitored by some hate group monitors.'
47 Eric Thomson, 'The Awakening', www.faem.com/eric/2000/et016.htm, accessed 21 Mar. 2007.

The reference to the Jews as 'Elders' here signifies a reference to the most notorious document in the history of anti-Semitism, *The protocols of the learned Elders of Zion*. This is the canonical text of the International Jewish Conspiracy, a book which, according to some accounts, first became public after it was daringly stolen from the chambers of Theodor Herzl, the father of modern Zionism – who was clearly acting in accord with the precepts laid out by the Elders, or was an Elder himself. It was required reading for Adolf Hitler and indeed all Nazi ideologues, who devoured and acted upon its every word. It is no exaggeration to say that Hitler's entire anti-Semitic philosophies were initially predicated on his reading of the *Protocols* somewhere around 1919, informing a worldview he did not substantially change thereafter. The *Protocols*, indeed, sold in huge quantities in Weimar Germany – especially among the professional classes. By Hitler's rise to power in 1933, it was in its thirty-third German edition.[48]

The argument of the *Protocols* is complex and repetitive, and often contradictory; but in essence runs as follows:[49] An international secret society of Jews, the Elders of Zion, has long been plotting global control and the subjugation of the Gentiles, the forthcoming reign of '*the King-Despot of the blood of Zion, whom we are preparing for the world*' (III:15 – this figure is obviously an analogue of the Antichrist). These Jews have, in fact, been 'bred and reared from early childhood to rule the affairs of the whole world' (II:2). Freemasonry has been used as a 'screen' for the activities of the Elders (IV:2), who have insinuated themselves or their representatives in or near the seats of power in all major institutions, and are now merely awaiting their moment to take final control: until such time, the Elders will remain 'invisible' to the world (I:15). The Elders operate through 'Force and Make-believe [...] bribery, deceit and treachery' (I:23). They have ensured that the young are inculcated into a set of beliefs which the Elders know to be false: 'Darwinism, Marxism, Nietzche-ism. To us Jews, at any rate, it should be plain to see what a disintegrating importance these directives have had upon the minds of the *goyim*' (II:3). Liberalism has replaced force as the dominant system of government in the West. This in turn has afforded the conditions wherein the Elders can exercise most control, as it is only a strong ruler who could have saved the Gentiles (I:6; X:10). The Elders have therefore plotted the downfall of aristocracy and fostered socialism, communism and anarchism (III:6–7); they were the guiding force behind the French Revolution (VI:14); indeed, '*We have in our service persons of all opinions, of all doctrines, restorating monarchists, demagogues, socialists, communists, and utopian dreamers of all kinds*'

---

48 For the *Protocols* in Nazi Germany, see Norman Cohn, *Warrant for genocide: the myth of the Jewish world conspiracy and the protocols of the Elders of Zion* (1967; London, 1996), pp 138–237. 49 *Protocols of the learned Elders of Zion*, trans. Victor E. Marsden, (1922; London, 1941). The *protocols* are presented in numerical order, 1–24, with further numerical subdivisions within each of them, like Biblical chapters and verses. References are given here in this way, incorporated into the main body of the text.

(IX:4). In fact, the Elders secretly have a hand in all international decisions already (V:5). They plan to rig elections and put in place puppet-presidents with exploitable weaknesses (X:13).

The real coup of the Elders has been to dismantle extant structures and institutions of authority – the monarchy, the aristocracy, the Church. They have worked to secularize the West, to replace Christianity with the dictates of industry and economic necessity: '*it is indispensable for us to undermine all faith, to tear out of the minds of the GOYIM the very principle of Godhead and the spirit, and to put in its place arithmetical calculations and material needs*' (IV:3). Western policy will further be destabilized by terrorism (VII:6), and by a series of specifically economic wars engineered by the Elders:

> It is indispensable for our purpose that wars, as far as possible, should not result in territorial gains: war will thus be brought on to the economic ground, where nations will not fail to perceive in the assistance we give the strength of our predominance, and this state of things will put both sides at the mercy of our international *agentur*; which possess millions of eyes ever on the watch and unhampered by any limitations whatsoever. Our international rights will then wipe out national rights, in the proper sense of right, and will rule the nations precisely as the civil law of States rules the relations of their subjects among themselves. (II:1)

This is a prelude to the calculated economic crisis the Elders will then bring about, causing the ruination of the Gentiles, who have placed all of their energies in the capitalist system, unaware that it was being manipulated all along by the Jews, who control the financial world (I:27). The Gentiles will be further exhausted by a series of terrorist measures: 'dissension, hatred, struggle, envy, and even by the use of torture, by starvation, BY THE INOCULATION OF DISEASES [that is, by germ warfare], by want' (X:19). Having achieved this, the plan is to create a 'Super-Government Administration' to seize political control with overwhelming force (V:11; XI:3). Gentile intellectuals and leaders will be exterminated (VI:7); the rest of the Gentiles will become a *lumpen proletariat* incapable of political thought, who will 'bow down before us, for no other reason but to get the right to exist' (VI:6). Having gained power, the Elders will control the definition of freedom through rigid control of the press and other organs of communication, although a sham dissent will be permitted, on preordained topics, to keep the proletariat controlled by fostering the illusion of freedom of speech. (One assumes that Orwell was aware of the contents of the *Protocols*, and that *1984*'s Emmanuel Goldstein – whose Book, which Winston Smith reads, is often very similar to the *Protocols* – is himself a version of an Elder of Zion. When he is inducted into the Order, Earl Turner is given a similar secret book to read.)

When Earl Turner describes the Jews as 'Satan's spawn', he is not speaking figuratively.[50] The neo-Nazi movement has an underpinning theology, which they call Christian Identity, or more simply Identity. Central to Identity belief is what is known as the 'Devil's Seed' theory, which states that Original Sin was born with the birth of Cain, who was the product of a sexual liaison between Eve and the serpent. Humanity is thus split into two bloodlines, the descendents of Adam (through Seth), and the descendents of Satan (through Cain). There is some tenuous scriptural authority for this: in Genesis 3:15, God says to the serpent, 'And I will put an enmity between thee and the woman, and between thy seed and her seed', while in Genesis 4:25 Eve discusses the birth of Seth: 'For God [...] hath appointed me another seed instead of Abel, whom Cain slew'. The former passage is taken to mean that the seed of the serpent forms a distinct branch or division of humanity (rather than, as I had always taken it to mean, snakes, since, as the verse goes on, 'it shall bruise thy head, and thou shalt bruise his heel'). The Jews, Identity believes, are the descendents of Cain, and thus literally 'Satan's spawn'.[51] This is a belief widely disseminated among the American far right. Richard Butler's Aryan Nations headquarters contains a library called 'The Ministry of Truth' (more chilling bad-Orwellianism), with publications including 'The Cain-Satanic Seed-Line', while the Aryan Nations website affirms: 'WE BELIEVE that there are literal children of Satan in the world today. These children are the descendants of Cain, who was the result of Eve's original sin, her physical seduction by Satan.'[52] The Posse Comitatus organization of fascistic militarists expands on this in their own website: 'Most, that call themselves jews [sic] today are in fact of the race of Lucifer through his son Cain. Cain was inherently evil from the beginning because he was of Lucifer's seed. Eve was beguiled by Lucifer and did, in the carnal sense, lay with him and begot Cain. It was a pair on the ground, not an apple on a tree! Eve was deceived by Lucifer and was lead [sic] to believe that she was laying with Yahweh God.'[53]

The modern origins of these notions are quite fascinating. They lie with the British Israel Movement, which flourished from the late-nineteenth to the mid-twentieth century.[54] Not primarily a racist organization, the British Israel Movement marshalled (and frankly abused) all the forces of nineteenth-century racial, physiological and philological theory to "demonstrate" that it was in fact the English, or sometimes the British, or sometimes Northern Europeans in general, who were in fact God's chosen people. The full panoply of British Israel thinking was

50 Macdonald, *The Turner diaries*, p. 199.   **51** For one version of the 'Devil's seed' theory, see Barkun, *Religion and the racist right*, pp 150–1. For the scriptural justification, see H. Ben Judah, *When? A prophetic novel of the near future* (1944; York, SC, nd), pp 69–70.   **52** Stern, *Militias*, p. 20; www.nidlink.com/~aryanvic/index-E.html, accessed 21 Mar. 2007.   **53** Posse Comitatus, 'Racial Identity', www.posse-comitatus.org.p2.html, accessed 21 Mar. 2007.   **54** For an account of the British Israel movement, and its connection with Christian Identity, see Barkun, *Religion and the racist right*, passim.

encapsulated towards the end of its life – yet again in an apocalyptic future fiction, *When? A prophetic novel of the near future* (1949), by the obviously pseudonymous H. Ben Juda. The following passage gives a good idea of the kinds of intellectual speculation (to put it kindly) to which British Israelism was given:

> We can therefore see that Ten-Tribed Israel migrated into the British Isles by tribes, as prophesied by the prophet Isaiah, and that the Angles changed the name to England after the Ephraim tribal insignia of the bull or calf, the Hebrew for which was Ngl, Angl, or Engl.
>
> It is further evident that after their deportation into Media, Ephraim changed their name to Ngl-Tzksons, meaning Bull Tribe of Isaac, which was later altered by time and the introduction of vowels into Anglo-Saxons. In Hebrew, Engl-ish would mean "Bull-man", which is probably the derivation of our John Bull.
>
> In the British Royal Coat-of-Arms, we still show the unicorn (or wild bull) of Ephraim, as referred to by Moses.[55]

Though clearly nonsense – this passage flagrantly commits what philologists call False Etymology, drawing connections between actually disparate words on the grounds that they happen to sound alike – *When?* was to become enormously influential in Identity thinking (as we have seen and will see, the inability to distinguish fact from fiction is a recurring feature of the radical right). In order to demonstrate that the English are in fact the chosen race, it is necessary to disprove the claims of the Jews, which 'Ben Judah' does by asserting that most Jews are not really semitic at all: while Sephardic Jews are indeed the descendents of Abraham, 'the Ashkenazim so-called Jew' is a relatively recent convert to Judaism, and thus the claim of Zionists (most of whom were Ashkenazim) to Palestine are groundless. To "prove" this, the author of *When?* draws on the work of Theodore Lothrop Stoddard, the influential 1920s racial theorist and author of books such as *The rising tide of color* (1920), who had argued that modern Jews were not in fact the descendents of Israelites but of Hittites. *When?* quotes Stoddard, here arguing from craniometry, as follows:

> Mankind is divided into two great races, the Dolicocephalic (long-skulled) and the Brachycephalic (round-skulled). The Ashkenazim are round-skulled, whilst the real semitic Jews are of long-skulled race. Racially, they are as far apart as the Poles, and their (Askenazim) claim to Palestine on historic grounds is therefore worthless.[56]

55 Ben Judah, *When?*, pp 37–8. 56 Ibid., p. 4.

Given that the Jews are in fact 'the spawn of Satan', it therefore follows that Jesus could not himself have been a Jew in the modern sense – indeed, the only one of the disciples who *was* Jewish was Judas Iscariot. *When?* quotes liberally from the *Protocols of the learned Elders of Zion*, interpreting them as a Zionist manifesto drawn up by the evil 'Synagogue of Satan', secretly plotting to control human destiny.

Of course, the *Protocols* are themselves a notorious forgery, largely plagiarized from Maurice Joly's *Dialogue aux Enfers entre Montesquieu et Machiavel* (1864), a covert criticism of the regime of Napoleon III in the form of a dialogue in which Montesquieu speaks for liberalism, Machiavelli for despotism: unsurprisingly, the *Protocols* are lifted from Machiavelli's speeches.[57] The origins of the document are still fundamentally mysterious, though they were fabricated in Paris, probably in 1897 or 1898, in the midst of the Dreyfus affair, by right-wing Russians – most likely, according to Norman Cohn, at the instigation of Piotr Ivanovich Rachkovsky, the head of the Okhrana, the Russian Secret Police, in Paris.[58] The *Protocols*, indeed, as Cohn has argued, come at the end of a century or more of shady anti-semitic writing, or of Jewish writing interpreted as incorporating or anticipating the diktats of the *Protocols*.

In August 1921, the *Times* produced its definitive account of the *Protocols* as a forgery. This killed off their reputation among all but a tiny hardcore in Britain, where their publishers, Eyre and Spottiswoode, declined to reprint them, though they continued to appear in small editions, often edited by the right-wing Russophile *Morning Post* journalist Victor Marsden. In Germany the damage was already done, while in the US Henry Ford declared himself a believer in the international Jewish conspiracy and by extension the *Protocols*, whose influence can be traced in two books published by or about Ford in 1922 – that is, a year *after* they had been revealed as a forgery – *The amazing story of Henry Ford* by James M. Miller and *My life and work* by Henry Ford in collaboration with S. Crowther.[59] In other words, the proof of forgery made little or no difference to belief in the absolute veracity of the document among committed anti-Semites. As I have already argued, rejected knowledge can be completely impervious to falsification, and this is what makes it so extraordinarily potent. As I hope this article has demonstrated, the far right are, to reiterate, characterized generally by a recurring inability to distinguish fact from fiction, and it is this very inability which the great liberal historian Richard Hofstadter has identified as an important feature of what he famously termed 'The paranoid style in American politics', a political mode which has resurfaced many times in American history (in living memory as McCarthyism, as politicized Evangelical Christianity, and as the militia movement), usually as a reaction against modernity, liberalism or cosmopolitanism

57 Cohn, *Warrant for genocide*, p. 8off.   58 Ibid., p. 113.   59 Ibid., p. 179.

(hence its continuing appeal, which we have noted, to the marginal or disenfranchised), whose exponents:

> regard a "vast" or "gigantic" conspiracy as *the motive force* in historical events. History *is* a conspiracy, set in motion by demonic of almost transcendent power, and what is felt to be needed to defeat it is not the usual methods of political give-and-take, but an all-out crusade. The paranoid spokesman sees the fate of this conspiracy in apocalyptic terms – the traffics in the birth and death of whole worlds, whole political orders, whole systems of human values. He is always manning the barricades of civilization. He constantly lives at a turning point: it is now or never in organizing resistance to conspiracy. Time is forever just running out.[60]

I said earlier that *The Turner diaries*, like many of the products of the far right, is a utopian text, springing from disenfranchisement and a consequent desire, however twisted, for a better world. But, as Karl Popper suggests in *The open society and its enemies* (1945), the problem with utopianism is that it is *inherently* fascistic – this, no doubt, is a significant part of its appeal for Macdonald and his readers.[61] Based as it is on Platonism – on a philosophy of ideal forms (of government, polity, society) – utopianism, the desire to remake the world wholesale according to a pre-existent plan, is a fundamentally *artistic* desire based on *aesthetics* and *perfectionism*, and is thus unable to accommodate the messy, complex realities of socio-political praxis except through apocalyptic violence. In 1959 Aldous Huxley, who knew more than most about utopias, looked back on the political history of his own lifetime, on the totalizing political systems and master-narratives, be they of the left or right, communist or fascist, and concluded that:

> the theoretical reduction of unmanageable multiplicity to comprehensible unity becomes the practical reduction of human diversity to subhuman uniformity, of freedom to servitude. In politics the equivalent of a fully developed scientific theory or philosophical system is a totalitarian dictatorship. In economics, the equivalent of a beautifully composed work of art is the smoothly running factory in which the workers are perfectly adjusted to the machines. The Will to Order can make tyrants out of those who merely aspire to clean up a mess. The beauty of tidiness is used as a justification for despotism.[62]

60 Richard Hofstadter, *The paranoid style in American politics and other essays* (New York, 1965), pp 29–30.
61 Popper, *The open society and its enemies, volume one: the spell of Plato* (1945; London, 2003). 62 Aldous Huxley, *Brave new world revisited* (1959; London, 1994), p. 31.

Popper, writing in the last year of the Second World War, made the same point, but more starkly: the 'out and out radicalism', he wrote 'of the aestheticist's refusal to compromise' means that the utopian politician 'must eradicate the existing traditions. He must purify, purge, expel, banish, and kill'.[63]

63 Popper, *The open society and its enemies*, p. 176.

Fear in an age without meaning

BILL DURODIÉ

Man is not destroyed by suffering;
he is destroyed by suffering without meaning.[1]

The search for meaning

On 11 May 2006 the British government published the *Report of the Official Account of the Bombings in London on 7th July 2005*.[2] This document examined what was known of the terrible events that had occurred the previous summer and which had led to the loss of fifty-two innocent lives, in addition to those of the four perpetrators. The preface to the report describes it as a 'narrative' and that is an apt and telling description for what follows. The document presents a step-by-step account of "what" happened, "where" and "when" it happened, by "who" it was carried out and even "how", but – despite investigations lasting almost a year and a section devoted to the issue – little explanation as to "*why*".

Yet it is precisely the "*why*" that is of particular interest. Without understanding why, there is little hope of precluding such incidents from happening again in the future. In addition, not being clear as to "*why*" allows all-manner of self-appointed experts, pundits and commentators – according to their pre-existing political persuasions – to project their own pet theory onto the situation with a view to shaping ensuing policy. Most common among these purported explanations has been the presumption that the attacks formed some kind of retribution for the British government having supported the US-led invasion of Iraq in 2003.[3] But oddly, the

---

1 Phrase attributed to the psychoanalyst and holocaust survivor Viktor Frankl, author of *Man's search for meaning* (Boston, 1959). 2 'Report of the Official Account of the Bombings in London on 7th July 2005'. Norwich: HMSO, HC 1087 (2006). 3 Such a view has become mainstream across the political spectrum, migrating from George Galloway's tirade against Tony Blair upon being elected MP for the Respect Party in the London Borough of Tower Hamlets in 2005, to the authors of 'Riding Pillion for Tackling Terrorism is a High-risk Policy', a paper in the Chatham House publication *Security, terrorism and the UK*, ISP/NSC

assumed ring-leader, Mohammad Sidique Khan, made no specific mention of Iraq in his so-called martyrdom video released soon after the bombings.

Others suggest the bombers to have been part of a resurgent and radical global Islamist movement, or extremist conspiracy. Accordingly, the presumed influences of madrasas, mosques and mullahs have come under scrutiny. Alternative explanations and justifications have been sought in the supposed social and economic backgrounds of the conspirators,[4] as well as their psychological profiles and educational performances. Much has been made of the fact that two of the four had travelled to Pakistan between November 2004 and February 2005, but the report indicates that who they may have met there 'has not yet been established'. In fact, the *Official Account* describes the backgrounds of the perpetrators of the London bombings as 'unexceptional', their purported links to al-Qaeda as lacking 'firm evidence', and their methods and materials as respectively requiring 'no great expertise' and being 'readily available'.[5]

We should not take the assertions of the bombers to have acted on behalf of other Muslims at face-value. A parallel *Report into the London Terrorist Attacks on 7 July 2005*, issued by the Intelligence and Security Committee also notes that the claimed responsibility for the attacks by Ayman al-Zawaheri was, 'not supported by any firm evidence.'[6] By interpreting the available information according to their own preferred models, many analysts have, in effect, been doing the terrorists' thinking and talking for them. They have helped to shape the vacuum of information and confusion otherwise left behind. These purported explanations may, in their turn, encourage and even serve as justifications to others intent on action. But are they right?

In truth, we will never know exactly what motivated the London bombers. Those truly responsible are no longer around to inform us. The publication of a rather limited 'narrative', rather than of an in-depth political analysis shows how difficult it has been for the authorities to establish the motives and drivers of those concerned. It suggests that much of the superficial speculation is not supported by any hard evidence. There is little to indicate that Khan, or his collaborators Shehzad Tanweer, Jermaine Lindsay and Hasib Hussain were particularly pious or held any deep appreciation of the Koran. Still less that they had direct relations to anyone in Palestine, Bosnia or Iraq. They did not bother to ask their families, friends or neighbours what they thought about such matters. That is why these were truly shocked by their actions. The bombers met in the local gymnasium rather than the local mosque, they went on outdoor activities together and, the day before the attacks, one of them played that quintessential English game –

Briefing Paper 05/01, London: RIIA.   4 R. Briggs, C. Fieschi & H. Lownsbrough, *Bringing it home: community-based approaches to counter-terrorism* (London, 2006).   5 'Report of the Official Account of the Bombings in London on 7th July 2005'. Norwich: HMSO, HC 1087 (2006).   6 'Report into the London Terrorist Attacks on 7 July 2005'. Norwich: HMSO, 13. Cm 6785 (2006).

cricket – in his local park. In the end, they acted alone – in isolation – a form of private gesture against a world they appeared to feel little connection with, let alone ability to influence. They took part in the ultimate 'not in my name' protest – a trend and slogan manifested by many other interest groups nowadays.[7]

The real truth, then, about the London bombings may be that they were largely pointless and meaningless. This would suggest a problem entirely opposed to that presented by politicians and officials, media and other commentators alike. The bombers were fantasists – want to be terrorists – searching for an identity and a meaning to their lives. They hoped to find it in a global cause that was not their own, but that appeared to give expression to their nihilistic sense of grievance. Islam was their motif, not their motive.

This interpretation may offer little solace to the relatives of those affected. Their demands, as well as those of others, for a public inquiry into the matter appear more like a desperate attempt to find a more substantial explanation or to attribute blame where, for now at least, none can be found.[8] That is hardly surprising, as the desire to understand the causes of, or to attach some kind of meaning to, adversity is a strong one. It can be deflating or confusing to discover that some event did not have the profundity originally attached to it, or that it was largely pointless. Nevertheless, we could all learn from the mother of Theo van Gogh, the Dutch filmmaker murdered by a similar, self-styled radical Islamist, who indicated in relation to her plight:

> What is so regrettable [...] is that Theo has been murdered by such a loser, such an incoherent person. Murder or manslaughter is always a terrible thing but to be killed by such a figure makes it especially hard.[9]

Recognizing the random and unpredictable character of her loss ensures it is not endowed with portentous meaning. It does not lead to a demand to reorganize society around the presumption of similar events occurring again. To do so would be to normalize extremes and thereby to marginalize what is normal. This would effectively 'do the terrorists' job for them',[10] by institutionalizing instability.

The usual rejoinder to this is to argue that terrorists 'only need to be lucky once',[11] while governments and their security agencies must counter them at all times if they are not to lose the public's support. But the evidence from the 7 July

---

7 'Not in my name' was the slogan used by many of those opposed to the Iraq war of 2003. Faisal Devji points to a growing usage of such non-political statements by a wide variety of groups encompassing environmental protestors and others in *Landscapes of the Jihad: militancy, morality, modernity* (New Delhi, 2005). 8 This is not to belittle the genuine grief of all those concerned, or indeed their understandable desire for support. 9 Cited in *De Telegraaf*, 26 July 2005. www.telegraaf.nl/binnenland/23285701/Moeder_Van_Gogh:_enige_juiste_straf.html, accessed 5 Mar. 2007. 10 A common warning from the Prime Minister, the head of the Security Service and many others. 11 A phrase attributed to the IRA after failing to assassinate the then Prime Minister, Margaret Thatcher in the bombing of the Grand Hotel in Brighton in 1984.

2005 bombings rather suggests this perception not to be true. Most people chose to go to work the following day.

As the quotation at the beginning of this article from the Holocaust survivor and philosopher, Viktor Frankl suggests, an absence of meaning is not just disorienting, it can be debilitating. Indeed, it is our failure to place things into an agreed framework that can readily make random events assume catastrophic proportions, thereby inducing a sense of fear and terror. The French political scientist, Zaki Laïdi, has suggested that the dissolution of the old – Cold War – world order was what in particular helped to create what he has coined to be 'A World Without Meaning.'[12] Accordingly, there is now a desperate and obsessive search for meaning and identity in society, even in situations that can be quite meaningless.

'What is it that can turn a young man from Leeds into a suicide bomber?' we ask ourselves. But this question, clear and logical as it seems initially, is itself a product of the times we live in. At the height of the Second World War nobody asked what turned young men from Berlin into aerial bombers. Within an assumed framework of meaning, or in pursuit of agreed goals, such events are understood and can be withstood – as was the case during the IRA's terror campaign on mainland Britain from 1973 to 1997. Today, in an age when nothing is, or appears, so obvious any more, everything is up for grabs.

The process of radicalization

To some, what is happening was predictable. The idea of a 'clash of civilisations', taken from the title of Samuel Huntington's 1996 book,[13] assumed that future conflicts would increasingly pit East against West in' a fundamental conflict over values. This thesis benefited from a renewed degree of interest in the aftermath of the attacks upon America in September 2001. But few have critically inquired into the true ideological origins of those perpetrating acts of terrorism in the name of Islam.

Others have been more circumspect in their pronouncements, but in essence the core assumption remains. In a speech on security to the Foreign Policy Centre in London, British Prime Minister Tony Blair argued in reference to the ongoing war on terror, that 'This is not a clash between civilizations. It is a clash about civilization. It is the age-old battle between progress and reaction, between those who embrace and see opportunity in the modern world and those who reject its existence; between optimism and hope on the one hand; and pessimism and fear on the other.'[14]

12 Z. Laïdi, *A world without meaning* (London, 1998).   13 S.P. Huntington, *The clash of civilizations and the remaking of world order* (New York, 1996).   14 T. Blair, *Not a clash between civilisations, but a clash about*

But the ideas and protagonists Tony Blair had in mind in this 'clash about civilization' are all foreign in their origins or, at least, externally-oriented and focused. He continued: 'The roots of global terrorism and extremism are indeed deep. They reach right down through decades of alienation, victimhood and political oppression in the Arab and Muslim world.'[15]

In a similar vein, the recently released British government document, *Countering international terrorism: the United Kingdom's strategy* (2006), identifies the need for a 'battle of ideas, challenging the ideological motivations that extremists believe justify the use of violence.'[16] This key strand of the strategy is described in terms indicating its having been solely conceptualized as affecting, or targeting, Muslims or Muslim communities. So while most politicians and officials have slowly reconciled themselves to the fact that many of the perpetrators of contemporary acts of terror are Western-born or educated, the glib assumption remains that what drives them is a foreign ideology or agenda that only Muslims can understand or address – a point reasserted by the Prime Minister in subsequent comments to the House of Commons Liaison Committee,[17] and again more recently by the Home Secretary, John Reid.[18]

But is the problem really a 'clash about civilisation' or even, as the Home Secretary proposed, that we are having to manage the consequences of some kind of conflict within Islam? In some ways it seems we rather face a more profound cultural crisis domestically. To recognize the problem as such, however, is discomforting for Western leaders and societies. It would require understanding the extent to which many of the ideas that inspire the nihilist terrorism we witness today are largely home-grown and inculcated. While conceding that many of the perpetrators and conspirators are increasingly turning out to have been Western in their origins most, including Tony Blair, still presume their guiding influences to have been reactionary ideas and ideologies from the East. Hence, a lazy empirical approach has been employed to identify so-called risk factors that may lead individuals to becoming 'radicalised'.[19] But this approach largely assumes a conclusion and then goes in search of the evidence to corroborate it. It is profoundly unscientific. Above all, it ignores the dominant social context within which most such individuals find themselves – that is, advanced Western societies.

civilisation. London: Foreign Policy Centre, 21 March 2006. fpc.org.uk/events/past/231, accessed 5 Mar. 2007. **15** Ibid. **16** 'Countering international terrorism: the United Kingdom's strategy'. Norwich: HMSO, 13. Cm 6888 (2006). **17** T. Blair, 'Uncorrected transcript of oral evidence to the House of Commons liaison committee', 4 July 2006. www.publications.parliament.uk/pa/cm200506/cmselect/cmliaisn/uc709-iii/uc70902.htm, accessed 5 Mar. 2007. **18** J. Reid, speech to Muslim groups in East London, 20 September 2006. press.homeoffice.gov.uk/Speeches/sp-muslim-group-20-09-06, accessed 5 Mar. 2007. **19** There is a burgeoning discussion on the causes of so-called radicalisation, emerging from a wide variety of organizations, little of which is peer-reviewed. One example was the recent BBC documentary by veteran broadcaster Peter Taylor; *Al-Qaeda: turning the terrorists* broadcast on 13 September 2006. The European Commission has also issued a Communication on *Terrorist recruitment: addressing the factors contributing to violent radicalisation* (COM (2005) 313 final).

Unsurprisingly, many researchers find their prejudices confirmed by using this method – that is what is wrong with it. Accordingly, listening to the inflammatory rhetoric of an obscure cleric or emanating from an impoverished background appears to be reasserted in their minds as 'radicalising' influences. All agree that a deep sense of injustice for affairs in the Middle East is also key.[20] But one could equally propose that being a billionaire, driving a white Mercedes or running the family business are significant risk factors. Certainly all three have featured in Osama bin Laden's life. Starting with an answer and then joining up the dots is child's play. It offers no insight beyond assumed conclusions.

The trial in London of the so-called 'Crawley Group', accused of plotting further terrorist atrocities through having acquired a large quantity of ammonium nitrate fertilizer is quite apposite in this regard. Their list of supposed targets included shoppers, drinkers, football fans and allegedly, 'slags' in nightclubs.[21] Such ideas appear to reflect those of contemporary policy-makers and their exaggerated fears of social disorder in certain sectors of society rather more than verses from the Koran. So, could paying too much attention to government policy be a radicalizing factor too?

In fact, as the American professor Marc Sageman has pointed out in the most authoritative study of people associated with al-Qaeda,[22] there are no clear radicalizing influences or predisposing risk factors that can be identified. If anything, these individuals are likely to a have a middle- or upper-class, secular background and to be reasonably well-educated. But that would put many of the critics and commentators at risk of becoming radicalized too.

In particular though, the individuals concerned were rarely recruited from above but rather they seem actively to have sought out terrorist networks or sects that they might join. Some only converted to Islam after this. This would seem to confirm their desire to be part of something, but more importantly it raises the issue as to why they are unable to find that something closer to home. The key is not what it is that attracts a minority from a variety of backgrounds, including some who are relatively privileged, to fringe Islamist organizations, but rather what it is about our own societies and culture that these fail to provide aspirational, educated and energetic young individuals with a clear sense of purpose and collective direction through which to lead their lives and realize their ambitions. Many such individuals are then left looking for meaning elsewhere, including, for some, among various arcane belief-systems.

In some ways the nihilist criminals that detonated their rudimentary devices in London in the summer of 2005, appear to reflect the sentiments of other dis-

20 WPSO6/5 (2006). *Towards a community-based approach to counter-terrorism*. www.wiltonpark.org.uk/ documents/conferences/WPS06-5/pdfs/WPS06-5.pdf, accessed 5 Mar. 2007. 21 'Gang planned to bomb London nightclub', *Guardian*, 25 May 2006. 22 M. Sageman, *Understanding terror networks* (Pennsylvania UP, 2004).

gruntled individuals and groups across the developed world today. Their acts seem more akin to the Columbine high-school massacre in April 1999 and other such incidents, where usually respectable young men, born and educated in the West, decide for various reasons – or none that we can work out – to kill themselves and scores of civilians.

Their ideas and influences appear to have far less to do with imams and mullahs, and far more in common with the dystopian views of numerous commentators who criticize Western society today. Indeed, a recently published compilation of Osama bin Laden's writings reveals how frequently he is inclined to cite Western writers, Western diplomats and Western thinkers.[23] At one point he even advises the White House to read Robert Fisk, rather than, as one might have supposed, the Koran.

It would be remiss to ignore the growing influence of a significant degree of what some have identified as a culture of self-loathing in the developed world. If one wants to discover anti-American views coherently expressed, or people who reject the benefits of science, progress and modernity, then one need not look far to find them. Such opinions are all around us. Indeed, less than two days had passed after 9/11 when Seumas Milne first used the term anti-American in a newspaper article for the *Guardian* entitled, 'They can't see why they are hated.'[24] On the same day, the Reverend Jerry Falwell, pastor of the 22,000-member Thomas Road Baptist Church of Lynchburg, Virginia, told US television viewers that God had given America 'what we deserve'.[25] Aside from such extremes, many others point to continued American intransigence over issues such as global warming and human rights as purported explanations for what happened.

It may be unpalatable or unpleasant to recall or recognize that a significant number of people, not all of whom were Muslim or even Asian, were not that saddened to see the Twin Towers in New York going down. A sense that America had it coming was quite widespread in some supposedly respectable quarters, where a barely concealed *schadenfreude* was in evidence. This may go some way towards explaining why it is that one of those arrested in the summer of 2006, after an alleged plot to use liquid explosives on airlines flying from London's Heathrow airport, has turned out to be the son of a UK Conservative party agent.

American consumerism is now widely viewed with contempt, but this reflects a broader view of human action in the world. Increasingly, Western intellectuals have come to portray this as being largely negative.[26] In certain quarters ambition has become portrayed as arrogant, development as dangerous and success as self-

23 O. bin Laden, *Messages to the world: the statements of Osama bin Laden*, ed. B. Lawrence & trans. J. Howarth (London, 2005). 24 S. Milne, 'They can't see why they are hated', *Guardian*, 13 Sept. 2001. 25 Cited in 'God gave U.S. "What we deserve" Falwell says', *Washington Post*, 14 Sept. 2001. 26 M. Bookchin, *Re-enchanting humanity: a defense of the human spirit against anti-humanism, misanthropy, mysticism and primitivism* (London, 1995).

ish. Even in America itself power has become presented as egotism, freedom as illusory and the desire to defend oneself as the act of a bully.

Western society today is replete with individuals and institutions that appear determined to criticize and undermine human achievements. The President of Britain's Royal Society called one of his latest books *Our final century: will the human race survive the twenty-first century?* (2003),[27] while the Professor of European Thought at the London School of Economics is comfortable describing human beings as being little more than a plague upon the planet in his book entitled *Straw dogs: thoughts on humans and other animals* (2003).[28] A recent edition of the prestigious UK science journal *New Scientist* speculated positively as to what the earth would be like without humans (and presumably without the *New Scientist*) being there.[29] Nor are such ideas limited to those of a few academics. Surely, when Michael Moore's *Stupid white men* became, in 2002, a best-selling book on both sides of the Atlantic – selling over 300,000 copies in the UK in its first year of publication alone – a few bright minds in the security world and beyond should have noticed the growing depth of cynicism and disillusionment in society and their potentially adverse consequences?[30]

It is this cultural malaise and pessimistic outlook that forms the backdrop, and inevitably shapes, contemporary terrorism. Increasingly, it appears that this is sustained by two elements – the radical nihilists who are prepared to lose their lives and those of others around them in their misguided determination to leave their mark upon a world that they reject, and the nihilist intellectuals who help frame a public discourse and culture of apocalyptic failure and rejection. Yet, the authorities appear determined to identify the causes as emanating elsewhere.

Social forces

As the UK in particular has had to confront the problems of conflict and terror before, it is readily assumed by many that all that is required now is to re-ignite a bit of the "Blitz spirit" to overcome today's enemies. Not only does this approach miss the internal drivers of the problem, it fails to identify the extent to which British society – as well as others in the developed world – has been transformed in less than a generation.

One of the best indicators of this is through our use of language. The sociologist Frank Furedi points to how certain words have exploded into popular consciousness in recent years, reflecting fundamental changes in society. For instance, references to the word "risk" in British broadsheet newspapers increased ten-fold

---

27 M. Rees, *Our final century: will the human race survive the twenty-first century?* (London, 2003).   28 J. Gray, *Straw dogs: thoughts on humans and other animals* (London, 2003).   29 *New Scientist*, 'Earth without people: what if we all disappeared tomorrow?' 14 Oct. 2006.   30 M. Moore, *Stupid white men … and other sorry excuses for the state of the nation!* (London, 2002).

over the course of the 1990s.[31] Presumably this is not because we actually face ten times as many risks as previously. Rather, it reflects developments in our perception of the world. Furedi notes that even the way in which we use the word risk has been altered. In the past it was often used in an active sense as in "taking a risk". This suggested possible benefits, as much as inherent problems, and indicated an engaged relationship between individuals and society. Today, more often than not, the word is used passively, as in "being at risk", thereby also pointing to a more disconnected orientation towards change.

This shift towards a passive and more individuated perspective on society is equally well brought out through the emergence of a growing therapeutic discourse. Words such as "stress", "trauma" and "vulnerable" have also recently emerged into popular consciousness, undergoing a similar ten-fold increase in use over a ten-year period.[32] At the same time, more active or social concepts such as "character" or "trade union" seem to have changed their meaning. The former now often refers to a personality in some kind of television soap-opera, while the latter, which used to conjure up thoughts of some kind of social solidarity with members of a community one might not even know, is today more likely to represent a mechanism to obtain individual perks or safeguard personal security.

Fear is often understood in narrow psychological terms.[33] It is usually taken to be a self-evident emotional response to an extreme or novel situation. But fear is also a social phenomenon. How people behave in specific circumstances depends upon wider cultural norms, expectations and beliefs.[34] That we become fearful as individuals or as a society is not simply dependent upon the threats that confront us, but also on our ability to make sense of those threats and the significance attributed to them.[35] In fact, how we as individuals, and as a society, define and respond to crises is only partly dependent upon their causal agents and scale. Historically evolving cultural attitudes and outlooks, as well as other social factors, play a far greater role. Our degree of trust in authority, in other human beings and in ourselves shapes our perceptions and determines whether we consider a particular problem to be a disaster in the first place.[36]

There is, for instance, a contemporary cultural proclivity to speculate wildly as to the likelihood of adverse events and to demand high-profile responses and capabilities based on worst-case scenarios. In the end, this only serves to distract attention and divert social resources in a way that may not be warranted by a more pragmatic assessment and prioritization of all of the risks that we face.

---

31 F. Furedi, *Culture of fear: risk-taking and the morality of low expectations* (London, 2002), p. xii. 32 Furedi, *Therapy culture: cultivating vulnerability in an uncertain age* (London, 2004), pp 4–5. 33 R.W. Dozier, *Fear itself: the origin and nature of the powerful emotion that shapes our lives and our world* (New York, 1998). 34 See for example C. Robin, *Fear: the history of a political idea* (Oxford UP, 2006) or J. Bourke, *Fear: a cultural history* (London, 2005). 35 D.L. Scruton (ed.), *Sociophobics: the anthropology of fear* (Boulder, 1986). 36 E.L. Quarantelli, *What is a disaster?* (London, 1998).

Technique and technology certainly help in the face of adversity, although the fact that particular societies both choose and have the capacity to prioritize such elements is also, ultimately, socially determined. More broadly, it is possible to say that resilience – loosely defined as the ability of individuals and society to keep going after a shock – is most definitely a function of cultural attitude or outlook. Cultural values point to why it is that, at certain times and in certain societies, a widespread loss of life fails to be a point of discussion, while at other times or in a different society, even a very limited loss can become a key cultural reference point.[37] This evolving context and framework of cultural meanings explains such variations as our widespread indifference to the daily loss of life upon our roads, as opposed to, for instance, the shock that ensued across the globe from the loss of just seven lives aboard the *Challenger* spacecraft in 1986.

The loss of *Challenger* represented a low-point in the cultural assessment of human technological capabilities. It was a blow to our assumption of steady scientific and technological progress that no number of everyday car accidents could replicate. It fed into and drove a debate that continues to this day regarding our relationship with nature and a presumed human arrogance in seeking to pursue goals beyond ourselves.

Hence, emergencies and disasters, including terrorist attacks, take on a different role dependent upon what they represent to particular societies at particular times, rather than solely on the basis of objective indicators, such as real costs and lives lost. In this sense, our response to terrorist incidents, such as that which occurred on 11 September 2001, teaches us far more about ourselves than about the terrorists.[38]

On the whole, the history of human responses to disaster, including terrorist attacks, is quite heartening. People tend to be at their most co-operative and focused at such times. There are few instances of panic.[39] The recent earthquake and tsunami in the Indian Ocean on 26 December 2004 serve as a salutary reminder of this. Amidst the tales of devastation and woe, numerous individual and collective acts of bravery and sacrifice stand out, reminding us of the ordinary courage, co-operation and conviction that are part of the human condition at such times. People often come together in an emergency in new, and largely unexpected ways, re-affirming core social bonds and their common humanity. Research reveals communities that were considered to be better off emotionally through having had to cope with adversity or a crisis.[40] Rather than being psycho-

37 E.L. Quarantelli & R.R. Dynes, 'Response to social crisis and disaster', *Annual Review of Sociology*, 3:1 (1977), 23–49. 38 B. Durodié, 'Cultural precursors and psychological consequences of contemporary western responses to acts of terror', in S. Wessely & V. Krasnov (eds), *Psychological aspects of the new terrorism: a NATO Russia dialogue* (Amsterdam, 2005), pp 37–53. 39 B. Durodié & S. Wessely, 'Resilience or panic? The public and terrorist attack', *The Lancet*, 360:9349 (2002), 1901–2. 40 Furedi, 'Disaster and contemporary consciousness: the changing cultural frame for the experience of adversity', *Draft report* (2004). www.terrorismresearch.net/finalreports/Furedi/FurediReportFull.pdf, accessed 5 Mar. 2007.

logically scarred, it appears equally possible to emerge enhanced. In other words, while a disaster, including a terrorist attack, destroys physical and economic capital, it has the potential to serve as a rare, if unfortunate, opportunity in contemporary society to build up social capital.

Of course, terrorists hope that their acts will lead to a breakdown in social cohesion. Whether this is so is up to us. Civilians are the true first responders and first line of defence at such times. Their support prior to, and their reactions subsequent to any incident, are crucial. Disasters act as one of the best indicators of the strength of pre-existing social bonds across a community. Societies that are together, pull together – those that are apart, are more likely to fall apart.

While there is much empirical evidence pointing to the positive elements of ordinary human responses to disaster, it is usually after the immediate danger has subsided that the real values of society as a whole come to the fore.[41] It is then that the cultural outlook and impact of social leaders and their responses begins to hold sway. These determine whether the focus is on reconstruction and the future, or on retribution and the past. Sadly, despite the variety of ways in which it is possible to interpret and respond to different emergencies, the onus today seems to veer away from a celebration of the human spirit and societal resilience, towards a focus on compensation and individual vulnerability. The recent trend to encourage mass outpourings of public grief, minutes of silence or some other symbols of "conspicuous compassion" is likely to be negative in this regard.

In the long run, cultural confusion as to who we are, what we stand for and where we are going undermines our attempts at building social resilience. Society today is less coherent than it was a generation or so ago, it may also be less compliant, but above all it appears less confident as to its aims and purposes. This can not be resolved by training ourselves to respond technically to disasters, but by a much broader level of debate and engagement in society – not just in relation to terrorism and other crises – but to broader social issues.

Presumably, people are prepared to risk their lives fighting fires or fighting wars, not so that their children can, in their turn, grow up to fight fires and fight wars, but because they believe that there is something more important to life worth fighting for. It is the absence of any discussion as to what that something more important actually is that leaves us effectively unarmed in the face of adversity today.

Social resilience

In September 1940, at the height of the Blitz, 5,730 people lost their lives in London alone. This is one hundred times larger than the number killed by the

---

41 R. Dynes, 'On disasters and popular culture', *University of Delaware Disaster Research Centre Preliminary Paper* (2000), 295.

London bombers on the 7 July 2005 and almost twice the figure killed on 9/11. By the end of the Second World War the final fatality count in London had reached 30,000. How could the British population be so resilient in the face of such adversity?

In his landmark study, representing the official interpretation of these events, Richard Titmuss suggested the key factors to have been clear leadership, equitable treatment and the provision of full employment to keep people occupied.[42] Others, such as Angus Calder have since questioned this interpretation, pointing to the existence of looting, a significant black market and juvenile delinquency as evidence that the famed 'Blitz spirit' was not all that it was cracked up to be.[43] Nevertheless, it is clear that the overall response was a remarkable display of fortitude. And while government motives may have been brought into question, at the time and subsequently, at least it is reasonably clear that it had some. During the Second World War, there was a clear sense of the need to carry on with normal life and to maintain everyday roles and responsibilities. Most of the population was actively engaged in the war effort and there was a particular focus on ensuring that people would not develop a 'shelter-mentality'.[44]

Such responses reveal a number of important lessons for today. It is assumed by some that the world has now been irrevocably changed by the events of 9/11 and 7/7; in other words, normalcy may never be restored. What's more, as the public can not be directly engaged in counter-terrorist activities they are largely encouraged to prepare themselves for the worst. However, one of the most striking changes in the disaster literature of the last fifty years has been in how it is assumed ordinary human beings react in a crisis.[45] Beyond the grossly distorted belief in the likelihood of panic lies a more subtle, yet unspoken shift in cultural assumptions, that in themselves undermine our capacity to be strong, both as individuals and as a society. That is, that in the past, the assumption on the whole, as born out by actual human behaviour, was that people were resilient and would seek to cope in adverse circumstances. Today, there is a widespread presumption of human vulnerability that influences both our discussion of disasters well before they have occurred, and seeks to influence our responses to them long after. A new army of therapeutic counsellors and other assorted professionals are there to 'help' people recover.[46] This presupposes our inability to do so unaided. Indeed, the belief that we can cope, and are robust, is often presented as outdated and misguided, or as an instance of being "in denial".

42 R.M. Titmuss, *Problems of social policy*. Nottingham: HMSO (1950).   **43** A. Calder, *The myth of the Blitz* (London, 1991).   **44** E. Jones, R. Woolven, B. Durodié, & S. Wessely, 'Civilian morale during the Second World War: responses to air raids re-examined', *Social History of Medicine*, 17:3 (2004), 463–79.   **45** Furedi, *Therapy culture*.   **46** S. Rose, J. Bisson & S. Wessely, 'A systematic review of single-session psychological interventions ('debriefing') following trauma', *Psychotherapy and Psychosomatics*, 72:4 (2003), 176–84.

In some ways, this latter element, more than any other, best exemplifies and clarifies some of the existing confusions and struggles that lie ahead. If self-reliance is old-fashioned and help-seeking actively promoted, for whatever well-intended reason, then we are unlikely to see a truly resilient society emerge. This cultural shift is reflected in the figures that reveal that whereas in the United Kingdom, in the period of trade union militancy and unrest known as the 'winter of discontent' of 1979, there were 29.5 million days lost through strikes; in 2002 there were 33 million days lost through stress.[47] As reflected in how the word "risk" is predominantly used, people have effectively shifted from being active agents of history to becoming the passive subjects of it. This may benefit social leaders lacking a clear agenda or direction. It may indeed be easier to manage the sick than those who struggle. But it also precludes the possibility of encouraging and establishing real resilience, resolve and purpose across society.

The standard way of dealing with disaster today is one that prioritises pushing the public out beyond the yellow-tape perimeter put up by the authorities. At best the public are merely exhorted to display their support and to trust the professionals.[48] Effectively, people are denied any role, responsibility or even insight into their own situation at such times. Yet, despite this, ordinary human beings are at their most social and rational in a crisis. It is this that should be supported, rather than subsumed or even subverted.

Handling social concerns as to the possibility of a terrorist attack is no easy feat. In part, this is because social fears today have little to do with the actuality, or even possibility, of the presumed threats that confront us.[49] Rather, they are an expression of social isolation and mistrust, combined with an absence of direction and an elite crisis of confidence. The starting point to establishing real resilience and truly effective solutions will be to put the actual threat posed into an appropriate context. This means being honest as to the objective evidence, as well as being able to clarify the social basis of subjective fears. The incessant debate as to the possibility and consequences of an attack using chemical, biological, radiological and nuclear weapons, is a case in point.[50] While Western societies have debated such nightmare scenarios as if they were real, terrorists have continued to display their proficiency in, and proclivity to use, conventional weapons, such as high explosives, car bombs and surface-to-air missiles.

Above all, if as a society, we are to ascribe an appropriate cultural meaning to the events of 11 September 2001 or 7 July 2005 – one that does not enhance domestic concerns and encourage us to become ever-more dependent on a lim-

47 C. Marsden & J. Hyland (2004), 'Britain: 20 years since the year-long miners' strike'. *World Socialist Web Site*. www.wsws.org/articles/2004/mar2004/mine-m05.shtml, accessed 5 Mar. 2007.   48 T. Glass & M. Schoch-Spana, 'Bioterrorism and the people: how to vaccinate a city against panic', *Clinical Infectious Diseases*, 34:2 (2002), 217–23.   49 P. Hubbard, 'Fear and loathing at the multiplex: everyday anxiety in the post-industrial city', *Capital and Class*, 80 (2003), 51–76.   50 B. Durodié, 'Facing the possibility of bioterrorism', *Current Opinion in Biotechnology*, 15:3 (2004), 264–8.

ited number of professionals who will tell the public how to lead their lives at such times – then we need to promote a far more significant political debate as to our aims and purposes as a society.

Changing our cultural outlook is certainly a daunting task. It requires people to clarify and agree on a common direction and then to win others to it. The reluctance to engage in this fundamentally political process and the clear preference to concentrate instead upon more limited, technical, goals leaves us profoundly ill-equipped for the future. It speaks volumes about our existing state of resilience and may actually serve to make matters worse. Bizarrely, few of the authorities concerned consider it to be their responsibility to lead in this matter. Nor do they believe such cultural change to be a realistic possibility. Yet, in the eventuality of a major civil emergency, they hope that the public will pay attention to the risk warnings they provide and alter their behaviour accordingly. By then it will be too late.

The Young Buddha's mystery trip

MARK O'SULLIVAN

Before I'd even begun to consider the notion of childhood fear in any depth, I'd already had my first reaction to it. An old song 'The Scottish soldier' came unbidden into my mind:

> There was a soldier, a Scottish soldier
> Who wandered far away and soldiered far away
> There was none bolder, with good broad shoulder
> He's fought in many a fray, and fought and won.[1]

Because I have neither the knowledge nor the language of the academic disciplines of Psychology or Literary Criticism and because the best I can do is to offer a personal perspective on childhood fear, I decided to follow this instinct, follow this Pied Piper's tune wherever it took me. In fact, I had an instinct too about where the tune would take me – stories often happen to mind like that. The destination? The Faery Land of Wordsworth's *Prelude*. But first, the journey. The *Mystery trip*.

As is so often the case, the song came with a very specific memory attached. A memory from my childhood of arriving back in my home town of Thurles at the end of a *Mystery trip* – a bus outing whose destination, easily guessed by the adults, was for the most part kept a thrilling secret from the children. Because we lived in Tipperary there were, of course, a limited number of possible destinations. Seaside resorts along the south coast. Tramore, Dunmore East, Youghal. Inland destinations to the west were common too; Killarney, Bunratty Castle in Co. Clare. It didn't really matter. In fact, I don't remember where we went to that day.

What I do remember is the muted singing of this song, 'The Scottish soldier', by our fellow passengers who'd sung their way along the journey. The brief unloosening of my shy reticence as I joined the chorus. The pleasure of contributing,

---

1 'Scottish soldier', Popular Song sung to the traditional Scottish March, aka 'Green Hills of Tyrol' (*c*.1853–56).

however meekly, to some greater harmony. I remember stepping from the bus out-side the Greyhound Stadium, the lighted windows along the street in the late dusk, the shivery chill of the night air on my sunburnt skin. Everyone seemed tired but happy and yet I wanted to cry. I felt a keenly visceral sense of desolation and dread.

> Because these green hills are not highland hills
> Or the island hills, they're not my land's hills
> And fair as these green foreign hills may be
> They are not the hills of home.[2]

Melodies are fictions abstracted from the world's cacophony of noises. The more memorable ones, often the simplest in construction, allow for the most complex of interpretations, such as projecting sweetness and sadness equally in their meas-ures. I think of Django Reinhardt taking old standards like 'After you've gone' or 'Rose room' and finding in his musical exploration of them an expression of the harsh, celebratory and peripatetic inner life of the Gypsy in all of us. The melody of 'The Scottish soldier' has the same potential, a major mode and yet a distinctly minor feel.

Lyrics are fictions too. Those of 'The Scottish soldier' speak of the melancholic loss experienced by a heroic figure. War has not depleted him but the journey has, and the distance from home. The song is the perfect vessel, then, in which to pre-serve this young boy's moment of heightened awareness. Pre-rational or, perhaps, sub-rational these are essentially felt moments. Even at eight years of age, as I was that day, I sensed a significance I couldn't have begun to explain back then. It seems to me that on that *Mystery trip* day, the unknown, the unknowable and ungovernable future threatened me with annihilation. I'm reminded of Temple Grandin's observations on cattle in her book *Animals in translation* (2004). Because cattle have, in effect, two-dimensional vision, a shadow across their path appears to them to be an abyss and sends them into retreat. The child experienc-ing existential fear is similarly halted in his tracks.

The fact that this *Mystery trip* memory was the first that occurred to me in relation to childhood fear struck me as quite odd in one sense. I realized that there were other more frightening episodes in my childhood that might have come to mind before this one. Outside the cocoon of our family home, the world tended to be harsher in many ways to children than it is now – perhaps I should say in different ways. One example will suffice. My first and, I have to say, last beating from a Christian Brother where I was punched and kicked along the ground on the aisle between the classroom desks. A very public humiliation at the hands of a representative of the God I still quite fervently believed in. Memorably confus-

2 Ibid.

ing stuff indeed and yet it doesn't seem to have registered on the same scale as that desolate evening a year or two before.

Many years later, someone showed me a poem in a religious magazine written by this man of the cloth towards the end of his life. Its tone was one of great fearfulness and self-contempt. Eternal damnation, it seemed, was very much on the cards. I don't think I've ever read anything so sadly, so naively revealing of a man's essential shallowness, his emotional lack of depth. I suspect that even as a child I recognized what he could not admit of himself. He was not a man. He was a caricature and, for that reason, easily enough identified and countered. My *Mystery trip* experience had already presented me with fears of far greater complexity.

So, when I thought about this instinctive choice of memory of mine, the *Mystery trip* day, I found myself making a layman's typology of fears. Physical fear – innate and environmental. Social fear – including familial and other inter-personal fears. And, finally, existential fear. Simplistic, I know, but my point is to indicate a certain hierarchy of fears that seem to me to become, at once, progressively less tangible and somehow more profound. For a child, existential fear is the most difficult because it requires a language he or she doesn't yet have to explain its significance. Instead, a child experiences this fear as raw sensation and that's what my story of *The Young Buddha's mystery trip* is about.

You will, I'm sure, be familiar with the story of the young Buddha's awakening. Born as Siddharta Gautama into a royal family on the Indian-Neplaese border, he lived a sheltered and overly-indulged life as a child in the royal compound. But, of course, paradise is never enough, not even for a child. Eventually, as a young prince, Siddharta sneaks out of the castle and on successive days encounters for the first time, vivid representations of sickness, old age and death. As the derivation of the word Buddha suggests, *he wakes up to reality*. The story guides us to an awareness of suffering, temporality and impermanence. But there's more to it than that, I believe.

The Young Buddha's reaction to the sick, the aged and the dead is a paradoxical one. He feels, at once, revulsion and pity. This is his introduction to the complex nature of human emotions, of those oppositions that he must learn to balance as he matures. Joy and sorrow, pleasure and pain, love and hate. It's his first step into the No-Man's Land between innocence and experience and, to quote William Blake, 'Soon spreads the dismal shade/Of Mystery over his head'.[3]

Like most true stories, *The Young Buddha's mystery trip* involves reconstruction, exaggeration, perhaps even fabrication. As Antonio Damasio writes in *The feeling of what happens* (2000), our 'unique personal episodes [...] are continuously reclassified in autobiographical memory.'[4] Like most true stories too, however, it's shaped

---

3 William Blake, 'The human abstract', *The complete poems*, ed. Alicia Ostriker (London, 1977), l.13–14.   4 Antonio Damasio, *The feeling of what happens: body and emotion in the making of consciousness* (London,

around a real, lived experience of insight. An event of such magnitude that it becomes a milestone along the largely forgotten path our lives have taken.

Why do we remember with such precision so little of our past? And why do some moments remain so vivid that they are not merely recalled but relived? Questions for the experts I suppose but I imagine that the answer to both questions is connected to the matter of sensory overload. Goethe it was who said, 'Man can bear anything but a succession of ordinary days'.[5] A succession of memorable days would, however, be a kind of autistic nightmare; an eternal, cumulative present obscuring any possibility of development. As for those epic moments we do remember, my guess is that our emotional sensitivities are so stimulated that our physical senses grasp and gather in every last signal we detect in that moment. I imagine this massive act of perception like a fireworks display in reverse. The sky fills itself with a remarkable pattern of flaming sparks that shoot explosively downwards to the latent firecracker that is our mind. Then we make a story of them. *The Young Buddha's mystery trip* is such a story.

The year is 1962. This Young Buddha is eight years old. He has a new baby brother and is delighted but somewhat fearful at his arrival. As the eldest child, he asserts his right to hold the baby in the back of the Ford Mini as they return home from the District Hospital and yet is terrified at its tiny vulnerability. For months now he's been uneasy about his mother's vulnerability too. Not yet thirty, she now has four sons. She's a vital, energetic woman who loves to sing but she's tired and, as in the course of any pregnancy, there have been ups and downs. The Young Buddha's father works long hours as an electrician in a factory outside town. To support his growing family, he needs to take every hour of overtime he can get. 'The dream of life', as Tolstoy characterized it, cannot be sustained without hard work, commitment, personal sacrifice.[6] As every child in time does, the Young Buddha senses among the shadows, the grinding machinery behind the grand and necessary illusion. And senses too that, like all machinery, it is susceptible to breakdown.

And there's a larger, darker shadow looming over him. His maternal grandmother is suffering from severe rheumatoid arthritis. She can walk only with great difficulty now and spends much of her time sitting or lying in bed. Her hands are already becoming misshapen. He's heard her say that she'd rather be dead than live like this. She is very angry and very bitter. They go to her house every day, walking from one end of the town to the other, so that his mother can do the housework that her mother can no longer do. His grandmother shows no appreciation of these efforts. There is only criticism, accusations of inadequacy. The Young Buddha has come to hate his grandmother and feels guilty for doing so. At

2000), p. 223. 5 Quote attributed to the German poet and novelist Johann Wolfgang von Goethe (1749–1832). 6 Leo Tolstoy, *Anna Karenin*, trans. Rosemary Edmonds (London, 1977), p. 16.

the same time, he feels her pain in his bones. Literally. Sympathetic pain but to him completely and confusingly real. His arms and legs ache every minute he spends in that house. In school, he's begun to have unexplained fainting fits. Unexplained, but he knows the cause – he's pretending. He doesn't, however, know why.

Every boy wants to be Superman, to put the world to right, to save all those in distress, to master this chaos over which no-one seems to have control. Failure to do so is unthinkable, the consequences unimaginably terrible for himself and for those he loves. And hates. Worse still, all of this is understood by him not in the rational sense but below the level of his consciousness. And so it is for the Young Buddha in that moment of heightened awareness. A series of disparate sensations have somehow coalesced below the surface and he's struck for the first time by existential fear. Proust in *Swann's way* (1913) writes 'What an abyss of uncertainty, whenever the mind feels overtaken by itself; when it, the seeker, is at the same time the dark region through which it must go seeking [...] It is face to face with something which does not yet exist'.[7]

His grandmother, because she's the slowest, is last to get off the bus. It's a difficult descent and he feels a spasm of pain at her every grimace but he knows he can't faint this time. They have to bring her across the street. He knows that the bus will have gone and all their neighbours too before they reach her house. The House of Pain. He knows that though they're all very tired, a walk of over a mile still awaits him and his mother and brothers. He knows that, of late, he is so afraid of the dark that he sleeps with the sheets over his head. He has always known but only recently absorbed the fact that the area he lives in was once the site of a great battle between Strongbow and the Irish chieftains and suspects that bloodied ghosts rule the night out there.

It is a strange feeling to be so overwhelmed by the vague echoes of questions only half-understood. A sense of having been in the dark for so long that the light creates a different kind of blindness in him. How long will all of this last? His grandmother's suffering, his mother's, his own. How will they survive? How will he survive? Will his mother's bones twist and bend obscenely with arthritis too? Will his own? Will his parents always have to work so hard? Will he, will any of them, ever be happy again? Will every song from here until eternity be a sad song?

It seems to me that this Young Buddha has been compelled to face the future in all its uncertainty. I think that when we become aware of the future, we simultaneously realize that the past is a lost world and our ability to live fully in the present is compromized. Even as children.

At the Jewish Cemetery in Prague, there's a permanent exhibition of drawings made by children in the Terezin concentration camp. My own quite ordinary

7 Marcel Proust, *Remembrance of things past*, vol. 1: *Swann's way*, trans. C.K. Scott Moncrieff & Terence Kilmartin (London, 1983), p. 49.

experience obviously pales in comparison to the terrors visited on these innocents. It's instructive, however, to look at the subjects of their drawings. They drew pictures of the world they came from – the Past. They made drawings of their present reality encompassing suffering, brutality and murder – what we might call the Present Negative. In other drawings of their present reality, however, a recurring motif is a signpost showing the way out of this hell – the Present Positive, so to speak. The final category of drawings comprised images of freedom in some paradise – the Future.

I remember reading once that there was some debate over the validity of these drawings. They were made during drawing lessons given to the children by the Viennese painter, Friedl Dicker-Brandeis. How much of the work reflected her intervention, how much was perhaps one child copying the work of another in a group situation, how much the fulfilling of expectations that children so often sub-consciously engage in to comfort and sustain us adults? Whatever about the merits of such arguments, another category beyond those I've outlined suggested itself to me. A category that could neither be doubted nor dismissed for lack of veracity. This category, I imagined, consisted of defaced or simply blank pages, scrunched up and cast aside not because there was nothing to draw but because even for a child there are certain intimations that are inexpressible. I imagined one of these children protesting – 'I can't draw. I won't draw. I don't want to draw. I want to go outside and play, run, fight, hide'.

The perceived depth of the unknown invites such confused exaggerations. Self-deprecation alongside self-assertion, the urge to rebel alongside the urge to retreat. And, similarly, on a less tragic scale, the Young Buddha of my *Mystery trip* story wakes not simply to reality but to an exaggerated reality. He challenges in extreme ways the reassuring narratives of logic, order, morality and hope he's been offered until now by parents, guardians, teachers perhaps, and by the fictional narratives he's so far encountered in whatever form. He no longer only lives but begins to play at living. He is no longer only himself but, little by little, allows the actor in himself to grow into the part.

The sense I'm trying to get at here is not of arrival at a new stage of development but of a new spur to the process of development. Heisenberg's Uncertainty Principle comes to mind – a bowdlerized version, no doubt, but nevertheless useful, I hope.[8] This principle talks about particle/wave duality. In the old physics, particles and waves were distinct and mutually exclusive. One is fixture, the other is flux. Their combination in one entity introduces the possibility of uncertain outcomes. In a similar way, the Young Buddha's view of the world before and after the onset of existential fear differs. The eternal present of childhood begins to

8 German physicist, Nobel laureate and one of the founders of quantum mechanics, Werner Heisenberg (1901–78) formulated the principle of uncertainty in March 1926, working in Niels Bohr's institute in Copenhagen.

recede and he lives in the temporal, unpredictable flow – no longer simply *being* but *becoming*.

So, the Young Buddha faints not simply as a cry for help under the impossible weight but to test the contention that when we fall, our loved ones will pick us up. He takes on his grandmother's pain not just to remove the cause of her bitterness but to pit himself against the power of pain. And in the aftermath of that *Mystery trip* day, he takes more and more to the streets not only to test himself against the world or to experiment with the trust invested in him by his parents but to prove to himself that there'll always be a place of welcome, that in the words of the Bob Dylan song, 'I came in from the wilderness, a creature void of form./ Come in, she said, I'll give you shelter from the storm.'[9]

Out on the street, this Young Buddha finds football where (even within the limiting rules of a game) he can express himself physically, hide the self in which he's become so insecure; try on new identities. Today, he can be Bobby Moore, tomorrow; George Best. He finds the more daring kids in the area, goes climbing orchard walls, goes playing Cops and Robbers, Cowboys and Indians in the wet, swampy reed-filled fields they call the Everglades down behind the Bishop's Palace – the thrill of danger and risk that marks the true spirit of enterprise. A year or so later he finds The Beatles. Another vivid but more singular memory. Running through Liberty Square after the Sunday matinee of *A hard day's night* – a film almost without narrative and racing along on boundless energy, unforgettable music and four adult kids, cheeky and irreverent and chased by a thousand girls.

And during this time he discovers something else. The world of books. Not fiction at first. *The Guinness book of records*, the *Rothman's football yearbook*, *Pears' cyclopaedia*. Facts, statistics and I wonder if that was about finding a counterbalance for the unknown in a wealth of measurable detail however obscure. The tallest man in the world. The most-capped player with Nottingham Forest. The rules of Lacrosse, a game he'll never play.

As for fiction, it wasn't a storyline or a particular character that made the first memorable impact on him. In the 1857 novel, *Coral Island* by J.M. Ballantyne there's a description of a coral reef whose clarity and vividness lit up a new place in his imagination. A first sense, perhaps, of the power of words to make something transcendent of the physical world and indeed to create fantastical worlds at once exciting and comforting in their endless and discoverable possibilities.

And fiction in whatever form serves another, more opaque, purpose in his wrestling with existential fear. In *The Prelude*, Wordsworth writes about 'The drowned man of Esthwaite'. It's a recollection of seeing his first corpse and his realization that the sight was not at all so fearful as he'd anticipated. He explains how;

9 Bob Dylan, 'Shelter from the storm', *Blood on the tracks* (Columbia, 1975).

> My inner eye had seen
> Such sights before, among the shining streams
> Of Faery Land.[10]

'Faery Land' and, in a later phrase from the poem, 'the forest of romance', refers to the worlds of myth, fairytale and fiction in which we encounter paradigms of life's journey, archetypes of its actors, dramatizations of its inevitable obstacles and our battles to overcome them.[11] In Wordsworth's words, existential fear is 'no soul-debasing fear' but a special kind of fear that triggers an imaginative response.[12]

In other words, a great creative outpouring expressed in gesture, behaviour, attitude has begun. Existential fear is in itself an expansion of consciousness in which imagination flourishes in positive as well as in negative ways. How it all pans out, what kind of balance will be achieved, will depend on many factors. Genetic traits, learned dispositions, home environment and all that entails, social obstacles and the greater imponderables still of chance and circumstance.

To whatever extent, every Young Buddha from that moment of heightened awareness onwards creates a vision of the world somewhere between reality and aspiration, between what is and what should be. But closer, I suspect, to aspiration, to what should be. At least in my case. That long-ago *Mystery trip* day, my *Satori in Thurles* so to speak, puts me in mind of these lines from Brendan Kennelly's poem, *The man made of rain* (1998):

> This little now
> is so beyond me
> I'd better make haste
> to invent
> eternity.[13]

---

10 William Wordsworth, *The prelude: the four texts* (1798, 1799, 1805, 1850) ed. Jonathan Wordsworth, (London, 1995) Book V (1850), l. 453–5. 11 Ibid. 12 Ibid., l. 451–5. 13 Brendan Kennelly, *The man made of rain* (Newcastle upon Tyne, 1998), 13, l. 28–32.

'Something under the bed is drooling': the mediation of fear through the rhetoric of fantasy in literature for children

AMANDA PIESSE

Mediating fear through fantasy relies heavily on the basic tenet that 'the fantastic must be so close to the real that you almost have to believe in it'[1] or, from the opposite direction, that 'the fantastic exists only against a background to which it offers a direct reversal'.[2] If the purpose of fear in literature for children is to offer a vicarious thrill, or a safe place in which to explore imagined dangers, or a place that 'stirs up dread on purpose for its own sake',[3] then the effectiveness of the experience will rely in large measure on the reciprocity between the reversal and the background. Like Bruno Bettelheim, without whose work, *The uses of enchantment* (1978),[4] no understanding of the archetypal tales rehearsed by Charles Perrault or the Grimm brothers is complete, Marina Warner champions the 'cultivation of dread as an aesthetic thrill.'[5] She makes clear why the original, unsanitized versions of the fairy tales, where ugly sisters get their eyes pecked out by crows for their unkindnesses; where wicked stepmothers dance themselves to death in red hot shoes; and where too-curious little red riding hoods get gobbled up by the wolf, are met with 'sighs of satisfaction at a grim and satisfying conclusion.'[6] Alternatively, fear might be a central part of telling a terrifying tale in a pacifying form (cautionary tales or indeed some lullabies fall into this group, where the rhythms or expectations of the form are at odds with a grisly content) or might be banished before gales of audience laughter by making mock – defeating fear with hilarity, mockery, exaggeration or grotesquerie.

1 Fyodor Dostoevsky, cit. Rosemary Jackson, *Fantasy: the literature of subversion* (London, 1981), p. 27. 2 Eric S. Rabkin, *The fantastic in literature* (Princeton, 1976), p. 216. 3 Marina Warner, *No go the bogeyman: scaring, lulling and making mock* (London, 2000), p. 4. 4 Bruno Bettelheim, *The uses of enchantment* (London, 1978). 5 Warner, *No go the bogeyman*, p. 4. 6 Ibid.

Fear, fantasy and the very young

In picturebooks for very small children, to whom stories are almost certainly being read by an older participant in the narrative contract, the tensions between danger and delight can be intensified or diffused by interplay between text and illustration. Frightening narrative might be offset by comical illustration, for example, and it is clear from basic research on children's attention to picturebooks, that the pre-literate consumer of picturebooks or illustrated texts will pay at least as much attention to the visual communication as to the aural communication.[7] Complicity between illustration and observer – where a figure looks directly out of the frame, engaging with the observer rather than with the other figures in the illustration – can also be used to create agency on the observer's part by suggesting that the figure in the illustration is seeking a response from the observer, relying on that response to validate or invalidate whatever is going on in the picture and thereby imbuing the observer with a sense of power. If that complicity is made comical – a moment of self-doubt on the part of the monster, or a complicit wink, perhaps, between an apparently endangered protagonist and the observer – then the moment can be seen to tip over into making mock. And the fact that the environment in which the texts are being read is probably secure – young narratee experiences vicarious danger in a secure adult presence – adds another dimension. In the first two texts I want to examine here, the fact that the story is probably being read aloud means that the alignment between the narratee and the protagonist in the story is never quite equal. The danger in which the protagonist in the text is placed depends largely on a lone small figure confronting a much bigger adversary. The child recipient of the text, however, while invoked into an identification with the protagonist through a shared relative smallness, is not confronting the danger alone because the story is being read out.

Tony Ross' *I'm coming to get you* (1984) is a picturebook with seventeen openings.[8] It shows a hairy 'loathsome monster', somewhere between a caveman and a yeti in appearance, hurtling through the universe on a spaceship yelling 'I'm coming to get you'.[9] After it conquers one planet, 'smashing their statues and destroying their books', chewing up the mountains, drinking the oceans, 'it gobbled up the whole planet, except for the middle, which was too hot, and the ends, which were too cold'.[10] The monster then homes in on 'a pretty blue planet called Earth' and a little teddy-bear-clutching boy, who, having got ready for bed, 'was listening to a story all about scary monsters'.[11] The spaceship finds earth, then Tommy's town, and then his house. Tommy, in the time-honoured tradition,

7 See, for example, Perry Nodelman, *Words about pictures: the narrative art of children's picturebooks* (Athens, CA, 1988) or Maria Nikolajeva & Carole Scott, *How picturebooks work* (New York, 2001). 8 'Opening' refers to a picturebook's double spread of pages from the end papers on. 9 Tony Ross, *I'm coming to get you* (London, 1984), opening 5. 10 Ibid., openings 6, 7, 8. 11 Ibid., openings 9, 10.

trudges fearfully up the stairs to bed, looking everywhere where a monster could hide before he gets into bed, and even starting fearfully when 'he thought he heard a noise outside his window'. The monster hides behind a rock and waits until dawn, hissing 'I'm coming to get you'.[12] The final two openings of the story run as follows: 'In the daylight, Tommy felt silly for having been so scared of monsters' but 'then, with a terrible roar, the monster pounced ...'. The last opening has no words at all, and we are as speechless as the narrator to discover that the terrible monster, which up until now has filled the frame of illustration at least as completely as Tommy has, is tiny, perhaps the size of a chestnut, the terrible club he has been wielding revealed, in this perspective, to be nothing more than a matchstick.

Ross' text plays a number of games, most of them invoking implicit intertextual experience and understanding on the part of the young reader. Generically, the story references the science fiction/superhero adventure, which generally has a hero overcome an extraterrestrial danger after a battle; it also implicitly invokes the Goldilocks story (with the planet that is not completely eaten up because of the middle that is too hot and the ends that are too cold) – a tale which probably holds few terrors for any child. Stylistically, it uses the repetition of the title line as a cumulative threat, but because the story is being read aloud, the narratee also has the option of taking control of the threat, joining in with the repeated growling of 'I'm coming to get you'. It builds tension (the monster gets closer and closer to the unsuspecting victim) but it also uses a standard trope of pantomime, where the audience can see the threat that the victim can't see, a "he's behind you" kind of motif, which underlines the clear distinction between the inhabitant of the fiction and the observer, and endows the observer with a certain degree of superiority. It uses comedy to relieve the tension; the planet that is destroyed is inhabited by 'the gentle banana people',[13] for example, and instead of checking under the bed, the traditional hiding place for monsters, Tommy peers into the toilet bowl to be sure the monster isn't hiding down there. The tale poses something of a threat to an audience hearing this as a bedtime story, because the potential victim in the text is also listening to a bedtime story, simultaneously fearing but ultimately disbelieving that he's about to be got, but it also uses the mild smiling face of the teddy, facing out into the audience as an intermediary between text and audience, to create a collusion between author and audience, a suggestion that this is all going to be all right (because otherwise teddy wouldn't be smiling).

Ross resolves the tension with a simple shift of perspective; the monster is revealed to be tiny, we laugh, and understand that a potential tragedy has become a comedy. The metaphoric message is clear to the sophisticated reader; in the clear

12 Ibid., opening 13. 13 Ibid., opening 12.

light of day the terrors of the night are tiny, and imagined monsters are only scary if they are not held in perspective.

Julia Donaldson and Axel Scheffler's *The Gruffalo* was the winner of the 1999 Smarties prize for children's books. It shows how wit, resourcefulness and use of the imagination – the use of fantasy by a protagonist within what is already a text of fantasy – enable the small and vulnerable to overcome the larger and more powerful. Mouse is confronted by a fox, an owl and a snake in turn; each wants to eat him, and, in the age-old trope, invite him to their house 'for lunch', 'for tea', 'for a feast'.[14] However, by invoking his imaginary friend the gruffalo, who has 'terrible tusks and terrible claws and terrible teeth in his terrible jaws'[15] (and whose favourite snacks happen to include roasted fox, owl ice-cream and scrambled snake) Mouse walks by the predators undisturbed. The cheerful rhyme of Donaldson's text is borne up by the bright daylight palette in which Scheffler's illustrations place the tale. It is clear that the terrible tusks and terrible claws, though illustrated for us, are emerging from Mouse's sunny imagination. But things take an unexpected turn – literally. As Mouse rounds a bend in the forest, we turn the page and his third celebratory soliloquy ('Silly old snake! Don't you know? There's no such thing as a gruffal -O!') turns into an exclamation of surprise, and the reader is left breathless as Mouse – and we – come face to face with a real live gruffalo.[16] Quick as a flash, though, Mouse tells the gruffalo that the most terrifying animals in the forest are all afraid of him, Mouse. To the gruffalo's initial astonishment and increasing uneasiness, as he follows Mouse through the forest, sure enough Fox, Owl and Snake, seeing the fearsome creature apparently deep in conversation with friend Mouse, flee the scene, and, afraid of so fearsome a mouse, the gruffalo too finally turns tail and runs.[17]

Here, text and illustration collude both to "lull" and to "make mock"; the terrifying imagery offset by the counterpoint of the jaunty rhythms and hyperbolic descriptions, and the gruffalo on its first appearance clearly possessed of a rather idiotic grin, in the tradition of the monsters created for Max to rule over in Maurice Sendak's modern classic *Where the wild things are* (1967).[18] *The Gruffalo*'s scariness is slightly dispelled too by the hyperbole produced by the page turn and the intake of breath. The monster, though slavering, is looking out of the picture in a somewhat self-conscious fashion rather than fixing its intended victim with a glittering eye, suggesting that it's more interested in being scary, and being seen to be being scary, than in actually eating Mouse. Any possibility of real fear is diffused by the tenor of the text and the agency of the reader in deflecting the gruffalo's attention from the Mouse. The bi-partite structure of the text helps too. Mouse's wit, having sustained him through encounters with real predators in the

---

14 Julia Donaldson & Axel Scheffler, *The Gruffalo* (Basingstoke, 1999), openings 4, 6, 8.   15 Ibid., opening 5.   16 Ibid., openings 9–10.   17 Ibid., openings 12–14.   18 Maurice Sendak, *Where the wild things are* (London, 1967).

first half of the text, leaves the reader with no reason to suspect it won't sustain him through the reversal; and the very repetition of the episodic meetings supports the "lulling" effect of the rhyme, even with the medial hiatus and then reversal. Anthropomorphism – the endowing of animals or inanimate objects with human characteristics – also places the fear at one remove, suggesting that, being both rational and aware of the meta-textual audience response, the gruffalo will respond to human and humane rationality rather than acting out of an entirely feral nature. Predictability, through repetition of rhyme and ultimately through a double repeated structure, bestows a degree of experience on the reader and/or narratee, and a moment of mock hyperbole, shared by the person reading the story aloud, the narratee and the mouse protagonist alike, reassures that a momentary shock need not be a fatal setback. Most of all, though, the controlled metre and the sustained bright palette allow for the confrontation of fear in a positive environment that belies the possibility of danger relayed by the narrative itself.

Picturebooks marketed for the young can also be more direct and confrontational, however. Antony Browne confronts fear of parental and sibling rejection in *Gorilla* (1983)[19] and *The Tunnel* (1989)[20] respectively. In each case, the narrative is sober and straightforward, with none of the gleeful, tension-releasing chanting available to the narratee in the texts I have just examined here. In Browne's work, the themes involve real emotional danger in relation to other real people. Within the text, this is not an enactment of a vicarious danger but the confrontation of real quotidian difficulty. Each text does contain a crossover from a realistic to a fantastic setting to help the protagonist work through the problem outside of real time, but each side of the fantasy/reality divide uses the same visual idiom. This exchange between fantasy and reality challenges the audience to sustain any declaration that what's worked out through the imagination is any less real than what's confronted in reality, removing the comfort derived from the clear demarcation between fantasy and reality in the process. Browne's texts are fundamentally disturbing, and are meant to be so; for our purposes, it is enough to observe that it is the absence of some of the alleviating techniques used by Ross, Donaldson and Scheffler that renders Browne's work so much darker, even if initially the format looks very similar. Similarly, John Burningham's *Granpa* (1984)[21] expects the very young audience for which it is marketed to revel in the apparently non-sequential exchanges between granddaughter and grandfather throughout and to understand, in that context, the speechless silence of its final frames to mean that there are some things (in this case the death of Granpa, made clear by a hunched up little girl looking at the empty space in Granpa's chair) for which there simply

19 Anthony Browne, *Gorilla* (London, 1983). 20 Anthony Browne, *The Tunnel* (London, 1989). 21 John Burningham, *Granpa* (London, 1984).

are no words and no resolution at all. This text addresses fear of loss only obliquely, representing the enormity of bereavement unapologetically, exactly as it is; a huge, inarticulable shock to be survived only by remembrance and silent contemplation. Such an unmediated moment is perhaps the best proof that the best picture books, like any other book worthy of a place in any canon, will grow in magnitude with the understanding of the reader or audience.

Mediating fear for the older child

The relationship between fantastic representation and rational experience (which includes real experience of fantastic texts) has so far been crucial to understanding how the young reader or narratee is encouraged to approach the problem of fear. The Bill Watterson *Calvin and Hobbes* cartoon from which this essay takes its title relies on the tension between fantastic and rational approaches for both its comic effect and for its enlightenment concerning why children's fears of the dark are so real. 'Don't turn out the light, dad! You didn't check under the bed for monsters!' cries Calvin; but his father, unmoved, simply replies, finger on switch, 'I'm sure there are no monsters under your bed. Go to sleep' and leaves the room without checking, secure in his own perception of things. The next frame shows Calvin and his toy tiger Hobbes tucked up in the darkened room, his father's final 'Goodnight' from outside the room being met with a wide-eyed, traumatized, pessimistically hyperbolic 'Goodbye' from the little boy. In the next frame, the cross-over into Calvin's worldview, always half in fantasy, is signified, as usual, by Hobbes being drawn as having come to life (he always looks like a stuffed toy if anyone else is around). And at this point Calvin's apparent hyperbole in his vale-dictory 'goodbye' is shown to be right. The monsters will not declare themselves when directly challenged, but when Calvin and Hobbes hold a loud conversation about how much nice lean weight Calvin has gained, and then peer over the side of the bed again, a pool of water is seen to be emerging, provoking Hobbes' 'Ugh. Something under the bed is drooling' and Calvin's resigned response, 'Start tying the sheets together. We'll go out the window'.[22]

What the cartoon does is to valorize the semi-fantastic point of view as dom-inant; there is tangible proof here that if you really know the nature of the beast (which children do and parents do not), you can provoke empirical proof of its existence. Something under the bed IS drooling, if you only know the right way to get it to show itself. Watterson aligns himself with the standard child fantasy that there's a whole world out there about which grownups know nothing. Calvin, the resourceful hero, has the means of escape ready, and is posited there-

22 Bill Watterson, *The essential Calvin and Hobbes* (Kansas, 1988), p. 150.

fore as experienced rather than naïve. Thus the cartoon turns the world upside down, making the imaginary the dominant idiom and dad's sophistication simply the blissfulness of ignorance. It takes fear seriously and acknowledges the reasons for its presence, but equips the protagonist with a means of escape and itself with a caveat. Such a danger only exists when the fantastic is allowed to dominate, the reality of that state of being in the present moment indicated by Hobbes' fully anthropomorphized state. Watterson's cartoons are for children and adults alike, the sophisticated play with states of being, the tension between the rational and the fantastic being clear from the very names of the characters: Calvin the fearful fantasist/pessimist, Hobbes the cheerful rationalist. But the cartoon does go some way towards illustrating again how engaging with a particular worldview can be used to show how fear depends on context and the degree to which participants have power over that context – precisely the same movement as we saw in *The Gruffalo*. The fantasist reader of Calvin and Hobbes, because he or she participates in that worldview, will be subject to its fears; the rationalist reader, who stands absolutely beyond fantasy, will not. Whether we, like Watterson, align these states with childhood and adulthood respectively, is a subjective matter.

Placing the intellectually superior but physically vulnerable child at the mercy of an irrational adult world is a staple characteristic of the writing of the twentieth century's most popular children's writer, Roald Dahl. In the fantasy mode which Colin Manlove has described as 'the English penchant for play' or for 'throwing opposites together in little worlds of wit',[23] *James and the giant peach* (1967), *George's marvellous medicine* (1981), *The Witches* (1983), *The Twits* (1980) and *Matilda* (1988)[24] all work out of this fundamental position, *Matilda* being the novel which relies least on the supernatural and most on the protagonist's own resources to bring about her own rescue. While Matilda's parents are basically ghastly, the headmistress of her school is the real figure of fear in the text, and it is interesting to see how each of Warner's three kinds of response to fear are marked off in the single paragraph that introduces the horror:

> Miss Trunchbull, the headmistress, was something else altogether. She was a gigantic holy terror, a fierce tyrannical monster who frightened the life out of the pupils and teachers alike [...] when she marched along a corridor you could actually hear her snorting as she went, and if a group of children happened to be in her path, she ploughed right on through them like a tank, with small people bouncing off her to left and right. Thank goodness, we don't meet many people like her in this world [...] if you ever do, you

---

23 Colin Manlove, *The fantasy literature of England* (Basingstoke, 1999), p. 5.   **24** Roald Dahl, *James and the giant peach* (London, 1967); *The Twits* (London, 1980); *George's marvellous medicine* (London, 1981); *The Witches* (London, 1983); *Matilda* (London, 1988).

should behave as you would if you met an enraged rhinoceros out in the bush – climb up the nearest tree and stay there until it has gone away.[25]

It is clear how this kind rhetoric works up 'the cultivation of dread as an aesthetic thrill.'[26] It creates an extreme image either by direct comparison ('a fierce tyrannical monster', 'snorting', 'like a tank') or by implication ('tyrannical' is reminiscent of 'tyrannosaurus'), but undermines it immediately by creating images of slapstick rather than real injury ('bouncing off her to left and right') and an incongruous, and therefore highly unlikely scenario, that of encountering a rhinoceros and having to climb a tree, which tips the danger into the safe realms of fantasy. But it also suggests a very experienced voice behind the text, and one which, through its direct address to the reader, is in collusion with its audience, in a verbal replication of the picturebook illustration staring out of the frame to reassure the audience. Once again, then, scaring, lulling and making mock are working together to provide fearful experience within a safely contained environment.

J.K. Rowling uses similar devices in her invocation of 'dread [...] for its own sake',[27] and her appropriation of Dahl's trademark grotesquerie is only one of a series of broad intertextual resonances in her novels. Her use of both the standard genres of school story and the heroic battle of good against evil are mapped onto each other seamlessly. Her representation of Hogwarts in the first four books works out of a standard pattern of school life; there are uniforms, house teams, lessons, rules, regulations, punishments and rewards which, posited within a framework of a normal working day in the life of a trainee wizard, provide a framework of predictability and carefully contained danger and fear. It is when that framework is threatened by a maverick teacher, or the encroachment of an exterior order on the school, that the secure framework begins to creak under the pressures of real danger.

The use of extreme description to undermine situations of extreme unpleasantness is evident from the beginning of the sequence of novels. Early in the series, when Harry has to confront danger head-on, it is within the confines of the school or grounds, and it is with the assistance of friends, or under the supervision of an adult. The reader in turn is initially protected by the Dahlesque use of hyperbole and grotesquerie. The episode in The philosopher's stone (1997) where Ron and Harry defeat the troll, for example, is made fascinatingly comic by the sheer impossibility of the creature ('It was a horrible sight. Twelve feet tall, its skin was a dull, granite grey, its lumpy body like a boulder'). That 'the smell that was coming from it was incredible' and the delightful detail that Harry confuses it by inadvertently sticking his wand up its nose, thus allowing Ron to knock it out with its own club, serves further to counterpoint danger with delight in the unspeakable.[28] The end of this first serious test of loyalty and capability dissolves into relieved, bathetic laughter, not a little tinged with hysteria.

Later in *The philosopher's stone* we see again the juxtaposition of horror and comedy, but with a very different effect. The school is once again under attack, this time from someone or something which is turning the inhabitants into stone. The movement this time is from comedy tinged with horror to real concern, since the first target of petrifaction in the text is Mrs Norris, Filch's cat that nobody likes anyway; next is Colin Creevey, who has been a figure of fun and some annoyance; but the list goes on to include Hermione, one of Harry's two best friends, and then Ginny, his other friend's little sister, a figure carefully set up as vulnerable by virtue of being small, young and female. The full horror of Harry himself being suspected of the petrifactions is pointed up by Peeves the poltergeist's jingle; *'Oh Potter you rotter oh what have you done? / You're killing off students, you think it's good fun.'*[29] Here the notion of lulling works in heartless counterbalance to the general feeling in the school, and there is a sense that the mode is utterly out of place, the horror beyond redemption of this kind.

Given the danger for the students, and their fearfulness at being vulnerable within the confines of the building itself, lessons that have been fascinating for their eccentricity and fantastical nature are now in deadly earnest. This is one place where Rowling clearly demonstrates the fascinating connection between fear and delight. In *Harry Potter and the prisoner of Azkaban* (1999),[30] Lupin's inspired teaching of the Riddikulus spell is a masterpiece of swift oscillation between danger and near-hysterical hilarity as each student in turn conjures up what he or she fears most, and then confronts it and banishes it by turning it into something ridiculous. Timing is of the essence, however, and some students are almost trapped by their own inability to relieve themselves of what they themselves have conjured. In the film version of the book,[31] the episode takes place to a record that the master in charge sets playing on an old-fashioned gramophone. 1930s-style music, that slightly manic inter-war flapper sound, a burlesque motif beloved of directors (compare with Julie Taymor's *Titus* when Titus is presented with the severed heads of his two sons as part of a travelling cabaret act, or at the end of Richard Loncraine's *Richard III* as Ian McKellen's Richard tumbles from a gantry into hellish flames to the music of 'I'm sitting on top of the world')[32] perfectly conjures up the atmosphere of bravery in the face of hellish odds. Here too then, implicit ideas of lulling and making mock come into absolute collision.

Rowling's fourth book, *Harry Potter and the goblet of fire* (2000), diffuses further the demarcation of the boundaries between the primary and secondary

28 J.K. Rowling, *Harry Potter and the philosopher's stone* (London, 1997), p. 129. **29** Ibid., p. 152 (Rowling's italics, to signify song). **30** J.K. Rowling, *Harry Potter and the prisoner of Azkaban* (London, 1999), pp 94–106. **31** *Harry Potter and the prisoner of Azkaban*, dir. Alfonso Cuarón Oroczo, 2004. **32** *Titus*, dir. Julie Taymor, 1999; *Richard III*, dir. Richard Loncraine, 1995.

worlds. The text falls in to three sections, and in each, the rapprochement between the two worlds is clear. The dark lord of the series, Voldemort, hitherto of limited power only in the wizarding world, is present in, and has a physical effect on, the non-magical world, recorded in chilling detail in the account of the murder of Frank Bryce. Horrid fascination and the anticipation born of superior readerly knowledge each play their part, as Frank, hiding behind the door of the room in which we know Voldemort to be seated, overhears an account of a murder. His disbelief is made comical ('Frank inserted a gnarled finger into his ear and rotated it. Owing, no doubt, to a build-up of earwax, he had heard the word 'Quidditch', which was not a word at all')[33] and then too awful for explicit description:

> And then the chair was facing Frank, and he saw what was sitting in it. His walking stick fell to the floor with a clatter. He opened his mouth and let out a scream. He was screaming so loudly that he never heard the words the thing in the chair spoke as it raised a wand. There was a flash of green light, a rushing sound, and Frank Bryce crumpled. He was dead before he hit the floor.[34]

The rollercoaster ride from horror to comedy that was so readily observable in the earlier books is now in reverse.

There are also texts of fantasy that deal with fear unrelieved by comedy. Ursula Le Guin in her *Earthsea* books,[35] Susan Cooper's work in her *The dark is rising* sequence,[36] and Philip Pullman, too, in his *Dark Materials* trilogy,[37] all show us fear in a handful of dust with very little relief. Each of these texts ask their heroes to confront the unknown and to act beyond their knowledge and strength, sometimes with the aid of superior guides and sometimes not. In Cooper's novel *The dark is rising* (1973), fear is mostly produced by the notion of the creatures of the dark being about to burst in upon a primary world largely blissfully unaware of the dark forces surrounding it. At the same time, 11-year-old Will's vulnerability as hero comes about largely because he is one of only a handful of people in a position to be aware of the danger and to experience the fear that goes with it. In Le Guin's sequence, written over a period of more than thirty years, the central figure Ged is absolutely broken by playing beyond his strength, and the fear evoked early in the series is the common one of trying to enter into combat with

33 J.K. Rowling, *Harry Potter and the goblet of fire* (London, 2000), pp 12–13.   34 Ibid., p. 19.   35 Ursula le Guin, *A wizard of Earthsea* (London, 1971); *The tombs of Atuan* (London, 1972); *The farthest shore* (London, 1973); *Tehanu* (London, 1993); *The other wind* (London, 2002).   36 Susan Cooper, *Over sea, under stone* (London, 1965); *The dark is rising* (London, 1973); *Greenwitch* (London, 1974); *The grey king* (London, 1975); *Silver on the tree* (London, 1977).   37 Philip Pullman, *Northern lights* (London, 1995); *The subtle knife* (London, 1997); *The amber spyglass* (London, 2000).

something elusive. In Pullman's work, the two child protagonists are actually placed in mortal danger by deliberately cynical, criminally negligent or woefully inadequate parental action, and such adult guidance as they receive is given momentarily or episodically by fellow-fighters against the dark on an ad hoc basis rather than in any systematic way. In all three sequences mentioned here, the notion of the inadequately equipped hero facing a generally unperceived danger calls up a fundamentally raw and fearful response to isolation and misunderstanding in the reader.

Among contemporary writers, Robert Cormier's uncompromising accounts of the darkest side of young human nature (*The chocolate war* [1974], *Tenderness* [1997], *The rag and bone shop* [2001])[38] are perhaps the most unrelieved, because they dispense with all notions of fantasy as an alternative battleground, positioning the universal fearful struggle between good and evil squarely in the real world and placing the protagonists, like those of the fantasy texts, in isolated opposition to general social perception. In *The rag and bone shop*, a 7-year-old girl, Alicia, has been murdered; the last person to see her alive is her 12-year-old friend Jason. Jason is called in to assist the police in their enquiries, not realizing for one moment that he is a suspect; the novel, which is brief and brisk, is largely taken up with the interrogation that elicits a false confession from him, the validity of which is overturned when Alicia's older brother turns up and volunteers his own confession.

The novel allows the reader privileged access to both the interrogator's methods and his ability to persuade himself of the veracity of things he knows to be untrue:

> And in a blazing moment, Trent knew irrevocably that the boy was innocent, knew in the deepest part of his being, past all doubt and deception that Jason Dorrant had not murdered Alicia Bartlett. Trent had witnessed too may evasions and heard too many protestations in all his interrogations to have any doubt about it [...] Maybe I'm wrong, he thought. Maybe for once my instincts aren't accurate [...] Trent had dreaded the day he'd meet a subject who would be the epitome of deception, outwitting him in the game of questions and answers, thrust and parry, an idiot savant who would somehow outguess and outflank him.[39]

It portrays brilliantly the fear and disorientation experienced by the protagonist:

> 'Let me emphasise the situation, Jason. Outside this door, there are officers waiting to charge you with the murder of Alicia Bartlett. Once you step outside, you will have no protection. Your age won't save you. There's a law

---

38 Robert Cormier, *The chocolate war* (New York, 1974); *Tenderness* (New York, 1997); *The rag and bone shop* (New York, 2001). **39** Cormier, *The rag and bone shop*, pp 131–2.

now that allows a juvenile like yourself to be tried as an adult. Which means life in prison, without parole, or worse. And you'll be looked upon as a murderer. Without any defenses. But there's a way to mitigate that outcome.'

'What way?'

'By showing that you are not a cold-blooded murderer, by showing that you did not mean to harm Alicia, that you are sorry that it happened …'

'But I didn't kill her.'

'I know, I know. Denial is part of the defence mechanism. Because you didn't mean to do it translates in your mind to the belief that you didn't do it. That's entirely understandable, Jason. What you did in one blinding moment gets blotted out in your memory and you convince yourself that you didn't do it.

'But I didn't.'

'You see? You are still in denial. And that's the worst thing you can be at the moment. You must turn away from that denial. And then you'll have a better chance …' […]

Trent could see the despair in the boy's eyes, his body drooping with weariness, the trembling of his chin, the tears staining his cheeks. He sensed the imminent moment of success, felt the sweet thrill of triumph, everything cast aside for the moment, all doubts gone. This was what he was hired to do, this was what he was born to do.[40]

Here then we see the classic notion of disempowerment as the fear at the centre of the text. But here there is no clear distinction between reality and fantasy. The hero is persuaded that fantasy – the state of being that would make the situation safe for the participant, to say nothing of the reader, in a text of the fantastic – is the product of his own mind and is the very thing that renders him guilty. But most chillingly of all, it shows how the innocent at the centre of the story can be persuaded that the heroic thing to do is to submit to a superior social wisdom which overpowers his own sense of self. The role of the mythic hero is absolutely reversed. Self-doubt as a version of self loss is the real centre of fear in this text then, and the reader has no recourse to a return to reality in order to relieve the fear of being caught up in a similar socially disempowering situation. In fact, quite the contrary; the closing chapter of the text sees the released Jason turned utterly in on himself and unable at all to understand why he confessed to something he knew to be untrue, and the text closes like this:

40 Ibid., pp 139–42. 41 Ibid., p. 154.

So he ignored the heat now and wondered about what he should do next. If he was going to show what he could do and really did it this time instead of *saying* he did it when he didn't [...] A beautiful feeling of sweetness came over him. He lifted his head, let the feeling carry him for a while, like a fresh breeze in his heart. Then he went into the kitchen and took the butcher knife out of the drawer.[41]

Here, fantasy as a means of safe experimentation gives way to the fantasist – the deceiver who finally believes his own lies. Fantasy is not a safe, alternative testing ground but horrifyingly embedded in and inseparable from reality, and once the nature of fantasy has been fused to such a horrific reality, no amount of lulling or making mock will rescue anyone; the very media by which we might be rescued have become unavailable.

Don't turn around: the embodiment
of disorientation in Mark Z. Danielewski's
House of leaves

DARA DOWNEY

Traditionally, the notion of the uncanny – Sigmund Freud's best efforts to root it firmly in repression aside – contains within it a profound sense of disorientation. One of Freud's own sources, psychologist Ernst Jentsch, describes the uncanny as 'something one does not know one's way about in', and goes on to add that, 'The better oriented in his environment a person is, the less readily will he get the impression of something uncanny in regard to the objects and events in it.'[1] Indeed, uncertainty lies at the very heart of the concept, since, as Anthony Vidler suggests, the uncanny 'would be characterized better as "dread" than terror, deriving its force from its very inexplicability, its sense of lurking unease, rather than from any clearly defined source of fear – an uncomfortable sense of haunting rather than a present apparition.'[2] It is these two elements of the uncanny – disorientation and amorphous dread – rather than the traditional psychoanalytical sources of fear associated with the term which, as I shall demonstrate, form the backbone of a particularly postmodern form of fear, formulated by Mark Edmundson as 'where's my car? where's my room? who am I? – the stuff of current-day anxiety dreams.'[3] What this quotation suggests is a sort of symbiotic relationship between the inability of the postmodern subject to pinpoint the source of his or her ambient unease, and the disorientation which Frederic Jameson sees as a central characteristic of that subject's experience of the spaces of the postmodern world.[4] As I shall argue, it is this relationship which constitutes one of the central themes of Mark Z. Danielewski's novel *House of leaves* (2000), which

---

1 Sigmund Freud, 'The "Uncanny"' in *The standard edition of the complete psychological works of Sigmund Freud. vol. XVII, 1917–19: An infantile neurosis and other works*, trans. James Strachey (London, 1955), p. 221.
2 Anthony Vidler, *The architectural uncanny: essays in the modern unhomely* (London, 1992), p. 23.   3 Mark Edmundson, *Nightmare on Main Street: angels, sadomasochism & the culture of the gothic* (London, 1997), p. 48.   4 See Frederic Jameson, *Postmodernism, or, The cultural logic of late capitalism* (London, 1991).

posits as inextricably bound up with one another the process of becoming lost, the disintegration of the individual and the flickering between presence and absence of a monstrous haunting (or indeed, haunting monster), which is only rendered more uncannily frightening by its refusal to haunt.

House of leaves is a book about a book about a film about a house that changes continually, growing endless (and endlessly shifting) corridors made of stone older than the solar system, and a staircase that is, on occasion, longer than the diameter of the earth. On a formal level, the text could be seen as being arranged in concentric diagetic circles, although the boundaries between these levels are far from impermeable. The innermost narrative tells the story of renowned filmmaker and award-winning photographer Will Navidson, his partner Karen Green and their two children, Chad and Daisy, who move into an apparently ordinary suburban house, on Ash Tree Lane in Virginia. When a shelf mysteriously falls down, Navidson's DIY efforts reveal that the inside of the house is one quarter of an inch larger than the outside. Then, overnight, a door inexplicably appears where there was never one before, which turns into an equally inexplicable corridor. This in turn becomes a labyrinth, which constantly and unpredictably reorganizes itself, and which Navidson and a group of other men set out to explore – an expedition which ends in death for several of the party.

This chain of events, however, is only related to the reader through a work of academic criticism, written by a man called Zampanò, analyzing but more often simply describing the film called *The Navidson record* which Navidson makes of their time in the house. The film starts off as a simple document of his attempts to reunite his crumbling family, recorded (in a startling echo of *The Blair Witch project*, released in 1999, just one year before *House of leaves* was first published) by means of hand-held cameras and others mounted on walls all over the house. Zampanò's unfeasibly detailed work of criticism, itself called *House of leaves*, is found in manuscript form by the narrator, Johnny Truant, a disaffected young man with a traumatic family history. Johnny is awoken in the middle of the night by a friend, who brings him to see the body of a man who died suddenly in his apartment block – that is, Zampanò – and who is found, without any visible injuries, next to three long and worryingly deep gouges in the floorboards. In this room, Johnny finds a trunk containing pages and pages of text, on various kinds of paper, typed and in handwriting, with multiple revisions and amendments and crossings out. Some pages are made illegible by stains, burns or age, and Johnny (as we find out in a series of extended, type-written footnotes, which appear in Courier font) sets out to piece it all together, while falling prey to severe psychological disturbance, which may or may not be caused by the unsettling nature of the material with which he is working. Moreover, in the process, he finds out that *The Navidson record* does not in fact exist, nor do many of the critical works to which Zampanò refers. Outside of Johnny's own narrative and editorial comments are the interjections of the "editors", which often correct Johnny's own amendments, and which include footnotes, a highly unreliable index, appendices in the form of collages, photographs, poems and letters from Johnny's mother while she is in a mental institution. In turn, all of this cannot be disentangled from the fact that Danielewski's *House of leaves* also exists in hypertext form, and has spawned an online message-board, featuring multiple "links" and "threads" which lead dizzyingly back to one another, or off on what are often seemingly unrelated tangents.

On the level of form as well as of content, then, the text is labyrinthine. By taking an unsolvable maze as its core subject matter; by bringing together a multitude of actual and fictional academic sources and authorities; by ensuring that every element of the narration is mediated through one of several different forms of representation or technology; and by including clues that the various narrative levels may be linked, the book never permits either the reader or the characters to gain a stable footing, or to find a coherent centre of meaning. The text therefore performs as well as represents the experience of space as frighteningly disorientating. That all of this has particular relevance for the configuration of the individual subject becomes evident when a precedent, if not necessarily an explanation, for the nature of the house on Ash Tree Lane is provided by Zampanò, in the shape of explorers' journals from the famous Jamestown Colony in Virginia, upon the remains of which the house is supposedly built. The journal entries, transcribed with endearing typographical fidelity by Zampanò and Johnny Truant, run as follows:

> 20 Janiuere, 1610
>
> More fnow. Bitter cold. This is a terrible Place we have stumbled on. It has been a Week fince we haue fpied one living thing. Were it not for the ftorm we would have abandoned it. Verm was plagued by bad Dreames last night.

> 21 Janiuere, 1610
>
> The ftorme will not break. Verm went out to hunt but returned within the houre. The Wind makes a wicked found in the Woods. Ftrange as it muft feem, Tiggs, Verm, and I take comfort in the found. I fear more the filence here. Verm tellf me he dreamt of Bones last night. I dreame of the Sunne.

> 22 Janiuere, 1610
>
> We are dying. No food. No fhelter. Tiggs dreamt he faw all fnow about us turn Red with blood.

And then [Zampanò and Truant transcribe] the last entry:

23 Janiuere, 1610

Ftairs! We have found ftairs!⁵

The moment takes on added significance when read in conjunction with the discussion of being lost in Kathleen M. Kirby's critical study *Indifferent boundaries* (1996), which quotes very similar journals, written by early explorers of the New World. What distinguishes these journals from the accounts in *House of leaves* is their initial confidence and objectivity. Kirby reads the impersonality of these accounts – the listing of geographical features, distances, heights and so on, in an attempt to achieve an objective description – as a means of creating a narrative situation in which, effectively, 'the subject is expelled from the landscape and becomes alien to it', by doing away with subjective reactions or even physical sensations such as cold, hunger or, most particularly, anxiety.⁶ Later passages, however, reveal a considerably less calm narrator in the face of fog, darkness and moving ice. In a passage that bears so remarkable a resemblance to those in *House of leaves* that it seems reasonable at least to suggest that it may constitute source material, the explorer, Samuel de Champlain, writes:

> The most self-possessed would have lost all judgement in such a juncture; even the greatest navigator in the world. What alarmed us still more [than the ice] was the short distance we could see, and the fact that the night was coming on, and that we could not make a shift of a quarter of a league without finding a bank or some ice.⁷

Such a dark, unstable, unfamiliar landscape, in which it is difficult to make definitive statements about distance or topography, due either to poor visibility, lack of maps, or both, does far more than simply force the explorers to admit that they are not entirely happy or in control. No longer able 'to ensure the uncontaminated primacy of the self' by setting up a clear distinction between exploring subject and explored landscape, the very ego boundaries of the exploring subject are placed under threat. As Kirby argues, 'Maintaining a stable space outside allows a subject to maintain his form even as he moves though it. Upsetting the distinctions of near and far, inside and outside, brings into question what is proper to the subject', which means that:

> This stance of superiority crumbles when the explorers' cartographic aptitude deteriorates. When they are lost, a different kind of subject emerges, a diffracted, porous self fused with a chaotic and mobile environment.

5 Mark Z. Danielewski, *House of leaves* (London, 2000), p. 413. 6 Kathleen M. Kirby, *Indifferent boundaries: spatial concepts of human subjectivity* (New York, 1996), p. 51. 7 From Samuel de Champlain, *The voyages of Samuel de Champlain, 1604–1618*, pp 199–200, quoted in Kirby, *Indifferent boundaries*, p. 51.

> To actually be *in* the surroundings, incapable of separating one's self from them in a larger objective representation, is, for the explorers, to be lost.[8]

The situation which Kirby is describing here has much in common with a form of psychosis known as legendary psychaesthenia, theorized by psychologist Roger Calliois in 1935 as a version of what happens to an insect when it mimics the background upon which it is resting. Merging itself with its surroundings, the status of the insect as 'figure-on-ground' is radically destabilized, an effect which Calliois refers to as '*depersonalization by assimilation to space*'. As he continues:

> [T]he living creature, the organism, is no longer the origin of the coordinates, but one point among others; it is dispossessed of its privilege and literally *no longer knows where to place itself* [...] The feeling of personality, considered as the organism's feeling of distinction from its surroundings, of the connection between consciousness and a particular point in space, [...] [is] seriously undermined.[9]

Kirby describes the psychological condition itself as follows:

> The subject afflicted with legendary psychaesthenia [...] exhibits a radical dysfunction in the order of space. He cannot affix himself to reality by establishing a predictable or reliable place in it. Noises and visions that seem objectively to fall outside the bounds of his body and psyche seem rather to occur within it; indeed, even his own consciousness may be detached from his body, drifting from its moorings on the inside to float outward into external space. He may see himself from the perspective of a doorway halfway across the room and really believe that's where he is.[10]

This is, essentially, a fairly accurate description of what happens to Johnny Truant, the young man who edits and makes typewritten comments around his reprinting of Zampanò's text. As he puts it himself:

> ```
> This much I'm sure of: I'm alone in hostile territo-
> ries with no clue why they're hostile or how to get
> back to safe havens, an Old Haven, a lost haven, the
> temperature dropping, the hour heaving & pitching
> towards a profound darkness, while before me my idi-
> ```

---

8 Kirby, *Indifferent boundaries*, pp 49, 53, 50 (emphasis Kirby's).   **9** Roger Calliois, 'Mimicry and legendary psychasthenia', trans. John Shepley in *October*, 31 (Winter 1984), 16–32, originally printed in *Minotaure*, 7 (1935), reproduced on www.generation-online.org/p/fpcaillois.htm, accessed 9 Jan. 2007 (all emphasis Callois').   **10** Kirby, *Indifferent boundaries*, p. 103.

otic amaurotic guide laughs, actually cackles is
more like it, lost in his own litany of inside
jokes, completely out of his head, out of focus too,
zonules of Zinn, among other things, having snapped
long ago like piano wires, leaving me with
absolutely no sound way to determine where the hell
I'm going, though right now going to hell seems like
a pretty sound bet.[11]

What this passage suggests is a fundamental breakdown in Johnny's ability to distinguish between events occurring in the outside world and those which occur
only inside his own head. This leaves him unsure of where he is going, unless it is
to hell – clearly a deliberate and complex irony, considering that an 'amaurotic
guide' (presumably, Zampanò himself, or at least his manuscript) is one who leads
a hero through hell and back out again, such as the Sibyl in Virgil's *Aeneid* and
Virgil himself in Dante's *Inferno*. As critic Jeremy Green argues, the unrepresentable, disunified nature of postmodern society gives rise to parallel distortions
to the configuration of the individual, bringing about 'the disintegration of the
subject, its dispersal among the codes and relays of information society.'[12] Green
continues:

> The difficulty for the novelist [in portraying the individual subject] lies in
> the immense gulf between the experience, agency, and cognitive capacities
> of the subject, and the large structures and processes that make up the
> postmodern world [...] the more compelling the account of structures and
> processes, [...] the weaker and more passive the individual will seem.[13]

Johnny *is* this subject, lost both literally and psychically; consumed by drugs, violence and sex; incapable of sorting out the events of his own childhood and even
his day-to-day experience, let alone the esoteric complexities of Zampanò's work
and his own relationship to it; and, eventually, so spooked that he holes himself
up in a dingy hotel room, afraid to come out, guarded by locks and guns. His
milieu – the tattoo parlours, night clubs and drug-fuelled pool parties of late
1990s Hollywood – might appear superficially to have little or nothing to do with
the howling wilderness that was pre-colonization Virginia, and he may not literally have lost his way. Nevertheless, postmodernity, with its unimaginably vast
networks and interconnecting systems of information, its disavowal of consensus
and centrality in all their forms, renders the world which he inhabits just as inco-
herent and impossible to navigate, epistemologically and indeed ontologically, as

11 Danielewski, *House of leaves*, p. 43. 12 Jeremy Green, *Late postmodernism: American fiction at the millennium* (New York, 2005), p. 188. 13 Ibid.

the virgin forest. What is more, because this alienating, labyrinthine cultural space – by which the self is dwarfed and rendered incapable of meaningful action – is represented, not mimetically, but metonymically, as an impossibly unstable house, a film that does not exist and a confusing and unsettling book written about that film, the reader is not permitted even the comfort of being able to situate this system reliably. Located everywhere and yet nowhere, in texts and places that hover between existence and non-existence, it slips constantly from the realm of the literal to the figurative and back again, eluding our grasp at every turn.

Frederic Jameson, in his essay 'Postmodernism, or, the cultural logic of late capitalism', reads Kevin Lynch's *The image of the city* (from which Zampanò also quotes) as suggesting the possibility of what he calls "cognitive mapping" as an antidote to the disorientation produced by postmodern urban, cultural and social spaces. Jameson states that Lynch's work:

> taught us that the alienated city is above all a space in which people are unable to map (in their minds) either their own positions or the urban totality in which they find themselves: grids such as those of Jersey City, in which none of the traditional markers (monuments, nodes, natural boundaries, built perspectives) obtain, are the most obvious examples. Dis-alienation in the traditional city, then, involves the practical reconquest of a sense of place and the construction or reconstruction of an articulated ensemble which can be retained in memory and which the individual sub-ject can map and remap along the moments of mobile, alternative trajec-tories.[14]

The purpose of cognitive mapping is 'to enable a situational representation on the part of the individual subject to that vaster and properly unrepresentable totality which is the ensemble of society's structures as a whole.' It is thus at once a local and a cultural project, a way of orienting oneself in a usable, if provisional, manner, while simultaneously admitting that full orientation is impossible. While a map provides an exhaustive picture of an area, allowing an almost infinite number of individual routes to be traced through it, a cognitive map or 'itinerary' is a highly subject-centred means of plotting the route of a specific journey, a dia-gram 'organized around the still subject-centred or existential journey of the trav-eller, along which various significant key features are marked – oases, mountain ranges, rivers, monuments, and the like.'[15] A particularly telling example of such an itinerary appears in H. Rider Haggard's late-Victorian blockbuster, *King Solomon's mines* (1885), the story of a group of English travellers' adventures in "darkest Africa". When it is viewed upside-down, a careful examination of the

14 Jameson, *Postmodernism*, p. 51. 15 Ibid., pp 51, 52.

map, drawn in blood, which the men use to find the legendary diamond mines, graphically, if crudely suggests a female body, complete with breasts, arms, navel and genitals. Indeed, the travellers' journey entails a figurative molestation of this body, as they travel over 'Sheba's Breasts' (which are described in detail and even feature nipples) and finally penetrate and despoil the hidden recesses of the treasure caves. Read in the context of Kirby's comments, the map can be read as literally embodying, through the coding of gender difference, the necessary distinction between the land to be explored and the men exploring it. At the same time, by depicting their route as a coherent, unified and recognizable figure, however schematic, they give graphic shape to their ability to comprehend and navigate that landscape. As Kirby puts it, 'Part of the function of mapping […] is to ensure that the relationship between knower and known remains unidirectional. The mapper should be able to "master" his environment, occupy a secure and superior position in relation to it, without it affecting him in return.'[16] Proudly displaying a clearly demarcated starting point and ultimate goal, the map enables the explorers to march confidently forward, male, English and triumphant, whatever difficulties they might encounter on the way.

This idea becomes somewhat clearer when read in conjunction with another of Kirby's sources, Yi Fu Tuan's *Space and place* (2001), in which he describes the experience of becoming lost as follows:

> I follow a path into the forest, stray from the path, and all of a sudden feel completely disoriented, space is still organized in conformity with the sides of my body. There are regions to my front and back, to my left and right, but they are not geared to external reference points and hence are quite useless. Front and back regions suddenly feel arbitrary, since I have no better reason to go forward than to go back. Let a flickering light appear behind a distant clump of trees. I remain lost in the sense that I still do not know where I am in the forest, but space has dramatically regained its structure. The flickering light has established a goal. As I move forward that goal, front and back, left and right, have resumed their meaning: I stride forward, am glad to have left dark space behind, and make sure that I do not veer to left or right.[17]

In Tuan's formulation, orientation is founded upon an exchange between the basic egocentric compass points of forward/backward, left/right and some external marker – or, to put it another way, between Self and not-Self. Confronted suddenly, in the absence of such a reference point, with the fact that the directions

16 Kirby, *Indifferent boundaries*, p. 50. 17 Yi Fu Tuan, *Space and place: the perspective of experience* (Minneapolis, 2001), p. 36.

created by the body are relative and subjective rather than absolute, with no workable correlative in the external environment, the subject is lost, no matter which way he or she turns. The ability to isolate some object from which one creates direction brings into being a "not-I", an Other, which allows the subject to retain a sense of where he or she is, by knowing where it is that he or she is not, even if location in the wider sense cannot be determined. At the same time, and in exactly the same way, the presence of this Other also serves to reinforce the identity of the subject, by allowing one to know who one is by taking the visible form of what one is not. In essence, it allows the subject to say, "that is that so I am me", and "that is there so I am here". It is for this reason, then, that the explorers in the passages quoted from *House of leaves* prefer the howling of the storm to total silence. Lost they might continue to be, but an identifiable sound, however horrific and frightening in and of itself, serves to reassure them of their separation from their environment, and so they can at least be certain that they have not lost their very selves. It is not, however, of much use as a form of orientation, since, by its very nature, the sound of a storm is neither fixed in place nor visible. From the abrupt end to which the explorers' journal comes (particularly in light of the fact that the 'Ftairs!' are one of the most dangerous features of Navidson's house, changing size and length rapidly and without warning) we can only assume that, ultimately, neither the wind nor the stairs perform as the light does in Tuan's description, but act in a similar manner to an *ignis fatuus*, tempting weary travellers deeper into uncharted territory and to their doom. In *House of leaves*, therefore, the very things which, under normal circumstances, serve to allow one to orient oneself, actually result in one becoming even more lost than before.

Indeed, in the novel as a whole, the ability of the individual to orient him- or herself in this manner is consistently undermined, and neither a coherent picture of their surroundings nor any real sense of direction is ever achieved by Navidson and his fellow explorers. Indeed, their efforts to chart the maze by creating landmarks prove futile. The men leave fluorescent markers at regular intervals along the corridors to remind themselves of turnings and to measure distance. On their return, however, these markers have been ripped to shreds, as if by a wild animal, although they have encountered none. This is one of the several altogether inconclusive pieces of evidence that the house might be inhabited by some sort of beast or monster. Other hints include the deep scratches next to Zampanò's dead body; the 'growl' that reverberates sporadically through the labyrinth, which may or may not merely be the sound of the walls shifting; and the claw of darkness which Zampanò describes as sweeping across the camera at one point, taking with it the dead body of Holloway, the self-appointed leader of the expedition. Overall, the signs of the Beast's presence never cohere to the point of demarcating some sort of trail, indicating the direction in which 'the Beast', as it comes to be known, has been travelling. Such a trail would provide a means by which the men could track it, and hence provide some sort of sense of orientation. Instead, these signs actually serve to make the men *more* disoriented, particularly as there appears to be no continuity or linearity to the marks which it leaves behind. In a sense, then, the Beast acts as the polar opposite to the female figure in Haggard's map. It destroys any attempts to plot or render stable the interior of the house, it is quite clearly mobile, and, insofar as it might simply be an indication that the house is changing shape, it serves as the sign and symbol of the house's physical volatility. Therefore, it acts neither as a fixed point by which one can get one's bearings, nor as a figure "fixed" by representation in a map. Instead, it actively embodies the negation of such locational security, and any efforts to navigate the corridors of the house end in complete disorientation, and, frequently, death.

Moreover, Danielewski's Beast cannot conclusively be distinguished from those who are exploring the environment it effectively personifies. Another way in which this protean monstrous figure manifests itself is in the form of the Minotaur, which features prominently in numerous footnotes in Zampanò's text, all of which are struck through with a black line. A monster in its ferocity and its hybridity, its terrible appetite for the flesh of Athenian youths and its transgression of the borders of what it is to be human, the Minotaur lacks the visual unity of the map in *King Solomon's mines*. It fails to be either recognizably human or entirely animal, and so cannot serve as a clear-cut Other from which the exploring subject can distinguish and thereby reaffirm his or her Self, a point underlined by its sporadic blurring with the novel's primary male characters. Deliberate typographical errors and phrases repeated and echoed on different levels of narration, suggesting that these levels are not in fact distinct, not only hint that Johnny, or possibly Navidson, might be Zampanò's son, or even Zampanò himself, but also that Zampanò's son might be the Minotaur. *House of leaves* therefore takes the notion of the Minotaur's disturbing proximity yet distance from humanity to its logical extreme. It is no wonder that no-one in the novel is able to navigate the corridors of the house, since, as the corporealization of the characters' trajectory through space, the Beast fulfils none of the functions usually fulfilled by such figures in exploration narratives.

One of the most vivid evocations of this idea comes in Johnny Truant's narration. Having become obsessed but also terrified by the manuscript, he finds himself gripped by what may or may not be nightmarish hallucinations or hallucinatory nightmares, and screams regularly in his sleep. The following passage recounts what happens when he goes alone into an empty room at the back of the tattoo parlour where he works, and he becomes gradually convinced that there is something behind him. He tells the reader:

```
[F]ocus on these words, and whatever you do don't
let your eyes wander past the perimeter of this
```

page. Now imagine just beyond your peripheral
vision, maybe behind you, maybe to the side of you,
maybe even in front of you, but right where you
can't see it, something is quietly closing in on
you, so quiet in fact you can only hear it as
silence. Find those pockets without sound. That's
where it is. Right at this moment. But don't look.
Keep your eyes here. Now take a deep breath. Go
ahead take an even deeper one. Only this time as you
start to exhale try to imagine how fast it will
happen, how hard it's gonna hit you, how many times
it will stab your jugular with its teeth or are they
nails?, don't worry, that particular detail doesn't
matter, because before you have time to even process
that you should be moving, you should be running,
you should at the very least be flinging up your
arms - you sure as hell should be getting rid of
this book - you won't have time to even scream.

Don't look.

I didn't.

Of course I looked.

I looked so fucking fast I should of ended up
wearing one of those neck braces for whiplash.

My hands had gone all clammy. My face was burning
up. Who knows how much adrenaline had just been
dumped into my system. Before I turned, it felt
exactly as if in fact I had turned and at that
instant caught sight of some tremendous beast
crouched off in the shadows, muscles a twitch from
firing its great mass forward, ragged claws slowly
extending, digging into the linoleum, even as its
eyes are dilating, beyond the point of reason, completely obliterating the iris, and by that widening
fire, the glowing furnace of witness, a <u>camera
lucida</u>, with me in silhouette, like some silly Hand
shadow twitching about upside down, is that right?,
or am I getting confused?, either way registering at
least the sign it must have been waiting for; my own
recognition of exactly what has been awaiting me all
along - except that when I finally do turn, jerking
around like the scared-shitless shit-for-brains I
am, I discover only a deserted corridor, or was it
merely a <u>recently</u> deserted corridor?, this thing,
whatever it had been, obviously beyond the grasp of

```
my imagination or for that matter my emotions,
having departed into alcoves of darkness, seeping
into corners & floors, cracks & outlets, gone even
to the walls […] as I keep spinning around like a
stupid top spinning around on nothing, looking
everywhere, even though there's absolutely nothing,
nothing anywhere.¹⁸
```

The paradox here is that, if the Beast is the embodiment of disorientation in the novel, then it is waiting for Johnny to turn around so that it can confront him with the vision of how lost he is, not because there *is* a hideous monster lurking in the shadows behind him, but because there isn't. Indeed, since he is lost already, and deeply unsettled by the subject matter, rampant contradictions and jargon-heavy academic impenetrability of Zampanò's manuscript, and only becomes more so after this incident, the Beast *cannot* be behind him, since an apparition, no matter how hideous, would act as a visible point of orientation. For Tuan, when one is lost, and turns around to see the flickering light (or conceivably, anything at all), self and Other come into being at the same moment, in that the subject seizes upon that external object so as to define and locate him- or herself in opposition to it. Gloating in anticipation of what Johnny will see when he turns to face it, the Beast is at once a monstrous inversion of this object, and its total absence, in that, in the absence of such an Other, to turn around is to be trapped within the basic directions created by the body, to literally lose oneself. With nothing against which to define forwards and backwards, right and left, such subjective directions become useless, and Johnny is left spinning in a geographical and existential void. The fear that the Beast induces – fear of getting lost – therefore depends upon its absence, and Johnny is confronted with (or rather, *not* confronted with) an impossible situation in which each alternative – to turn around or not to turn around – can only generate terror.

The year before the publication of *House of leaves*, saw the emergence of two rather different texts positing the ease with which one can become lost in the forest as their locus of terror – *The Blair Witch project* and Stephen King's *The girl who loved Tom Gordon*. Both texts, I would argue, feature moments which are the exact opposite of Johnny's failed encounter with the Beast. *Blair Witch*, an infamously realistic film allegedly (and falsely) based on video tapes found in a North American forest where three teenagers had gone missing, has much in common with *House of leaves* stylistically, in that the jerkiness and jump cuts characteristic of its less-than flawless camera work closely resembles Zampanò's descriptions of *The Navidson record*. The film convincingly portrays the fear of the three main characters as they become aware, not only of an unseen presence which stalks

18 Danielewski, *House of leaves*, pp 26–7.

them, but also that they are without a map and hopelessly lost. Underlying the overall premise is a sense that the fear created by this presence actually causes or at least exacerbates their disorientation. That the film differs fundamentally from *House of leaves* becomes clear, however, at the very end, when it is suggested (albeit in a confused and confusing manner) that the characters become victims of a psychopathic child molester who has been mentioned early on. What is notable about this murderer (who haunts the urban legends of the surrounding town and who never appears within the camera frame except in the expressions of terror registered on the faces of the teenagers) is that he or she, it is rumoured, always forces one victim to face the wall while killing another. The sight of Mike facing the wall in a house which he and Heather encounter in a clearing is almost the last thing that we see before the camera falls to the ground amid screams of fear and pain. To an extent, then, the film climaxes with a failure to turn and look upon the monstrous presence even greater than Johnny's, since Mike never turns around and Heather's camera never points in the direction of whoever is in the room with them. On the other hand, there is definitely a monster in *Blair Witch*, albeit a human one, and he or she is undoubtedly both corporeal and dangerous. Nonetheless, by providing its audience with information, however inconclusive, and with a fixed human explanation for all that happens, the narrative is stabilized and re-oriented epistemologically, even if its characters never find their way out of the woods and are themselves never found.

King's *The girl who loved Tom Gordon,* the story of a pre-pubescent girl who loses her way in the woods, is even more optimistic and far less ambivalent about the possibilities of counteracting disorientation and the role played by a monster in that process. Gradually becoming convinced that she is being stalked by something that is not human, the little girl, Trisha, finally hears the monster coming out of the trees behind her, and 'Slowly, both with terror and with a strange sort of calm inevitability, Trisha turned to face the God of the Lost.' What she sees, however, provokes a certain disappointment rather than fear:

> It emerged from the trees on the left side of the road, and Trisha's first thought was: *Is that all? Is that all it ever was?* Grown men would have turned and run from the *Ursus americanus* which lumbered out of the last screen of bushes [...] but Trisha had been prepared for some awful horror torn from the underside of the night.[19]

In this case, then, turning around actually serves to *reduce* fear and aid in orientation, as the reference to left and right serves to highlight; and indeed, Trisha is found and brought home shortly afterwards. Moreover, when she turns 'She

19 Stephen King, *The girl who loved Tom Gordon* (London, 1999), pp 71, 70 (all emphasis King's).

had seen the bewilderment in its face, had seen its fear of her', implying that looking the thing in the face has, as Tuan's model would suggest, serves to reaffirm her
selfhood.[20] King's monster, even more so than the killer in *Blair Witch*, fails to be
properly monstrous in the same sense as Danielewski's Beast, in that to gaze upon
the God of the Lost is to orient rather than disorient the subject and to reinte-
grate rather than disintegrate individual identity. What Trisha sees is not the
simultaneous monstrosity and evanescence of the postmodern uncanny, but
simply a very dangerous beast. According to Kirby, 'one of the most representative
features of postmodernism, as Jameson describes it, is its erasure of lines that had
previously kept separate phenomena and objects apart. Postmodernism cannibal-
izes everything into its own dizzying productive circuit.'[21] In these terms, the contemporary world is itself a sort of devouring monster, literally consuming
everything and spitting it back out again in unrecognizable fragments. *House of
leaves* can therefore be seen as a model of postmodern culture, in that it incorpo-
rates the explorers' journals, not for their own sake, but in order to throw light on
the *status quo* several centuries later. Indeed, the contents of the journals also con-
veniently serve to explode any suspicions that the novel might be positing the
American past as a time of wholeness, when the subject *wasn't* lost and leaky.
Vidler employs a somewhat similar analogy between culture and monstrosity in
reference to postmodernist architecture, which has seen, he notes, a return to the
body as the basic model of design. However, contrary to that which forms the
basis of classical humanist design:

> this body no longer serves to center, to fix, to stabilize. Rather, its limits,
> interior or exterior, seem infinitely ambiguous and extensive; its forms, lit-
> eral and metaphorical, are no longer confined to the recognizably human
> but embrace all biological existence from the embryonic to the monstrous;
> its power lies no longer in the model of unity but in the intimation of the
> fragmentary, the morselated, the broken.[22]

Both mirroring and producing the fragmentation of the postmodern subject,
such buildings (of which Navidson's house and its elusive Beast are only slightly
hyperbolic paradigms), themselves both symptoms and representations of contemporary culture, have a profound effect upon the viewer. As Vidler puts it:

> the owner of a conventional body is undeniably placed under threat as the
> reciprocal distortions and absences *felt* by the viewer, in response to the
> reflected projection of bodily empathy, operate almost viscerally on the
> body. *We* are contorted, racked, cut, wounded, dissected, intestinally

20 Ibid., p. 284. **21** Kirby, *Indifferent boundaries*, p. 58. **22** Vidler, *Architectural uncanny*, pp 68–9.

revealed, impaled, immolated; we are suspended in a state of vertigo, or thrust into a confusion between belief and perception. It is as if the object actively participated in the subject's self-dismembering, reflecting its internal disarray or even precipitating its disaggregation.[23]

On the other hand, as Elisabeth Bronfen would argue, the sight of such mutilation also serves to reassure the viewer of his or her own integrity, whether physical or psychic.[24] Bereft of the assurance provided by the sight of a monster, Johnny Truant, Will Navidson, Zampanò and indeed, we as readers, are faced with nothing more than the uncanny spectre of our own dissolution and the thought that, wherever we go and whichever way we might turn, we are all, ultimately, lost.

23 Ibid., pp 78–9. 24 See Elizabeth Bronfen, *Over her dead body: death, femininity & the aesthetic* (Manchester, 1992).

The erroneous Elemental:
(de)constructing the legend of Leap

KATE HEBBLETHWAITE

Widely believe to be one of the most haunted houses in Western Europe, Leap
Castle stands between the town of Birr in County Offaly and Roscrea in County
Tipperary, Ireland. Situated at the foothills of the Slieve Bloom mountains, Leap's
geographical location – a veritable house on the borderland – symbolizes its long-
standing imaginative role as a gateway to the spirit world. Now inhabited by the
folk musician Sean Ryan, Leap (pronounced "Lep") has experienced a turbulent
and blood-soaked history, the repercussions of which are said to have left an
indelible paranormal mark. Indeed, the castle is widely believed to be haunted by
an impressive roll call of supernatural entities. These include a cloaked monk, an
old man dressed in a green cut-away coat, knee breaches and buckled shoes (who
is sometimes accompanied by a lady in similar old-fashioned costume), and a
woman in a red dress.[1] The most famous of these ghosts, however, is that simply
called "The Elemental". First described in 1908 by the then lady of the manor,
Mildred Henrietta Gordon Darby (1869–1932), an elemental is not a ghost, but
rather a creature that has never lived – an entity composed of primeval malignant
forces. It is characterized by an exceptionally foul smell, is usually invisible and,
at Leap, is said to lurk around a turn of the spiral staircase leading to the chapel
at the top floor of the building. It is with this entity and, more particularly, its
deconstruction that this essay is concerted.

That such a thing as a primeval malignant Elemental *could* haunt the halls
of Leap is not entirely beyond the bounds of credibility if one believes in the
power of a room – or building – to retain the spiritual echo of physical actions
that have once taken place there. If this *is* possible, then the bloody history of
the castle is the perfect environment for the corporeal manifestation of such
psychic vibrations.

1 John D. Seymour & Harry L. Neligan, *True Irish ghost stories* (1914), www.gutenberg.org/files/14099/
14099.txt, accessed 20 Mar. 2007

The history of the castle is dominated by two families: the O'Carrolls, and the Darbys. The O'Carrolls seized the lands from its previous owners, the O'Bannions in the fifteenth century and, it is said, mixed the mortar for the castle's foundation stones from the blood of their defeated enemies. First built some time before 1514, in 1541 (following a period of intense in-fighting) Leap Castle passed into the hands of Tadgh O'Carroll. This earned him the bitter envy and hatred of his older brother Thaddeus – himself considered incapable of the necessary ruthless leadership of the clan because of his priestly status. Thaddeus relentlessly undermined Tadgh's position by colluding with his political enemies. In response, Tadgh invited his brother to pray in the chapel at Leap Castle where Tadgh then slit Thaddeus' throat. With all rivals out of the way Tadgh embarked upon a campaign of ruthless consolidation of his position. One of the most notorious of these acts was a dinner party thrown for a neighbouring clan, the O'Mahons, under the guise of extending overtures of peace. Drugged food and wine was served at dinner and, as the O'Mahons succumbed to the effects, Tadgh had them carried to the chapel, situated at the top of the central keep of the castle. In the chapel's wall (and still there to this day), Tadgh had built a long shaft known as an *oubliette*, which dropped vertically to the basement of the castle. The prisoners were thrown down the shaft and were either killed outright or left to die in agony from wounds incurred from the fall. The *oubliette* remained sealed until the mid-1920s; when it was finally excavated, four cartloads of human remains were taken away.

In the mid-sixteenth century, the castle passed into the Darby family through the marriage of John Darby, an English Officer, to Finola O'Carroll. Leap was enlarged and modernized by Jonathan Darby in the mid-eighteenth century when the central tower keep was given a two-story high one-bay wing with battlements either side of it, Georgian gothic windows and a Gothicized Venetian doorway. The castle was destroyed by fire on 30 July 1922, during the Irish Civil War (1922–3), and stood in a near-derelict condition for the next half a century. It was eventually bought by a young Australian, Peter Bartlett, in 1974 and has since undergone something of a structural rehabilitation. As a result of such violent occurrences, and the folklore that subsequently gathered around them, Leap garnered an increasingly sinister reputation. Describing the castle in *Dance of the quick and the dead* (1935), Sacherverell Sitwell remarked:

> Perhaps there is no house in the world that holds so many suggestions of the supernatural. Leap Castle has to be seen to be believed. It may be regarded as the Escurial of the demi-world. Even the most unbelieving will come away from it a little shaken in their denials. The intensity of this strange place exceeds in its details anything that the most dramatic mind could imagine.[2]

2 Sacherverell Sitwell, *Dance of the quick and the dead: an entertainment of the imagination* (London, 1935),

It is important to note, however, that it was not until Mildred Darby wrote about
the ghosts of Leap at the start of the twentieth century that the castle itself began
to acquire a degree of notoriety. Formerly known as Mildred Dill, she had married Jonathan Darby of Leap in 1889 – a cause for much celebration among the
local community, 'On each window [of the castle] were placed horse shoes to
bring luck and to keep away ghosts, for Leap Castle has a host of traditions, even
of ghosts.'[3] Darby herself was a keen writer and the first – and fullest – account
of the Elemental was her own, published in the December 1908 edition of the
Occult Review. The article, written under the pseudonym Andrew Merry and entitled 'Kilman Castle, the house of horror', was a very thinly disguised description
of Leap Castle and its spectral entities. The most memorable ghost was an entity
simply called 'The Thing':

> The Thing was about the size of a sheep, thin, gaunt and shadowy in parts.
> Its face was human, or to be more accurate, inhuman, in its vileness, with
> large holes of blackness for eyes, loose slobbery lips and a thick saliva-drip-
> ping jaw, sloping back suddenly into its neck! Nose it had none, only
> spreading cancerous cavities, the whole face being one uniform tint of
> grey. This too was the colour of the dark coarse hair covering its head, neck
> and body. Its forearms were thickly coated with the same hair, so were its
> paws, large, loose and hand-shaped; and, as it sat on its hind legs, one
> hand or paw was raised ready to scratch the paint.
>
> Its lustreless eyes, which seemed half decomposed in black cavities and
> looked incredibly foul, stared into mine, and the horrible smell which
> before had offended my nostrils, only a hundred times intensified, came
> up into my face, filling me with a deadly nausea. I noticed that the lower
> half of the creature was indefinite, and seemed semi-transparent – at least,
> I could see the framework of the door that led into the gallery *through* its
> body.[4]

Aside from this description of the Thing/Elemental, the article enumerates a veritable smorgasbord of ghostly goings-on, from a mysterious indelible damp patch
in the main bedchamber, to a drunken steward rolling barrels down the stairs, a
shrieking damsel in a scarlet dress pursued by two lustful brothers and a groaning
nobleman stuck up a chimney to name but a few. It is the Elemental, however,
which has gathered the most interest in the literature on Irish ghosts subsequently
written, with books featuring Leap dedicating the majority of their material on
the castle to it.

pp 99–100.   **3** 'Rejoicings at Leap Castle', *Midland Tribune*, 8 Nov. 1889.   **4** Andrew Merry, 'Kilman
Castle: the house of horror', *Occult Review* 8 (Dec. 1908), p. 344.

Despite such fascination in this reeking spectre, this essay will contend that, possibly unlike the other more "ordinary" ghosts of Leap, the Elemental was fundamentally fabricated by Mildred Darby's imagination. This is not to say that the vision itself was necessary untrue – an issue which Darby alone was categorically able to resolve. 'Kilman Castle' was the first account of the Elemental; to a certain extent, then, this was the *author's* ghost, a personal phantom which spoke of, and to, very personal fears. Its subsequent appeal as *the* defining ghost of Leap Castle in turn demonstrates that the unease which it obviously evoked in Darby is universal, its notoriety a direct result of the disquiet which it continues to evoke. Indeed I would argue that, in describing the Elemental, Mildred Darby identified and encapsulated aspects which are common causations of fear. The importance of Mildred's envisagement of this apparition, then, lies less in determining whether or not it was real, than in discovering what it illustrates about factors intrinsically fearful to the human imagination. It is these universal "flash-points" of fear that many writers and artists have in turn exploited in their creation of tales and images of the macabre.

The first issue to take into account when deconstructing the legend of Leap is Mildred Darby herself. In her history of the building, *Leap Castle: a place and its people* (2001) Margaret Freeman-Attwood (Mildred's granddaughter) recounts the years of isolation, frustration and unhappiness that Mildred endured as lady of Leap. Trapped in an unhappy marriage to an overbearing, bullying husband who resented her wit and vivacity, and attempted repeatedly to curb her creative talents, Darby also suffered the unhappy loss of her first child in 1892, just four weeks after he was born. Although Mildred and Jonathan went on to have four more healthy children, 'not one of her children shared her tastes or measured up to her intellect'. Indeed, speculating on her grandmother's mental state, Freeman-Attwood concludes that:

> From all accounts, my grandmother [...] was a woman to whom no one at home listened [...] Nobody, it seems, came half-way to meet the person seething within that neat Edwardian exterior. Milly was a creative woman shut inside herself, whose friends and relations mostly lived in England. Scorned and abused by her husband, she was never afraid of him [Mildred ...] was fighting all her married life for the survival of her identity, and insisting on the validity of the ghosts was a vital part of her struggle.[5]

In 1909, following the publication of 'Kilman Castle', Jonathan Darby forbade his wife from writing any more stories, ostensibly because of the humiliating sensationalism of her account of the family home. Denied any kind of creative output,

5 Margaret Freeman-Attwood, *Leap Castle: a place and its people* (Norwich, 2001), pp 100–8.

as Freeman-Attwood suggests, such a naturally rebellious person may well become addicted to the idea of spectral goings-on, willing them into being.

Invariably, the spectre of psychological inquiry will loom over any ghostly narrative. In 1879 the Austro-German psychiatrist, Richard von Krafft-Ebing, argued that 'protracted states of hysterical delirium' could induce hallucinatory visions: 'The most frequent and important are delusions of sight, smell, and touch. The visual hallucinations are mostly visions of animals, funerals, fantastic processions swarming with corpses, devils, ghosts and what not.'[6] He gives the example of a 24-year-old servant girl, regarded as insane, who experienced paranormal visions: 'She sees ghostly figures prophesying disaster, processions of spirits, caravans of strange and terrifying beastlike forms, her own body being buried, etc'.[7] The Elemental's reeking human/animal form certainly corresponds with Krafft-Ebing's checklist for hallucinatory insanity. Moreover, the argument that the repression of Mildred's natural character by a forceful husband subsequently lead to ghostly visions as a projection of psychic energy is a compelling one.

In the first decades of the twentieth century, psychoanalysts were by degree both fascinated and perturbed by the role that ghosts, telepathy and other such phenomena played in the construction – and deconstruction – of the human psyche. In 1933, Sigmund Freud's seminal essay 'Dreams and occultism' argued that the mind's urge to invent is fundamental: 'From the very beginning, when life takes us under its strict discipline, a resistance stirs in us against the relentlessness and monotony of the laws of thought and against the demands of reality-testing.' In such a way, 'the employment of psychoanalysis may throw a little light on other events described as occult.'[8] C.G. Jung likewise argued for a close connection between the unconscious and the occult in a number of essays, including his doctoral dissertation 'On the psychology and pathology of so-called occult phenomena' (1902), and his later works, 'The psychological foundations of belief in spirits' (1920) and 'Psychology and spiritualism' (1948). Although Jung purposely avoided the question of whether ghosts exist in themselves, declaring that 'there is not a single argument that could prove that spirits do not exist', he concluded that:

> These phenomena exist in their own right, regardless of the way they are interpreted, and it is beyond all doubt that they are genuine manifestations of the unconscious. The communications of "spirits" are *statements about the unconscious psyche*, provided that they are really spontaneous are not cooked up by the conscious mind.[9]

6 Richard von Krafft-Ebing, *Text-book of insanity* (1879), p. 498.   7 Ibid., p. 495.   8 Sigmund Freud, 'Dreams and occultism' in *New introductory lectures on psychoanalysis*, trans. & ed. James Strachey (London, 1973), pp 62, 69.   9 C.G. Jung, 'Psychology and spiritualism' in *Psychology and the occult* (London, 1987), p. 139.

In her account of the castle's history, Freeman-Attwood also tells of her grandmother's favourite game, Muckski. This would involve 'collecting mud, dirty water, old leaves, pond slime, spilled motor oil and worse; anything really mucky we could find.' The concoction was then mixed in a bucket after which, 'The climax to this delightful occupation consisted in stealing a paintbrush from the potting shed and carrying out the solemn ritual of plastering every door and gate within range with the oozy, greyish liquid.' The author then recounts the opinion of a 'psychologist friend' who 'sees Milly as projecting her fury and resentment at her lot in this life into this essentially dirty and disruptive, if harmless, ritual.'[10] If this aspect of Mildred Darby's behaviour has been regarded as so manifestly a projection of her deep-seated unhappiness, then her description of the Elemental certainly has the potential to be similarly considered. Described as 'slobbery', 'cancerous' and 'decomposed', one could argue that the Elemental is as much an unconscious projection of Mildred's recognition of the injurious effects of her family life as it is a supernatural entity in its own right.

Psychoanalytic theory, however, is a matter all too easy to oversimplify. Rather than make swift assumptions about such a multivalent topic, I shall leave the question of the Elemental as the physical or psychological manifestation of Mildred Darby's unconscious an open one. In fact, what I am arguing here is not that Mildred was necessarily insane, hysterical or even mildly depressed. Nor that her vision of the Elemental was the outright projection of psychological problems. What is more interesting is the idea that the projections of ghosts in general have historically been determined as denoting aspects of deep-seated human unease. Moreover, as Jung argued, the greater the intensity of the vision, the more stimulated the mind that has conjured it: 'The same primitive fear of ghosts is still deep in our bones, but it is still unconscious. Rationalism and superstition are complementary [...] in other words, the more rationalistic we are in our conscious minds, the more alive becomes the spectral world of the unconscious.'[11] Real or not, the fear of ghosts is deep in our bones, and rooted in our psyche. As such, the images of decay, death, or animal/human chimeras that ghosts are often said to take actually implies more about the universals of the human mindset than a single individual's state of mind. For fear, unease or despair to be envisaged (or believed to be envisaged) as an oozing, decaying, boundary-disrupting spectre surely testifies to a degree of universality in what humans in general find disquieting.

The universality of a "fear factor" is more pervasively demonstrated in the manipulation of the emotion in literature. Mildred Darby herself was a published author of fiction. Her first short story appeared in 1898 and, by the time 'Kilman Castle' appeared, she had written a large number of stories as well as three novels, two of them about life in Ireland. Often she took life at Leap as her subject and,

---

10 Freeman-Attwood, *Leap Castle*, p. 109.   **11** Jung, 'Psychology and spiritualism', p. 144.

while by no means triumphs of literary skill, her stories display a degree of deft observation and imaginative talent. 'Kilman Castle', although describing the ghosts of Leap, is itself framed as fiction, the whole being narrated by one Captain Gordon. The setting is a weekend shooting party at the castle, at which both ghost stories are told, and ghostly experiences are undergone by the visitors, which furnish an account of almost every ghostly manifestation ever heard of at Leap. The Elemental is quickly rendered the most terrifying, however, and the reader's first, indirect, encounter is a description by the lady of Kilman Castle, Betty O'Connoll:

> Suddenly, two hands were laid on my shoulders. I turned round sharply, and saw, as clearly as I see you now – a grey 'Thing' standing a couple of feet from me. I cannot describe in words how utterly awful the 'Thing' was, its very undefinableness rendering the horrible shadow more grue-some. Human in shape, a little shorter than I am, I could just make out the shape of big black holes like great eyes and sharp features, but the whole figure – head, face and all – was grey – unclean, blueish grey, some-thing of colour and appearance of common cotton wool.[12]

Although Darby/Merry claims that 'This is a true story of facts that have occurred, and that are occurring',[13] such a narrative, consciously framed as fiction and deliberately designed with a penchant for the sensational, almost requires a spectral apogee – and the Elemental does not fail to deliver. It is the last ghost to appear in the story and, with its charnel-like stench and indefinable form, the very "thingness" of the Elemental easily surpasses anything the other ghosts have to offer. So successful was this ghost, that when Mildred Darby retold her story for inclusion in John D. Seymour and Harry L. Neligan's *True Irish ghost stories* (1914) almost six years later, the description retained a close correspondence with that of Betty O'Connoll:

> But of all the ghosts in that well-haunted house the most unpleasant is that inexplicable thing that is usually called "It." The lady of the house described to the present writer her personal experience of this phantom. High up round one side of the hall runs a gallery which connects with some of the bedrooms. One evening she was in this gallery leaning on the balustrade, and looking down into the hall. Suddenly she felt two hands laid on her shoulders; she turned round sharply, and saw "It" standing close beside her. She described it as being human in shape, and about four feet high; the eyes were like two black holes in the face, and the whole

12 Merry, 'Kilman Castle', p. 330. 13 Ibid., p. 308.

figure seemed as if it were made of grey cotton-wool, while it was accompanied by a most appalling stench, such as would come from a decaying human body.

Demonstrative of Mildred Darby's imaginative power, since the publication of 'Kilman Castle', each one of the ghosts she discusses has become part of the fabric of the castle's history, surfacing repeatedly (with variations) in allusions to the place. As such, what in fact was *first* collated and described with such gusto by Darby in the twentieth century had assumed the character of timeless folklore: the Elemental being the apex of this fiction-as-fact phenomenon.

Regardless of its factual veracity, the literary value of the Elemental was confirmed by its subsequent advent in the works of W.B. Yeats, Oliver St John Gogarty and Sacherverell Sitwell. None of these writers, as far as has been gathered, actually had any direct contact with Mildred Darby, each relying on anecdotal evidence to furnish the details of their accounts. In Book III of *A Vision* (1937), Yeats describes what he saw as the six states of the spirit's transition from death to rebirth. For Yeats, steeped in the world of myth and magic, the Elemental illustrated a complex point about the soul's progress towards reincarnation. Accepting that the spectre was half-human, half-beast he nevertheless filters out its innate paranormal horror:

> In the third discarnate state [the spirit] may renounce the form of a man and take some shape from the social or religious tradition of its past life, symbolical of its condition. Leap Castle, though burnt down during our Civil War and still a ruin, is haunted by what is called an evil spirit which appears as a sheep with short legs and decaying human head. I suggest that some man with the *Husk* exaggerated and familiar with religious symbolism, torn at the moment of death between two passions, terror of the body's decay with which he identified himself, and an abject religious humility, projected himself in this image.[14]

In his essay comparing Yeats and Gogarty's use of the Elemental, 'Yeats, Gogarty and the Leap Castle ghost' (1972), Grover Smith makes much of the 'abstract, allegorical, meaning' drawn by Yeats in comparison to Gogarty's 'far bolder and more definite' macabre overtones.[15] Certainly, although Gogarty concurred with his friend, Yeats, about the composite nature of the Elemental, for him the spectre was unconditionally conceived in sorcery and had more than a little predisposition to the conventions of gothic horror. *A week end in the middle of the week, and*

14 W.B. Yeats, *A Vision* (New York, 1961), p. 224.   15 Grover Smith, 'Yeats, Gogarty and the Leap Castle Ghost' in *Modern Irish literature*, ed. Raymond Porter & James D. Brophy (New York, 1972), p. 130.

other essays (1958) contains a chapter dedicated to Leap, 'The most haunted house of them all'. This opens with Gogarty's recollection of a haunting: 'There are haunted houses everywhere. There is that college in Cambridge in which a divinity student lived [...] the back room of which was haunted by something so evil that the student resolved to exorcise it himself.' Brandishing a crucifix before him, 'he was seized by something invisible and the crucifix was all but torn from his grasp.' Demonstrably failing in his attempt at exorcism, the student is also discovered 'to have lost his reason' in the process.[16] Prefaced by this tale of a God-defying ghost, Gogarty's subsequent account of the Leap hauntings is thus inferentially tainted by the idea of defiance of religious sensibility. This additional dimension of the negation of the divine, it could be argued, is a deliberate attempt to heighten his readers' anxiety prior to the "main attraction" of the Elemental itself.

As suggested in the chapter's title Gogarty also makes much of the castle and its surrounds, suggestively rooting it in the "haunted house" literary tradition: 'The landscape round Leap Castle is bleak enough though the land itself is rich, for its richness depends on the rains that sweep the countryside, making it look desolate and inhospitable.'[17] Indeed, Mildred Darby's own tale of ghostly events – a group of friends staying for a weekend in a castle in the country – is also, by now, an almost clichéd condition of the ghost story. Her description of the building, meanwhile, 'a sombre-looking bare building, consisting of a square keep tapering slightly to the top, looking in its grim grey strength, as if it could defy time itself',[18] almost obligates an equally impressive legend be attached to it. Castles are the natural places for intrigues, pathos, lunacy, ignominy and illusory security and, as Anthony Vidler argues, '[have] been a pervasive leitmotiv of literary fantasy and architectural revival alike since the early nineteenth century.'[19] The image of the haunted house is perhaps the most palpable embodiment of the passage from *heimlich* to *unheimlich* – literally from the "homely" to the "unhomely" – itself a critically well-worn concept.

The disruption of the known and supposedly safe, or the gradual transformation of a sense of security and freedom from fear to the ominous dimensions of its apparent opposite, has been analyzed most famously by Sigmund Freud in his essay 'The Uncanny' (1919), although the state was first identified by Ernst Jentsch in his 1906 essay 'On the psychology of the uncanny'. Two years later Mildred Darby herself would describe the Elemental as an 'uncanny spook' in her preface to 'Kilman Castle'.[20] At once a psychological and an aesthetic phenomenon, the subtle distortion of the supposedly safe into the unbearably fearful (the passage from *heimlich* to *unheimlich*) has been a trademark feature of the house

---

16 Oliver St John Gogarty, 'The most haunted house of them all' in *A week end in the middle of the week, and other essays* (New York, 1958), p. 202. **17** Ibid., p. 203. **18** Merry, 'Kilman Castle', p. 315. **19** Anthony Vidler, 'The architecture of the uncanny: the unhomely houses of the romantic sublime', *Assemblage* 3 (July 1987), 7. **20** Merry, 'Kilman Castle', p. 308.

in the gothic novel. From Horace Walpole's pioneering *The castle of Otranto* (1764) to Edgar Allan Poe's 'The fall of the house of Usher' (1839) and Bram Stoker's *Dracula* (1897) and, in the twentieth century, such movies as *The house on haunted hill* (1959), *The legend of hell house* (1973), and *The Haunting* (1999), the castle (or imposingly large house) has been as much a locus of horror as its inhabitants. It may be a cynical, yet logical, hypothesis to propose that the imaginative possibilities of the spectral increase in direct proportion to the dimensions of its surroundings. This cynicism was deftly articulated by Jane Austen whose *Northanger Abbey* (1818) gently satirized those who judged apparitions by the architecture they inhabited. Catherine Morland, an avid reader of gothic novels, is entranced by the prospect of visiting an abbey, 'and she could not entirely subdue the hope [...] of some awful memories of an injured and ill-fated nun':

> As they drew near the end of their journey, her impatience for a sight of the abbey [...] returned in full force, and every bend in the road was expected with solemn awe to afford a glimpse of its massy walls of grey stone, rising amidst a grove of ancient oaks, with the last beams of the sun playing in beautiful splendour on its high Gothic windows. But so low did the building stand, that she found herself passing through the great gates of the lodge into the very grounds of Northanger without having discerned even an antique chimney [...] The breeze had not seemed to waft the sighs of the murdered to her; it had wafted nothing worse than a thick mizzling rain.[21]

Sacheverell Sitwell's account of Leap Castle deliberately appeals to this shivering delight in uncanny spaces, drawing effect from the physical entity of the building rather than an adumbration of its spectral inhabitants: 'Legend brings the dogs from every village within sound of their baying; but no man dares go near the castle, and it stands in the moonlight at its windows and the sound of life within.' Although brief mention is made of the 'suggestions of the supernatural', the description adheres almost exclusively to the castle itself, 'The intensity of this strange place exceeds in its details almost anything that the most dramatic mind could design'.[22]

In contrast, Oliver St John Gogarty's sketch of the castle is a mere foreword to the Elemental. When Gogarty finally describes this spectre, all the tags of the ghost story are evidenced: the unexpected night visitor, the half-seen Thing, the foul stench, and the clandestine suggestion of sexual violation:

> At dusk, after the candelabra had been lighted, a visitor was ascending the great stair. He felt two weights suddenly laid upon his shoulders, which

21 Jane Austen, *Northanger abbey* (London, 1995), pp 125, 140–1.   22 Sitwell, *Dance of the quick and the dead*, pp 97, 99, 100.

tended to press him down. He could not turn about; but on looking at his shoulders he saw a hoof on each, and, as he bent, he could see behind his knees the hindquarters of a gigantic black ram. The same story about the smell was repeated; but there was this detail. When at last the mounting animal let him go, he turned and saw no more than the legs of which he had already caught a glimpse; but he heard the scamper of hoofs.

Over and above this account, which closely corresponds to Darby's 'Kilman Castle', Gogarty gives his own original addition, describing an encounter with a local who suggests that the Elemental 'is someone who was partially metamorphosed into an animal body and is seeking release.' Gogarty elaborates on this idea, suggesting 'Probably [Leap] was the centre of obscene rites. Some king perhaps had handed over his wife to be punished by magicians with a fate more horrible than any torture that ends in death.'[23] An entirely new aspect to the Leap legend, Gogarty's supplement is not traceable to any of the previously existing stories surrounding the castle. In these three very different manifestations of the same ghost, then, it is possible to detect the strong influence of personal preoccupation and intent upon textual representation for literary ends.

Even in the twenty-first century, the Elemental has been co-opted as a representational spirit. In his 2004 article on the function of castles in Ireland's Celtic Revival, Andrew Tierney argues that the Elemental symbolizes the re-eruption of the resurgent Celt, 'which as both man and beast draws on a long line of colonial imagery of the native Irish body stretching all the way from Geraldus Cambrensis right up to the English newspaper caricatures of Mildred's own day.' The remodelling of the castle along prescribed "gothick" lines in the mid-eighteenth century, which included the blocking off of rooms and stairways effectively suppressed the castle's original Irish medieval gothic character 'within the formal constraints of classical rules.'[24] Herself no native of Ireland (she had moved to Leap Castle from her home in England), the Anglo-Irish Mildred Darby was uncomfortable with her role as "lady of the castle". Tierney contends that her published stories reveal this disquiet as they often attempt to reconcile the strongly Protestant Leap Castle with its Celtic heritage. In 'Kilman Castle', for example, the setting is displaced from the midlands (the actual location of Leap) to the north west coast of Ireland, thus redefining the building along lines more attune with the conventional Celtic Revival novel.[25] Her local researches into the famine years in Ireland which culminated in her 1910 novel, *The Hunger*, also display elements of this desire for iden-

---

23 Gogarty, 'The most haunted house of them all', p. 208. 24 Andrew Tierney, 'The gothic and the Gaelic: exploring the place of castles in Ireland's Celtic revival', *International Journal of Historical Archaeology* 8:3 (Sept. 2004), 197, 191. 25 '[T]he setting of the Celtic Revival novel was almost exclusively a west of Ireland one, subscribing not only to a romantic notion of the untamed wilderness but also an exotic sense of "the other".' Ibid., 190.

tification with the nationalist aspirations of the area's indigenous residents. A similar desire for integration may be discerned in Mildred's ensuring that her children became known as "O'Carroll-Darby" rather than the English-sounding Darby. The 'acute colonial guilt'[26] which Tierney thus diagnoses in Mildred Darby may therefore have lead her to create the Elemental as a deliberate inversion of the processes of containment and isolation which she felt the castle – and the Darby family – was in danger of succumbing to. In "allowing" (nay, promoting) the re-emergence of indefinable gothic horror, Mildred was, in a way, realigning the soul of the castle itself with the Celtic Revival spirit, deliberately overturning the anglophile influence of Enlightenment architectural formality and religious apartness that had been imposed on Leap since its possession by the Darby family. In other words, fear of isolation had led Mildred to seek commonality in a more overwhelming – and definably Irish – object of fear.

The literary elasticity of the Elemental that Yeats, Gogarty and even Tierney reveal is likewise exposed in Mildred's own description of the Elemental which tallies closely with many examples of contemporary ghost stories. I have already mentioned the predilection by writers of the gothic for atmospheric buildings. In addition, the lengthy description of the apparition itself from 'Kilman Castle' is almost an exemplary instance of the calculated inducement of unease, playing upon those precise factors most inclined to disturb. The Elemental is described as neither fully human, nor fully sheep: a matted hairy creature that has both paws *and* hands, the ghost muddies the boundaries between beast and man, invoking a nightmare of human/animal miscegenation, or indeed deliberately playing on the unease incurred by revelations that man was not specially created. Moreover the Elemental carries a suggestion of inherent deformity, and descriptions of slime, decay, foetid odours and bodily secretions also abound. In short, the Thing is so frightening *because* of its very "thingness": it straddles the divide between life and death, solid and ethereal, human and animal. Neither one thing nor the other, its location on the very periphery of definability marks it apart as something unnatural – something to alarm. Such indefinable border creatures are a key feature of the very best ghost stories and gothic horror narratives. The title of one of Fitz-James O'Brien's most successful short stories is 'What was it? a mystery' (1859); James Hogg's *The private memoirs and confessions of a justified sinner* (1823), likewise, recoils from a full explanation of the mysterious Gil-Martin figure – is it a ghost, a devil or the projection of insanity? Similarly, M.R. James' short stories abound with such nameless, faceless horror creatures that are never fully exposed or explained. 'Canon Alberic's scrap-book' (1895), for example, is the story of an ancient book with an unsettling illustration. In its details, the description of the figure within the picture is actually very similar to Mildred Darby's description of the Leap ghost, given at the start of this essay:

26 Ibid., 194.

The shape whose left hand rested on the table was rising to a standing posture behind his seat, its right hand crooked above his scalp. There was
black and tattered drapery about it; the coarse hair covered it as in the
drawing. The lower jaw was thin – what can I call it? – shallow, like a
beast's; teeth showed behind the black lips. There was no nose: the eyes of
fiery yellow against which the pupils showed black and intense, and the
exalting hate and thirst to destroy life which shone there, were the most
horrifying features in the whole vision.[27]

Unsettling reality rather than pushing the boundaries of credibility, James' creatures (like the Elemental) are also for the most part passive spectres who threaten
more than they act. As such, their horror exists largely in the potential for action,
in the imaginative sphere that we, the onlooker, create for them: and they are all
the more terrifying for it. Moreover, as demonstrated effectively in Ridley Scott's
Alien (1979) and indeed the best of gothic fiction and film, the object of fear
itself or any kind of rational explanation for its inception always lies partly out
of reach, or camera shot – our overactive imagination being invited to fill in the
gaps.

The foul smell and nauseatingly slimy lips and jaw of the Elemental are also
key elements in much gothic horror. In Bram Stoker's *Dracula*, Jonathan Harker
is revolted by the rank breath of the vampire Count, while the infamously unsettling opening of Oscar Wilde's *The picture of Dorian Gray* (1890) is due largely to
its emphasis on olfactory appeal. Slime as the nexus of horror has a similarly long
tradition in horror. Utilized as a means of establishing unnaturalness, writers
employ the slimy to physically objectify elements of intellectual unease. Xenophobic anxiety is revealed in Richard Marsh's *The Beetle* (1897) as its Egyptian nemesis
is ultimately reduced to a pool of goo. In Bram Stoker's *The lair of the white worm*
(1911), sexual apprehension is suggested as the female protagonist's lair is characterized by its foul foetid odour, reminiscent of bilge water and death – itself suggesting monstrous and corrupt genital secretions. Likewise, Arthur Machen
peppered many of his tales with bizarre beings whose tendency to dissolve into
rancid slime compounded their unnatural unhumanness. To take just one of
many examples, *The great god Pan* (1890) – Machen's invective against the *fin-de-
siècle* New Woman – ends with its *femme fatale* finally being hunted down and
killed. In dying, however, the woman reveals her innate abnormality in the revelation of her dissolution 'to the depths, even to the abyss of all being':

The skin, and the flesh, and the muscles, and the bones, and the firm
structure of the human body that I had thought to be unchangeable, and

27 M.R. James, 'Canon Alberic's scrap-book' in *Casting the runes and other ghost stories*, ed. Michael Cox
(Oxford, 1999), pp 10–11.

> permanent as adamant, began to melt and dissolve [...] and at last I saw
> nothing but a substance as jelly.[28]

Fear of the slimy is still something which creators of modern horror utilize: *The Blob* (1958), for example, had a giant amorphous slime-ball as its nexus of horror; *Ghostbusters* (1984) typified its ghosts by a trail of slimy ectoplasm; and, returning to *Alien*, the extraterrestrial creature is often depicted with slime-dripping jaws, while the birthing pods themselves are caked with goo. Dissolution into primordial slime, or indeed being inherently slimy, embodies the liminality of existence itself. Neither solid nor liquid, slime embodies the crossing of boundaries of perception to the extent that, as both Jean-Paul Sartre and Mary Douglas have argued, sliminess, the ultimate in abjectivity, negates even life itself, instead invoking the putrefaction that follows death.[29]

The turn of the twentieth century, with its craze for spiritualists, mediums, table-tilting, séances, table-rapping, ghost clubs and the Society for Psychical Research, was an accommodating historical period for ghosts. While it is not wholly beyond the bounds of possibility that Mildred Darby's Elemental was, and is, real (in the loosest sense of the term), its deconstruction reveals components that are almost too expedient to be denied. By no means am I suggesting that Mildred Darby's account of the Elemental was intentionally designed with an eye to maximum literary effect. Her account of the ghost, however, displays all the hallmarks of those narratives which *are* deliberately intended to do precisely that. The Elemental is a boundary-crossing entity, a miscellany of those elements most designed to frighten us – and as such, despite its contrived status, it remains the most "successful" ghost at Leap Castle. In short, the triumph of the Elemental is not necessarily in its realness, but in its formation from the conventions of imaginary fear.

Despite its capability for deconstruction, the validity of Leap Castle's Elemental is not necessarily threatened by its fictional facets. Ascertaining whether Mildred Darby's ghost was a deliberately constructed über-ghoul to trump the notoriety of her husband's castle's ethereal inhabitants, or indeed a very real projection of paranormal phenomena (either from Mildred's unconscious or the house's own psychic memory) is not the point. Descriptions of the spirit by its various witnesses and chroniclers in fact reveals something far more fascinating than a crude "is it real?" verdict on the spirit itself. Primary fears are perpetuating; hard-wired into the human psyche. When one reaches into the metaphorical mental store-cupboard for expressions of fear that will touch the multitude –

---

28 Arthur Machen, *The great god Pan* (London, 1996), pp 114–15.   **29** Mary Douglas, *Purity and danger: an analysis of the concepts of pollution and taboo. Mary Douglas, collected works: vol. 2* (London, 2003); Jean-Paul Sartre, *Being and nothingness: an essay on phenomenological ontology*, trans. Hazel E. Banks (London, 1977), pp 606–7.

whether their intended manifestations be political, fictional, psychological or paranormal – that, time and again, the same images of boundary dissolution and decay recur says much about the egalitarian nature of fear itself. Humanity may be divided by the fears which are externally imposed, through tribal, national, religious or political divarication; a fact attested by the near-destruction of Leap Castle itself by disgruntled nationalist insurgents. However, when it comes to the innate fears of the individual, the frequent recurrence of elemental aspects of unease, all of which are embodied in Leap Castle's own "Elemental", ultimately reveals fear's capacity not only to divide but also to unify.

Dead ends: the decline of the recent American horror movie

BERNICE M. MURPHY

The years between the release of George A. Romero's *Night of the living dead* (1968) and Wes Craven's *A nightmare on Elm Street* (1984) marked a pinnacle of commercial and critical success for the American horror film that has yet to be equalled. After decades lurking in the shadows of pop culture, horror cinema had at last become a truly mainstream phenomenon. As one recent overview of the genre has put it:

> In terms of output, the horror film was at its zenith in the 1970s. Arguably, it also reached an artistic peak unscaled since the early 1930s. Though there were still any number of formula genre pieces and each tentpole film would inspire a flurry of similar efforts, the '70s horror film attracted ambitious and interesting filmmakers as well as play-it-safe schlockmeisters. It was possible for a work as unusual and diverse as, say, Harry Kümel's *La rouge aux lèvres* (*Daughters of darkness*, 1971), John Hancock's *Let's scare Jessica to death* (1971), Gary Sherman's *Death line* (*Raw meat*, 1972), Nicolas Roeg's *Don't look now* (1973) and Robin Hardy's *The wicker man* (1973) to find their place in cinemas, exciting critics and fans, perplexing and perhaps shocking those who'd turned up expecting something more conventional.[1]

Although several of the films cited here are European, there can be no doubt that American writers and filmmakers played perhaps the greatest part of all in reinvigorating a genre which had in previous decades become distinctively moribund. One only has to cite a few of the best known movies of this era to appreciate the contribution made by American and American-based genre innovators. Besides Romero's genuinely groundbreaking reinvention of the zombie movie in

1 James Marriot & Kim Newman, *Horror: the definitive guide to the literature of fear* (London, 2006), p. 113.

Night of the living dead (1968), the decade which followed also saw the release of Roman Polanski's *Rosemary's baby* (1968), Wes Craven's *Last house on the left* (1972) and *The hills have eyes* (1977), William Friedkin's *The Exorcist* (1973), Tobe Hooper's epoch-defining endurance test *The Texas chain saw massacre* (1974), Brian De Palma's baroque psychic power/high-school massacre movie *Carrie* (1976), John Carpenter's prototypical slasher flick *Halloween* (1978) and Stanley Kubrick's supernatural masterpiece *The Shining* (1980). In addition to the palpable originality and energy of the films cited here, much of the success experienced by the genre during this period can be attributed to the fact that, for many critics, readers and cinemagoers, horror seemed to capture the zeitgeist – the turbulent mood of a chaotic and often disturbing era which encompassed events such as the civil rights struggle, widespread civil unrest, the Vietnam war and the oil crisis – in a way that no other genre could manage. If this is indeed the case, then I will suggest here that it has categorically failed to do so since.

Film critic Robin Wood (who did much to help establish modern horror cinema as a valid topic of academic debate in his well-known article *The American nightmare: essays on the horror film* [1979]) has suggested in his introduction to a recent collection of genre criticism: 'Aside from *Day of the dead*, is there any American horror film made since 1980 that could be championed as any sort of radical statement about our impossible (so-called) civilisation?'[2] While one may perhaps disagree with Wood's insistence that *Day of the dead* (1985) is the best horror movie of the past thirty years – although it must come close – the essence of his point remains the same; the fact that, with a few notable exceptions, the American horror movie in its current incarnation is in a sorry state indeed. It seems less than probable that genre enthusiasts and critics in decades to come will speak of nastily inventive but derivative fare such as James Wan's *Saw* (2004) and Eli Roth's *Hostel* (2005) with the respect which is generally now afforded to unmistakably innovative movies such as *The Texas chain saw massacre* and *The Exorcist*, both of which helped establish horror cinema as a means of expressing gnawing and otherwise largely unacknowledged contemporary anxieties and pre-occupations.

This is not to say, however, that we should unthinkingly canonize *every* horror film that emerged during the 1970s and early 1980s. Anyone who has sat through a representative selection of movies from the period will know that there were many derivative, shoddy and downright awful films made. At the same time, it was not entirely unlikely that one could come across a horror film worth watching for all the *right* reasons at one's local cinema; because there were more than a few filmmakers at work who were, intentionally or otherwise, truly interested in

2 S.J. Schneider (ed.), *The horror film and psychoanalysis: Freud's worst nightmare* (Cambridge, 2003), p. xviii.

stretching the possibilities of the genre. Apart from the occasional film of genuine interest, the years since this high-point have unfortunately seen a depressing reduction in both quality and impact, a trend that no doubt has much to do with the commercial and imaginative decline of so many of the directors behind the original boom – including once vaunted but now much diminished figures such as John Carpenter, Tobe Hooper and William Friedkin.

If we consider for a moment the sub-standard roster of American horror films which have received a mainstream cinema release in the United States during 2006, we get some indication of rather sorry state the genre currently finds itself in. 804 movies were released during this period, of which around twenty-five were American horror films.[3] The most popular horror film of 2006 was *Saw III*, the latest instalment in the most successful horror franchise of recent times (*Saw II* was the most popular horror film of 2005 while the original *Saw* was one of the surprise hits of 2004). Eight of the twenty-five films received a PG-13 rating, while the remainder were rated "R" for restricted entry (meaning only audiences over the age of eighteen could see them). Surprisingly, given the trend of previous years, there was only one outright video game adaptation (*Silent hill*); there were however four remakes of well-known 1970s films (*The hills have eyes, The Omen, When a stranger calls* and *Black Christmas*). Four other movies were either sequels or prequels to previous movies (*The Texas chain saw massacre: The beginning, Final destination three, Saw III* and *Underworld: evolution*) while another film, *Pulse*, was a distinctly underwhelming adaptation of the Japanese film *Kairo*. This means that only *eleven* entirely original American horror films have been released during 2006, of which five were rated PG-13. This roster included decidedly unimpressive efforts such as the disastrous Sci-Fi tinged vampire flick *Ultraviolet*, the derivative slasher *See no evil* (starring monosyllabic WWF wrestler Kane), *Slither* (yet another film about alien parasites taking over a small town) and the similarly unsuccessful teen-oriented warlock movie *The Covenant*. All in all, it is a formula-reliant, remake and sequel oriented line-up very similar indeed to that seen in 2005, 2004, 2003 and 2002.

The reasoning behind the disheartening trend that has seen so many ill-advised remakes is presumably grounded in the belief that if a concept was commercially successful once, it will prove so again. The fact is that the intelligent, provocative horror film – the horror film made for adults, and *not* primarily for audiences under the age of eighteen – is becoming a rarity nowadays and one that can usually only be found in the work of European and Asian film makers. It is true that arguably some of the most frightening horror movies ever made feature very little violence or sexual content at all, so I am not suggesting that a film must

---

3 All box-office statistics cited here come from: http://www.the-numbers.com/market/2006/Horror.php, accessed 20 Feb. 2007.

have scenes of an explicitly violent nature in order to be effective, worthwhile or, for that matter, adult. But what this consistent trend towards lower-rated and overtly teen-oriented films of decidedly poor quality does tell us is that most horror films being made in the studio system today are significantly restricted by the demands of the young audience they are supposed to be catering for. This, in part, explains the glut of video game adaptations released since *Resident evil* appeared in 2002, based on a game *itself* much indebted to Romero.[4] It may also help explain the all-pervasive drive towards remaking as many old films as possible. After all, if the studios target an audience that is too young to have seen the original anyway, what's the harm in cynically repackaging the concept in a shiny new movie specially made for the kids of today?

Just to make sure these remakes will prove a hit with their target audience, they generally feature a roster of interchangeably bland teenage stars who have already gained a following on the small screen. For instance, *Buffy the vampire slayer* star Sarah Michelle Gellar has featured in more than her fair share of forgettable teen-oriented horror movies, among them *Scream 2* (1997), *I know what you did last summer* (1997), *The Grudge* (2005) (a remake of a successful Japanese film), and most recently, *The Return* (2007). *Smallville's* Tom Welling, turned up in *The Fog* remake (2005), *Malcolm in the middle's* Frankie Muniz starred in dire "evil computer game" movie *Stay alive* (2006) and *Seventh heaven's* Jessica Biehl fought off cannibalistic rednecks while wearing an implausibly tight T-Shirt in the woeful "re-imagining" of *The Texas chain saw massacre* (2003). If you're really lucky, like the producers of *The house of wax* (1953; 2005), you can even persuade the likes of "socialite" Paris Hilton to allow herself to be gorily dispatched. In addition to the atrocious, plodding new versions of classics like *The Texas chain saw massacre,* and *The wicker man,* this dubious honour of a remake has also been paid to a number of fairly mediocre movies, such as *When a stranger calls, The Omen* and *The Amityville horror.* It seems a film doesn't even to have been all that *good* to warrant a new version: perhaps those essaying such remakes feel that they could do a better job, although the results so far have suggested otherwise.

American horror cinema at the present time appears to be in the thrall of its past successes, in a manner that fatally stifles innovation and originality. As many have observed before this crisis in originality, horror has always been a highly self-aware and imitative genre, and much of the pleasure in watching a certain type of movie can lie in its formulaic nature. Even the infrequent horror viewer has learned what kind of trouble to expect when a group of naïve city dwellers becomes stranded in the countryside (*The Texas chain saw massacre, Deliverance* [1972], *Wrong turn* [2004]); when a family moves into a house with an unsavoury

---

4 Horror films based on games since this time include: *Alien versus Predator* (2004), *Resident evil: apocalypse* (2004), *Doom* (2005), *Blood rayne* (2005), *House of the dead* (2003) and *Alone in the dark* (2005).

past (*The Amityville horror* [1979], *Poltergeist* [1982]), or when a masked killer begins to stalk a group of rebellious teenagers (*Halloween*, *Scream* [1996]). The interest here lies in seeing how, despite working within a well established set of narrative conventions, the filmmaker will upend or subvert our expectations. For example, classic 1960s horror movie *The Haunting* (1963), delightfully bizarre Richard Matheson adaptation *The legend of hell house* (1973) and Kubrick's *The Shining* all demonstrate that it is a *very* bad idea to bring somebody with psychic powers into a haunted house. But although all three films pivot upon the same basic premise, the execution and consequences in each case are very different indeed: formula has provided a starting point rather than a rigid blueprint. However, beginning with the tedious pre-eminence of the slasher movie during the 1980s, the unthinking and opportunistic repetition of elements which had already proved popular in earlier films began to dominate proceedings in a manner that became stifling, and ultimately, as Wes Craven's *Scream* demonstrated, ripe for post-modern parody.

The irony here is that Craven's witty depiction of pop-culture-saturated teens terrorized by killers as media savvy as themselves *itself* became a prime illustration of the law of diminishing returns. The series eventually petered out with a duo of mediocre sequels which further highlighted the depressingly franchise-reliant nature of modern Hollywood. The *Scream* trilogy's initially invigorating but later insufferably smug sense of self-awareness may have all but extinguished the lingering embers of the slasher phenomenon – 1980s horror's most consequential (and analyzed) development – but it did leave many wondering what direction the genre would or, indeed, could take next. The answer is that it failed to develop at all, and instead took a giant leap backwards, to the extent that supposed "homage" to the past has today become an excuse for a lamentable lack of new ideas.

The *Scary movie* franchise (2000–6) – originally a spoof of *Scream* which was actually a loosely linked series of "comic" skits based on other, better movies – is the by and large unfunny but entirely logical next step for a genre that has so comprehensively cannibalized its own back catalogue; a cannibalization that has now begun to encompass material from other countries. At least when the most recognizable elements of both classic and recent horror movies are spoofed by the latest *Scary movie* instalment (as in *Scary movie 4*, which opens with an admittedly amusing spoof of the first high-concept *Saw* film starring television agony uncle Dr Phil and Basketball player Shaquille O'Neal), the audience knows that originality and innovation is not the point here. Rather, in this instance, crude parody and the tiresome repetition of familiar plot lines and character types are what matter. Unfortunately, the ceaseless recycling of tropes and situations from older, better films is present in much more than the *Scary movie* franchise. As the statistics indicate, it is becoming increasingly difficult to find an American horror film release in recent times which isn't an outright remake, a prequel, a sequel, a computer game adaptation or an English-language version of an Asian movie.[5]

So what else has caused this catastrophic downturn in a genre that was once so relevant and so innovative? One factor often overlooked with relation to the 1970s horror boom is the extent to which the horror movie successes of that decade relied upon literary antecedents. As genre critic Noel Carroll has pointed out, with reference to the substantial commercial success of novels such as Ira Levin's *Rosemary's baby* (1967), William Peter Blatty's *The Exorcist* (1971) and Thomas Tryon's *The Other* (1971), 'The relationship between horror film and horror literature has been quite intimate in the current horror cycle, both in the obvious sense that often horror films are adapted from horror novels; and in the sense that many of the writers in the genre were deeply influenced by earlier horror movie cycles'.[6]

Following the considerable impact of William Peter Blatty's *The Exorcist*, one author in particular would gradually become a goldmine for producers and directors. The steady succession of Stephen King adaptations which began in 1976 with Brian De Palma's *Carrie* has yet to dry up, but with the notable exception of *Carrie*, *The Shining* and Rob Reiner's version of *Misery* (1990), King's cinematic legacy has encompassed considerably more misses than hits. Certainly, anyone who has seen the dismal adaptations of *Cujo* (1983), *Dreamcatcher* (2003), or worst of all, *Maximum overdrive* (2006) (which King made the great mistake of directing himself) will have their reservations about the worth of his contribution to Hollywood.

Despite this dubious antecedent, the 1970s golden age in American horror cinema was, to a considerable extent, kick-started by the popular and commercial success of literary horror and by the emergence of a number of key new names – among them Ira Levin, Peter Straub and William Peter Blatty – who all had film versions of their work made during the decade.[7] As the most prominent of these newcomers, Stephen King was one of the first genre authors to be consciously marketed as a brand-name, reaping million dollar advances, signing immensely lucrative multi-book deals and benefiting from the intensive marketing drive that now characterizes the best-seller list. Thirty years after his publishing debut, King remains the biggest name in commercial horror fiction. Anyone browsing through the typical bookshop's horror section will be hard-pressed to find any fiction at all by new or unfamiliar authors, so comprehensively do King, Dean Koontz, Richard Laymon and their low-rent British counterparts James Herbert and Sean Huston dominate the bookshelves. Unfortunately, this tendency among

5 Such as: *Ring* (1998; 2002), *The Grudge* (2003; 2004), *Pulse* (2001; 2006) and *Dark water* (2002; 2005).
6 Noel Carroll, *The philosophy of horror* (London, 1990), p. 2. 7 Such as, for example, the film versions of Blatty's *The Exorcist*, Straub's *Ghost story* (1979; 1981) and Levin's *Rosemary's baby*, *The Stepford wives* (1972;1975) and *The boys from Brazil* (1977; 1978).

publishers to invest a great deal of money and effort in one author has helped create the situation today, whereby a few panned-out big names from the previous generation still dominate at the expense of untried new talent. There are interesting and original horror writers out there – such as Dennis Etchinson, Jack Ketchum, Caitlin R. Kiernan and Lisa Tuttle – but the problem is it is very difficult for the average member of the public to actually *find* them unless they are familiar with small presses and obscure specialist journals.

With the commercial horror novel in such a state of decline, there are much fewer literary antecedents for film to feed off. Significantly, the most important horror novel of the past decade, Mark Z. Danieleweski's *House of leaves* (2000), a dizzyingly self-referential variation on the traditional haunted house novel, is considered virtually unfilmable. There has only been one American horror film based upon a literary adaptation since 2002, and that was Gore Verbinski's Americanized remake of *Ring*, which drew on Hideo Nakata's 1998 film version much more than Koji Suzuki's source novel.

There is an argument to be made, therefore, that the video game has replaced the novel as the source text of choice for American horror directors, and with less than stellar results. The fact is, playing a game differs quite substantially from watching a film unfolding on screen. On the most obvious level, game playing is active and immersive, requiring the enthusiastic participation of the gamer, who to a certain extent creates their own experience. Film-going is, rather, like reading a novel – a passive medium in which one is exposed to someone else's imaginative processes: we may strongly identify with the protagonist, but unlike when playing a computer game we do not *become* them. Film adaptations of video games so far seem to have been made with the assumption that if the *mise-en-scene* and general look of the game is replicated, the audience, already familiar with the source, will be satisfied. However, because so many video games are already much indebted to earlier, better films, what we're actually getting is a third-hand reimagining of someone else's concept (as in the Romero-indebted *Resident evil*). In addition, game play and immediacy is more important in a game than coherent plotting. The original (game) version of *Silent hill* had six possible endings, none of which made all that much sense, but this did not detract from the effectiveness of the game. In the film adaptation, however, such narrative indeterminacy proved disastrous. Only the likes of David Lynch can persuasively get away with this kind of thing, as the labyrinthine *Mullholland Drive* (2001) testifies.

Video game adaptations aside, another notable development in the recent American horror film is the release of a number of films which have, as their main selling point, prolonged scenes of extreme violence and gore. It may seem heartening that someone is making horror films for a supposedly "adult" audience and actively seeking to gain an 18-certificate rather than the more lucrative lower rating of the films previously discussed but this isn't always such a positive indication. There is something rather bleak about the suggestion, enthusiastically expressed by both the creators of such films and many reviewers, that because a film depicts torture, mutilation and a nihilistic attitude towards human life, it is therefore "daring" and "shocking", and thus represents a welcome return to the values of the so-called "real" horror film.

Films such as *Saw*, *Saw II* and *Saw III*, Eli Roth's *Cabin fever* (2002) and *Hostel*, Rob Zombie's *House of a thousand corpses* (2003) and *The Devil's rejects* (2005) and the recent Alexandre Aja remake of *The hills have eyes* (2006) showcase decapitations, eye gouging, lashings of gore and any number of nastily inventive death scenes, each calculated to appeal to the appetites of the "hardcore" horror fan. Overtly influenced by the early work of directors such as Wes Craven, Tobe Hooper and George A. Romero, as well as the more recent work of Japanese directors such as Takeshi Miike, these films tend towards the depiction of brutally realistic violence rather than fantastical or supernatural happenings. Indeed, the overtly supernatural horror film now seems to have been relegated for good to the dreaded universe of the PG-13 flick, a realm inhabited by the expensive looking but light-weight likes of *The exorcism of Emily Rose* (2005), *What lies beneath* (2000), *The Gift* (2000) and *An American haunting* (2005) all of which take their cues from M. Night Shayamalan's manipulative crowd pleaser *The sixth sense* (1999).

Recent films by Roth and former punk rocker Rob Zombie openly proclaim their indebtedness to envelope-pushing American films of the past, as well as, in Roth's case, to Asian horror directors such as Miike. Zombie even set his deeply cynical, derivative debut *House of a thousand corpses* in the 1970s, and in both this and his follow-up *The Devil's rejects* reused many of the situations and even bit-players from famous horror films of this era (such as the murderous clan trope from *The Texas chain saw massacre*). His films, like *Saw* and *Hostel*, also have much in common with the kind of horror films which came from Italy in the 1970s and 1980s.[8] Like the often-critiqued cannibal movie/zombie sub-genres, they display a decidedly one-dimensional fixation upon graphic scenes of bodily dismemberment and physical anguish. They also tend to feature bland, unlikable protagonists whose only reason for existing is to die violently.

Hostel, perhaps the most infamous example of this type of horror film, is about two arrogant American college boys, Paxton and Josh, who spend their summer backpacking around Europe. Along with an Icelandic buddy, they are lured to a small Slovakian town by the promise of girls, booze and drugs. Naturally, this is actually a horrific trap, and within the first forty-five minutes of the film Josh is tied up in a fetid torture chamber being systematically hacked to

---

8 The most notorious films of this oft-criticised subgenre include *Cannibal holocaust* (1980), *Cannibal ferox* (1981) and *Zombie flesh eaters* (1979).

pieces by an effete German businessman who has paid handsomely for the privilege. As the film progresses, we get to see scenes of people literally vomiting with fear, fingers and toes being cut off, eyeballs removed, and a traumatized Japanese girl messily hurling herself in front of a train, to name but a few of the more notable moments. In one of Roth's distinctly ham-fisted attempts to make some sort of vague comment on global relations following the invasion of Iraq, it seems that rich Western Europeans will pay more money to torture an American. Many critics also thought they detected some allusions to the Abu Ghraib prisoner abuse scandal here,[9] but the fact that this is an entire film about naïve Americans being set upon by evil foreigners would seem to significantly complicate this assessment. Indeed, Roth's commentary on current affairs seems no more insightful than this: 'You know, we live in really crazy, fucked-up times, and usually it's not Ok to just freak out. With a horror movie like this though – a crazy, intense bloodbath – you can walk into a room with a bunch of strangers and just scream and go nuts'.[10]

The original *Saw* movie is similarly concerned with confronting the audience with scenes and situations of a distinctly unpleasant nature, although it must be said that the premise is rather cleverer than the simplistic "sadistic Eurotrash versus innocent Americans" dynamic utilized by Roth. At the beginning of *Saw*, two men, neither of whom is known to the other, awaken to find themselves chained up at opposite sides of a grubby bathroom. A corpse lying in the middle of the floor clutches a tape recorder and a hand gun; when they play the tape they are told by their unseen captor that one must kill the other by six o'clock that evening or dire consequences will ensue. It gradually transpires that a sadistic serial killer named 'Jigsaw' is kidnapping carefully selected victims and forcing them into situations in which they must do great harm to themselves or to others to escape – one woman is, for instance, forced to manually extract a key from the intestines of a corpse which opens the bear-trap style device placed around her head; another protagonist will later have to saw off his own foot. It all concludes with a nasty twist and the inevitable promise of a sequel. In a trend that first emerged during the 1970s, the ability to graphically depict scenes of death and torture has all too often become the *raison d'etre* of such films, which means that special effects are showcased at the expense of old-fashioned ingredients such as genuine originality, vision and characterization. Famously, once he received financial backing for his satirical masterpiece *Dawn of the dead* (about a small band of survivors who seek shelter from a world overrun by zombies in a luxurious shopping mall), George Romero sent a terse telegram to his special effects supervisor,

9 Such as Jack Mathew's review in the *New York Daily News*, 7 Jan. 2006, or Nev Pierce's review of the film for BBC, www.bbc.co.uk/films/2006/03/13/hostel_2006_review.shtml, accessed 1 Mar. 2006. **10** Roth interview by Andrew O'Hehir, Salon.com/ent/movies/review/2006/01/05/btm/print.html, accessed 20 Feb. 2007.

Tom Savini, which simply said: 'Start thinking of ways to kill people'.[11] Sure enough, the finished film has scene after scene in which zombies (and humans) are dispatched with shotgun blasts, machetes, baseball bats and even helicopter blades. But while it is possible on the most basic level to view such scenes in the film as a kind of gruesome slapstick, Romero has also placed them within the context of a scathing and genuinely intelligent critique of consumerism and the insular, materialistic nature of contemporary American society.

Excessive amounts of blood and vomit do not a daring film make, and gore is not in itself radical or interesting. The overwhelming feeling one gets from watching films like *House of a thousand corpses* and *Hostel* is one of desensitized indifference; whereas but a single moment of intelligent and thought provoking violence in another instance might have more impact upon the viewer than both films put together.

If we consider as a brief example Austrian director Michael Haneke's recent art-house hit *Hidden* (2005), about a middle-class Frenchman whose comfortable, insulated existence is fatally compromised when an unknown stalker begins filming his every move. Either deeply intriguing or frustratingly inconclusive, depending upon your perspective, the film still manages to create in its audience, from the outset, a feeling of steadily escalating fear and suspense. Towards the end of the film, there is one brief moment, of sudden, shocking bloodshed, which elicited, from the audience I was, with gasps of genuine horror. This act of violence was all the more effective for having been used so precisely and so effectively in an otherwise bloodless film. In contrast to the type of horror film that rests upon the depiction of technologically impressive death scenes but is otherwise all too often lacking in anything interesting to say, *Hidden* demonstrates quite effectively that a film need not rely on effects or on gratuitous acts of violence to be truly shocking. It is a lesson that many of the great horror directors of the 1970s knew already. For example, any close viewing of *The Texas chain saw massacre* will reveal that despite the movie's infamously gory reputation, it is actually a relatively bloodless film. The horror here comes more from what is implied by the nightmarish setting and the sheer grotesqueness of the premise than by what is actually shown. Surely few sights in modern horror cinema are more disturbing than that of the bone- and feather-strewn living-room seen in the film, which comes complete with lampshades made of human skin and the decidedly disturbing sight of a clucking chicken crammed into a cage much too small for it? One of the most shocking scenes, in which mask-wearing grotesque Leatherface suddenly appears from behind hidden doors and bludgeons his helpless victim with a sledgehammer, and then slams them shut again, happens so quickly that like the protagonist, the audience barely has a chance to comprehend what has happened. It is a

---

11 Quoted in Adam Simon's documentary *The American nightmare* (2000).

moment ten times more chilling than the excruciatingly prolonged scenes of tor-ture and mutilation seen in *Hostel* and *House of a thousand corpses*, both of which obliquely draw upon Hooper's movie but fail to *learn* from it. To paraphrase Romero, they can think of ways to kill people, but not much else.

Another symptom of the same kind of imaginative indebtedness to the past is the trend which saw a spate of zombie-themed movies slowly shuffle towards the box office. The trend began with Danny Boyle's *28 days later* (2002), and was fur-thered by Zack Snyder's 2004 remake of *Dawn of the dead* and Edgar Wright's witty British hit *Shaun of the dead* (2004). It may be that fictive depictions of soci-etal breakdown and mass death have greater popular appeal at times of consider-able political and social unease. Certainly, this would seem to make sense, especially when one considers the manner in which the original trilogy of *Dead* films directed by George Romero, each, in their different way, acted as a chilling commentary on the mores of contemporary American society.[12] Another, rather less elevated factor may be that the zombie film, relying as it does upon a set of fairly straightforward conventions directly lifted from Romero – in other words, that a band of disparate survivors must battle a mindless horde of reanimated corpses – is especially appealing to young filmmakers as a concept, because it requires so little in the way of original thought, or, perhaps just as importantly, money. The Irish horror industry, small as it is, recently saw the release of not one but *two* comic zombie films – Conor McMahon's *Dead meat* (2004) and Stephen Bradley's *Boy eats girl* (2005). However, encouraging as it is to see cinema horror emerge from a local context, one cannot help but wish that most of this spate of young pretenders had left this sort of thing to Romero. His witty comeback in *Land of the dead* (2005), though by no means up to the standard of his earlier masterpieces, may well be the best mainstream B-movie in years, as well as a typ-ically incisive but less-than-subtle critique of the social and economic divides of present-day America (the movie depicts an insular, sky scraper dwelling elite who have seized the opportunity presented by years of zombie-related conflict to con-solidate their own wealth and influence, while ignoring the plight of the desperate underclass who actually do all the fighting).

Romero's return to the big screen in 2006 highlighted not only the lapse into obscurity of most of his contemporaries (save for a few underwhelming instal-ments of the television series *Masters of horror*), but also the extent to which the current American horror movie has comprehensively failed to productively engage with the social, political and economic realities of the present day. An exception

12 For instance, *Night of the living dead*, in which Romero virtually invented the modern horror film, can be said to have dramatized Cold War apocalyptic anxieties, fears about the conformity of modern American society, and issues related to the Civil Rights struggle; *Dawn of the dead*, as previously indicated, is a scathing satire on 1970s insularity and materialism, while *Day of the dead* has been seen by many as a bitter indictment of Regan-era militarism.

to this is, perhaps, the remarkably xenophobic *Hostel*, which, as already outlined, is founded upon the dubious premise that resentful Eastern Europeans will do practically *anything* to make a quick buck. One might of course argue that real-world events have, in a sense, overtaken the horrors that fiction is capable of, and that a world where one can download pictures of real-life beheadings to a mobile phone in a matter of seconds is a world where life has finally superseded art. This, I would argue, however, is an unconvincing get-out clause since much the same has been said, in one way or another, about every catastrophic world event since the French Revolution. Films should not always have to comment on real-world issues by any means, but at the same time it is deeply disheartening that the genre which only a generation ago captured more than any other a sense of the turbulent, often disturbing contexts of late 1960s and 1970s still looks to *that* era for inspiration rather than the equally turbulent present.

There has, however, been one gore-laden American film of late that does perhaps say a great deal about the times in which we live. Though it may not often have been reviewed as such, there is a good case to be made for the fact that the most commercially successful horror film of recent years is Mel Gibson's *The Passion of the Christ* (2004). After all, the film graphically depicts the agonizing torture and death of a man tormented by visions of Satan. The same man later rises from the dead. Ironically, the film was most acclaimed by right-wingers and conservative Christians, exactly the kinds of people who would have been queuing up to condemn such a gratuitous display of violence had it been utilized in anything but a biblical context. As well as demonstrating that there is a wider audience for films entirely in Aramaic and Latin than one would have previously supposed, the film also proved that mainstream audiences will sit through a great deal of gore and violence if it all serves religious ends (which intriguingly suggests that we may soon be seeing a boom in biblical slasher movies).

Still, the most significant horror icon of the past decade comes not from Hollywood, or the Bible, but from Japan, in the form of Sadako Yamamura, vengeful star of the highly successful *Ring* trilogy, which is about the angry spirit of a psychically gifted young girl who seeks to inflict her own suffering on the rest of the world. Yet typically, the kind of intelligent, provocative horror that has emerged from Japan, Hong Kong and South Korea in recent years – including exhilarating, chilling films such as *Old boy* (2003), *Audition* (1999), *A tale of two sisters* (2003) and *The Eye* (2002) – has failed to spur Hollywood into raising its own standards, but instead has become fodder for the ever-busy remake factory.

The ready availability of foreign horror films on DVD has transformed the genre, allowing directors and tropes previously unknown in the West to have a gradual but ultimately profound impact – a fact attested to by the sheer number of spooky little girls to be found in American horror films following the success of *Ring*. Most encouraging is the fact that horror fans in the West are becoming increasingly open to films from other traditions and cultures, a trend to which the recent success of Korean monster-movie *Host* (2005), Mexican director Guillermo Del Toro's Spanish-set masterpiece *Pan's labyrinth* (2006), and the French film *Them* (2005) attest. If it allows horror from other nations to gain a foothold in the West, perhaps the American horror film's decline in quality has in this respect been a good thing. Certainly, cinematic horror has also been enjoying something of a boom in continental Europe and in Britain as of late, as the release of films such as *Dog soldiers* (2002), *The Descent* (2005), *Wilderness* (2006), *The Ordeal* (2005), *Them, High tension* (2004) and *Severance* (2006) indicates.

The advent of digital filmmaking technology, which allows fledgling directors and producers to make and distribute movies much more cheaply than in the past, should also yield positive results. On balance, as the success of the (admittedly over hyped) *Blair Witch project* in 1999 demonstrated, with the right degree of marketing savvy, low budget, off-beat horror films *can* find their way to mainstream success. It must be hoped then that the "next big thing" in American horror comes soon, and that the film in question is made by people who shun the obvious route of an unnecessary remake, video-game adaptation, or gore heavy/story light concoction which makes the audience grimace but does little else. American horror cinema at the present time needs to stop relying so heavily upon the successes and preoccupations of the past and start worrying quite seriously about the future: only then, like Mel Gibson's much-abused Messiah, will it rise again.

Freud's nightmare

CHRISTOPHER FRAYLING

In 1926, the 43-year-old American writer and socialist Max Eastman visited Sigmund Freud in his office at Berggasse 19 – a street in the residential sector of Northern Vienna. Eastman had published, ten years before, one of the first popular non-specialist introductions to Freud's teaching for American readers, in *Everybody's Magazine*. He had also published a chapter on 'Marx and Freud' which Freud had judged to be 'really important; probably also correct'. So when he found himself in Vienna in 1926, Eastman made an appointment with the great man. His fact-finding tour of the Soviet Union a couple of years earlier had helped to shake his faith in Marxism – and he was also beginning to have serious doubts about Freud as well.[2]

He went up the stairs to the landing of Berggasse 19, turning right to the door of Freud's compact suite of offices. Then, through the foyer outside Freud's waiting room – with its metal bars on the doors, for security reasons – to the waiting room itself.[3] Eastman recalled his first impressions of the waiting room some sixteen years later in 1942, as part of a chapter on Freud – 'Visit in Vienna – the crotchety greatness of Sigmund Freud' – in the book *Heroes I have known* (1942):

> Berggasse 19 was a big roomy house full of books and pictures, the whole mezzanine floor padded with those thick rich rugs in which your feet sink like a camel's in the sand. I was not surprised to see hanging beside Rembrandt's *Anatomy lesson*, without which no doctor's office would be recognisable, a picture of *The Nightmare* – a horrid monster with a semi-evil laugh or leer squatting upon a sleeping maiden's naked breast. Freud's early speciality had been anatomy, and he had in him the hard scientific curios-

1 This essay was first given, as a paper in draft form at the *Fear* conference (Trinity College Dublin) on 19 May 2006, and as a lecture to the Friends of the Freud Museum, London, on 17 Nov. 2006. 2 Max Eastman, *Heroes I have known* (New York, 1942), pp 262–73. 3 For photographs of these locations, taken some twelve years later, see Edmund Engelman, *Berggasse 19 – Sigmund Freud's home and offices, Vienna 1938* (Chicago, 1981), plates 2, 7, 8, 9 & 10.

ity suggested by Rembrandt's picture. But then he had too, in my belief, a streak of something closely akin to medieval superstition [...] Freud's discovery that impulses suppressed out of our thoughts can continue to control those thoughts, both waking and sleeping, and also our actions and bodily conditions, was certainly a major event in the history of science. But what a lot of purely literary mythology he built around it! Mental healing always did and always will run off into magic.[4]

For Max Eastman, this big roomy house – actually an apartment – with its professional offices looking away from the street towards an inner courtyard, with its offices crammed to bursting point with books, journals, paintings, prints, photographs, antique sculptures and oriental rugs – an 'embarrassment of objects'[5] as Peter Gay was to call it – this environment was a kind of protection by a middle-class family against the world outside; it was also in some ways a metaphor for the psychoanalytical process itself. Freud had indeed likened his psychoanalytical work in the early text *Studies on hysteria* (1895), to 'clearing away, layer by layer, the pathogenic psychical material which we liked to compare with the technique of excavating a buried city.'[6] Eastman also thought there was something obsessional about Freud's collecting mania: so many objects and pictures crammed into such a small space. The two men discussed among other things whether the unconscious was a thing or a concept; the role of metaphor in Freud's science; the question of whether psychoanalysis was a science at all; the relationship between physical and psychological explanations; and why Freud seemed to dislike America so much – 'I don't hate America', Freud replied, 'I regret it'. From his one visit in 1909, he didn't like the rich food or the obsession with making money and he didn't like being turned into a fashion. After the meeting, which ended cordially, Max Eastman left the apartment convinced of two things. First, that Freud's dislike of America really had something to do with 'our rather hard-headed scepticism about some of the more mythological of his reported discoveries in "the Unconscious".'[7] Eastman much preferred the phrase "unconscious brain states" to the more usual "the Unconscious" because he felt the use of the word as a noun rather than an adjective made it seem too much like a thing rather than a concept, 'a scheming demon for which anatomy certainly finds no place'. Second, that Freud was at the same time a scientist and a latter-day demonologist:

> Freud would not let his discoveries be a contribution to psychology. They had to <u>be</u> psychology – "Freud's psychology". And there had to be quite a little of the infallibility of the Pope in his pronunciamentos.

---

4 Eastman, *Heroes*, p. 264.   **5** Peter Gay, *Freud – for the marble tablet*. In Engelman, *Berggasse 19*, pp 13–54. **6** Gay, *Freud*, pp 19–20. *Studies on hysteria* was written by Freud with Josef Breuer.   **7** Eastman, *Heroes*, esp. pp 215–66.

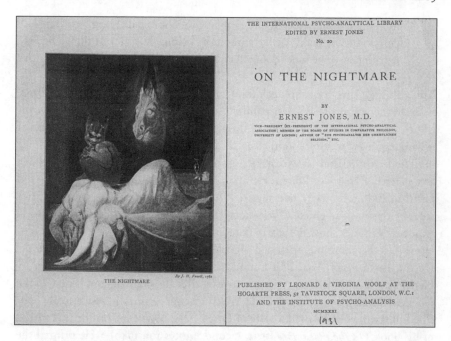

THE INTERNATIONAL PSYCHO-ANALYTICAL LIBRARY
EDITED BY ERNEST JONES
No. 20

ON THE NIGHTMARE

BY
ERNEST JONES, M.D.
VICE-PRESIDENT (EX-PRESIDENT) OF THE INTERNATIONAL PSYCHO-ANALYTICAL
ASSOCIATION; MEMBER OF THE BOARD OF STUDIES IN COMPARATIVE PHILOLOGY,
UNIVERSITY OF LONDON; AUTHOR OF "ZUR PSYCHOANALYSE DER CHRISTLICHEN
RELIGION," ETC.

THE NIGHTMARE   By J. H. Fuseli, 1782

PUBLISHED BY LEONARD & VIRGINIA WOOLF AT THE
HOGARTH PRESS, 52 TAVISTOCK SQUARE, LONDON, W.C.1
AND THE INSTITUTE OF PSYCHO-ANALYSIS
MCMXXXI

Title page of the first edition of Ernest Jones' *On The Nightmare*, published 1931, with a reproduction of the second version of Fuseli's *The Nightmare* (1790–1) erroneously dated.

Freud, concluded Eastman, was a man who veered from scepticism to credulity, a short-fused man who tended to see criticism as betrayal of the cause.[8] The whole of Eastman's chapter is in fact centred on these two levels of analysis: the science, the anatomy, the external symptoms, the measurable; and the metaphorical, the archaeological, the literary, the mythological – even the demonological. Which brings us to that framed print of *The Nightmare* which he saw hanging against the dark floral wallpaper of Freud's waiting room, and which he misremembered as of 'a sleeping maiden's naked breast'. It may also have been seen by "H.D." – Hilda Doolittle, the American poet and friend of Ezra Pound – who was in analysis at Berggasse 19 between March 1933 and December 1934, and who then published her *Tribute to Freud* in the mid-1950s:

> I waited as usual in the room, with the round table, the odds and ends of old papers and magazines. There were the usual framed photographs [...] There was the honorary diploma that had been presented to the Professor in his early days by the small New England university. There was also a bizarre print or engraving of some nightmare horror, a "Buried Alive" or

8 Ibid., pp 267, 272–3.

some such thing, done in Düreresque symbolic detail. There were long lace curtains at the window, like a 'room in Vienna' in a play or film. The Professor opened the inner door after a short interval. Then I sat on the couch.[9]

This '"Buried Alive" or some such thing' was almost certainly Fuseli's *The Nightmare* (rather than the Belgian painter Antoine Wiertz's *The premature burial* [1854], the best-known treatment of this theme, for which there is no evidence of it hanging in the waiting room).

The first question is: which version of *The Nightmare* by the Zurich-born artist Henry Fuseli – or Johann Heinrich Füssli, as he was originally called – did Eastman and maybe H.D. actually see? Of the original *Nightmare*s by Fuseli, two separate versions had entered Western culture. The first was exhibited at the Royal Academy summer show in 1782 (painted the year before), where it caused a sensation – as the ambitious artist had probably intended. This version is now in the Detroit Institute of Arts. The second, an upright replica painted to order by Henry Fuseli, was made in 1790–1, ten years after the original, and is now in the Goethe Museum Frankfurt. Freud's Welsh disciple, Ernest Jones, actually confused the two when he used a plate of Fuseli's *The Nightmare* on the title spread of his book *On the nightmare* (1931, second impression 1949).[10] He printed the Frankfurt version of 1790–1, and wrote below it 'by J.H. Fuseli 1782'; a surprising error because Jones also acknowledged the help of Professor Paul Ganz of Basle – a distinguished inter-war Fuseli scholar – in getting permission to reproduce the painting and 'providing assistance'.[11] To be fair, there were still muddles about the dating of the two pictures at the time.

But, which *was* the printed version hanging in Freud's waiting room? We know from Max Eastman that it was already there in 1926. It was probably there in 1933–4, when H.D. was in analysis. But it does not appear in Edmund Engelman's celebrated photographs of the interior of Berggasse 19, which he took in May 1938, the month before Freud left Vienna 'to die in freedom',[12] as the apartment was about to be dismantled. But the print *was* there in December 1937, when Freud's close friend and colleague Madame Marie Bonaparte (whom he always called "the Princess": she was Princess George of Greece) filmed some home movies – including footage of the waiting room – which were subsequently to be edited together for the American Psychoanalytical Association, after the raw footage had been unearthed by Anna Freud in the early 1970s. These home movies, slightly out of focus, contain two separate shots of *The Nightmare*, the first static, the second moving. The first, of five seconds, shows the framed print

9 H.D., *Tribute to Freud* (New York, 1974), 'Writing on the Wall', pp 60–1. **10** Ernest Jones, *On the nightmare* (London, 1931; reprinted London 1949), illustration opposite the title page. **11** Ibid. **12** Freud to his son Ernst, 12 May 1938, in English, cited in Gay, *Freud*, p. 13.

The location of Fuseli's *The Nightmare* in Freud's waiting room, behind an
antique jar. Frame enlargement from Marie Bonaparte's home movies, filmed Dec. 1937.
(Courtesy of the Freud Museum, London.)

The print of Fuseli's *The Nightmare* which hung in Sigmund Freud's waiting room.
Frame enlargement from Marie Bonaparte's home movies, filmed Dec. 1937.
(Courtesy of the Freud Museum, London.)

on the wall against the floral wallpaper; the second, of three and a half seconds, pans up a large jar from antiquity – probably Egyptian, designed to rest in the sand – which stands in front of the print, and which was presumably moved for the earlier shot. Anna Freud's voiceover, added later, explains that the shots with their French inter-titles were taken by Marie Bonaparte – who appears in one of them 'waiting for her analytic hour' – and that 'all the pictures in the waiting room [...] all these pictures are still there – that's all the waiting room. And the waiting room is now, in Berggasse, very much restored as it was then'.[13] Actually, *The Nightmare* is an exception to this. The version of the print hanging today in the Sigmund Freud house in Vienna was placed there in the 1970s. Maybe Marie Bonaparte was drawn to this particular image, because of her own interest in the psychopathology of horror, and in the works of Edgar Allan Poe about which she was to write a celebrated study. She had known Freud since 1925 when she first entered analysis in Vienna.

The print may have been given to Freud by Ernest Jones, who published some key works on the nightmare – essays written in 1909–10, while he was reorganizing the medical section of the University of Toronto library, expanded to book length in 1926 and first published as a book in 1931. Most of the 1931 book was written some twenty-two years earlier, by Jones's admission, and published (part one) as a long article in the *American Journal of Insanity* (66) and (part two) as *Der Alptraum* in a series of monographs called *Shriften* (no 14, 1912), edited by Freud himself.[14] Jones first met Freud towards the end of April 1908, at the Hotel Bristol in Salzburg, and first visited Freud in Vienna the following month. He later recalled that Freud said to him at the time 'what we most need is a book on dreams in English; won't you write one?'[15] So the second, and most attractive, possibility is that Jones saw the print of *The Nightmare* on the wall of the Berggasse apartment in May 1908, and that this – plus Freud's question – first aroused his interest in the subject. If so, the print was already there as early as 1908 – and it may no longer have been there in May 1938, unless Edmund Engleman omitted to photograph that particular angle of the waiting room. Engelman later recalled, of his single photograph of the waiting room, 'in my eagerness to get on into the "important rooms" I rushed through this one, stopping only for a quick shot of the pictures and diplomas on one wall.' He also recalled that the angles he chose were partly to do with 'the positions where Freud usually stood or sat', and partly with where he could place his bulky tripod without damaging anything.[16] So the print *may* after all have been there in May and June 1938. It is thought that Freud must have presented his framed print of Fuseli's *The Nightmare* to Marie Bona-

13 Anna Freud's voiceover to the home movies, screened as part of the permanent exhibition at 20 Maresfield Gardens.   14 See Brenda Maddox, *Freud's wizard – the enigma of Ernest Jones* (London, 2006), pp 68–89. Also Jones, *On the nightmare*, pp 7–8.   15 Maddox, *Freud's wizard*, p. 61.   16 Engelman, *Heroes*, pp 136–7.

Print, after *The Nightmare*, from the portfolio by Eugene Le Poitvin
Les Diableries érotiques, published in France in the 1830s. This was in Freud's
personal collection. (Courtesy of the Freud Museum, London.)

parte when he emigrated, which would explain two things: that it didn't travel to
20 Maresfield Gardens, his last refuge in Hampstead, London NW3; and that a
Fuseli print with a Freud dedication "to M.B." was auctioned in Geneva a few
years ago – where it was bought by a French psychoanalyst.[17] I like to think it now
hangs in *her* waiting room. Marie Bonaparte died in 1962.

Back to the print itself. Freud seems to make no mention of it in his published
works but he does refer to a collection which includes a related print. This print
was one of an undated folio of eighteen images in a small folder called *Le
Poitevin: les diableries érotiques*, which Freud had in his library. The collection –
by the French printmaker Eugene Le Poitevin (1806–79) – had first been published in 1830, in France – a series of images of devils, sometimes alone and sometimes in groups, enacting the erotic fantasies of young girls. The example which
related to *The Nightmare* shows a small devil lifting the nightdress of a woman
who lies half naked across her bed – a direct, and more obviously erotic, transcription of Fuseli's originals. Following the popular success of Fuseli's *The Nightmare*
in the 1780s, the image – especially the 1782 version – soon entered the blood-
stream of popular culture, and the result was a small industry of parody "night-

17 Communication from Michael Molnar, acting director of the Freud Museum, London, May 2005.

mares", in the form of political satires or erotic prints or illustrations to horror novels. Fifteen direct transcriptions have been unearthed, dating from between 1783 and 1823, not to mention less direct ones. Le Poitevin's take on the theme dates from a time when *The Nightmare* had become a popular inspiration for French book illustrations.[18] His "erotic sorcery" was a late example, before the craze petered out. It seems likely that Freud already possessed this folio in 1909, because he mentions the Le Poitevin collection in his case history of the 'Rat Man', published in that year. In the final section of his published case notes – called 'The father complex and the rat idea' – Freud describes how this highly intelligent 29-year-old lawyer called Ernst, who introduced himself in October 1907 and stayed in analysis for eleven months, was obsessed to the point of neurosis with a torture involving rats in a pot and open buttocks which, he'd been informed while serving in the army, was 'a horrible punishment in the East'. Freud then free-associates around some of the symbolic meanings and verbal connotations of rats: dread of disease, guilt about money ('*raten* = instalments'), fears of anal penetration and even the rat as penis. There is then this footnote: 'If the reader feels tempted to shake his head at the possibility of such leaps of imagination in the neurotic mind, I may remind him that artists have sometimes indulged in similar freaks of fantasy. Such, for instance, are Le Poitevin's *Diableries érotiques*'[19] which included the transcription of *The Nightmare*. It is worth noting here that in Freud's equally celebrated 1908–9 case history of the cheerful 5-year-old "Little Hans" (son of Freud's friend Max Graf) – the boy has a phobia about being bitten by a white horse, and about carriage-horses dropping down dead in the street.

Marie Bonaparte's footage of Fuseli's *The Nightmare* shows it to have been printed back-to-front – the opposite way round to all known official printed editions, for example the edition of January 1783, a stipple engraving by Thomas Burke. This was one which indelibly associated Fuseli in the public mind with *The Nightmare*, a bestseller at five shillings a time in a first edition of 2,000 copies which quickly sold out.[20] At first glance it looks as though this particular shot in the home movie must have been flipped – as sometimes happens – but the shot is

18 See Christopher Frayling, 'Fuseli's *The Nightmare* – somewhere between the sublime and the ridiculous' in Martin Myrone (ed.), *Gothic nightmares* (London, 2006), pp 13–15, 45–51. Also, David H. Weinglass, *Prints and engraved illustrations by and after Henry Fuseli* (Aldershot, 1994), section on *The Nightmare*, pp 55–72. A print resembling the Le Poitevin print, in the form of a small lithograph vignette attributed to Charles Ramelet (1805–51), from the journal *Macedoines* in 1830, is reproduced in Peter Tomory, *The life and art of Henry Fuseli* (London, 1972), plate 227. In this version, the devil is not lifting the victim's nightdress, which covers more of her right thigh. It is also left-to-right rather than right-to-left, another example of reversal. The Le Poitevin seems to have been an erotic parody of the Ramelet, which was presumably quite well-known at the time. 19 Sigmund Freud, *The case histories – 'Little Hans' and the 'Rat Man'. Standard edition of the complete psychological works, vol. X, 1909* (London, 2001), p. 214. The 'Rat Man' case is described pp 154–249, including that 'horrible punishment in the East'; 'Little Hans', pp 22–100. 20 See Myrone, *Gothic nightmares*, p. 49.

Henry Fuseli, *The Nightmare*. Stipple engraving by Thomas Burke, after Fuseli, published 30 January 1783 – the official engraving which made the artist famous. (Courtesy of the British Museum, London.)

the same way round behind the antique jar, and in neighbouring shots the writing is the correct way round, for example on the spines of books. The out-of-focus inscription is on the left side of the border, the more common position, with the writing aligned to the edge of the image. So this was probably a pirate version or even a photograph of the Fuseli print which had been reversed in the printing. The reversal made it look more like the 1790 version, which is also reversed, the victim's head on the left, nightmare on the right. There was something of a Fuseli revival in the early part of the twentieth century – with the attention paid to *The Nightmare* by the Surrealists (for obvious reasons), with the reinvention of Switzerland as a cultural non-sporty destination, and with the William Blake renaissance. This resurgence continued with the purchase of many of Fuseli's paintings by the Kunsthaus in Zürich, which became the biggest collection of this "local artist made good". So maybe this print was a part of that fashion. Maybe Freud purchased it in Switzerland. Or maybe it was purchased at a printsellers in London.

If it was, then it is likely that Ernest Jones purchased it; a gift to his master and teacher from Freud's closest British adherent – and one of his most uncritical disciples. Jones was part of the "inner circle" around Freud, the only colleagues from whom he was willing to take criticism. But – like Max Eastman – Jones was later (in his classic biography, published 1953–7) to recall that Freud could be a credulous as well as a good late nineteenth-century scientific positivist. In 1931, Ernest Jones's *On the nightmare* was published by Leonard and Virginia Woolf at the Hogarth Press. Jones was by then well in with the Bloomsbury set, via the writer James Strachey, brother of Lytton, who had contacted him in 1920 offering to translate Freud's writings into English. Jones had explained to Freud that the dynasty was 'a well-known literary family'.[21]

In *On the nightmare*, Jones outlined the various "explanations" of nightmares which had been in common currency from medieval times to the early twentieth century, and then contrasted them with 'the epoch-making work of one man – Professor Freud – on the psychogenesis of dreams and the relationship of them to the neuroses.'[22] For Jones, writers on the nightmare had for centuries mistaken the true *cause* of the malady for various superficial factors or symptoms 'that play a part, of varying importance, in the evocation of a given attack.'[23] In the Middle Ages, the causes tended to be projected outwards, onto "external personal agents" such as lewd demons or grimacing dwarfs, incubi visiting women by night and succubi visiting men by night. St Augustine, for example, in *The city of God*, wrote of fiends of hell tempting frail humanity. The more cynical Geoffrey Chaucer, in *The wife of Bath's tale*, preferred to observe that visits by incubi had become a lot rarer since mendicant friars started preaching in convents. Then, from the early seventeenth century onwards, the causes tended to be projected onto bodily processes or physical factors – non-mental and non-sexual – which physicians began seriously to study and classify for the first time. So, various writers in the Age of Enlightenment rejected the timeworn folkloric explanations as "superstitious" and instead debated which bodily process held the key to nightmares: sleeping on one's back or left side, eating difficult-to-digest or undigested food (favourites included cucumbers, West Indian pears and under-done pork), an over-full stomach, circulatory disturbances, breathing difficulties, menstruation and reading anxious-making books too late at night. All these were eighteenth-century "explanations" of the nightmare experience. The thing was to reduce the superstitions to "natural causes" and then explain them away.

21 See Maddox, *Freud's wizard*, p. 160.   22 Jones, *On the nightmare*, 'Pathology of the nightmare', pp 13–54.   23 Ibid., pp 30, 37, 50; section on 'medieval superstitions', pp 57–97.

Ernest Jones began *On the nightmare* with an epigraph from Erasmus Darwin, the physician, poet, and grandfather of Charles – the same literary epigraph the first four lines of which had appeared beneath the original print of Fuseli's *The Nightmare* in 1783:

> So on his Nightmare, through the evening fog,
> Flits the squat fiend o'er fen, and lake, and bog;
> Seeks some love-wilder'd maid with sleep oppressed,
> Alights, and grinning sits upon her breast –
> Such as of late, amid the murky sky,
> Was marked by Fuseli's poetic eye[24]

This was the folkloric version of the nightmare with a vengeance, originally part of Erasmus Darwin's scientific poem *The botanic garden*, subtitled 'The loves of the plants' (1789–91) – where it illustrated Darwin's thoughts on the suspension of the willpower in sleep, while the senses remain alert, so you experience the painful desire to exert the voluntary motions which leads to all sorts of imaginings: 'In vain she wills to run, fly, swim, walk, creep'.[25] Such thoughts were part of what was in the late eighteenth century known as "the new psychology" and show that the unconscious was already topical, if not yet so called. Darwin's lines were also a misunderstanding, or a misreading, of Fuseli's painting. He evidently thought the nightmare was the horse – 'so on his Nightmare [...] flits to squat fiend' – rather than the mara (a completely different word, from the old Teutonic for "devil" and the Anglo-Saxon for "crusher") squatting on the woman's breast. It was a confusion which has survived to this day, between a female horse (mare) and a "nightmare". In the painting, the sightless horse is the vehicle of the mara – it even wears a collar – and could just as well be a stallion: a blind creature leading the mara to random places. In what may well be a version of Fuseli's original drawing of March 1781, the horse isn't even there.[26] Perhaps Freud, unlike Jones, would not have fully comprehended this linguistic and gender confusion: he would have thought of *The Nightmare* as *Der Alptraum*. But Ernest Jones was fascinated by the connections between the two traditions – even if they were purely linguistic, especially to an English speaker – and his one explicit reference to Fuseli in the entire text is in a chapter on the mythology of horses, riders, human-animal metamorphoses and night-flights – which he sees as examples of "interchangeability". So he cites a Swiss folk legend, in which:

> the mara penetrates through the key-hole into the bedchamber in the guise
> of a steed, lays her fore-hoofs on the sleeper's breast, and with glowing eyes

---

24 Ibid., p. 5. **25** Continuation of Erasmus Darwin quote above, seventeen lines later. See Myrone, *Gothic nightmares*, p. 43. **26** Frayling, 'Fuseli's *The Nightmare*', p. 11. See Nicolas Powell, *The Nightmare* (London, 1973), pp 58, 97–8 for a reproduction and possible explanation. There is no bottle on the table either.

stares at him in the most alarming fashion – a description which might well have been written in reference to one of the versions of the frontispiece by Fuseli in the present volume.[27]

Actually, it might not. The steed in the painting is a background figure, the mara is either a monkey-like creature (in the first version) or a cat-like creature (in the second), the victim is female and the eyes are glaring out at the viewer rather than staring at the sleeper. So he was wrong on all counts. No version of the Fuseli painting remotely resembles Jones's account of the folk legend. And the "horse-mara" connection in the painting may even have been intended as a joke – as a visual pun on the word "mare". Fuseli did like macabre jokes.[28]

Less explicit references to Fuseli's painting occur in the many nineteenth-century quotations about the nightmare experience cited by Jones – though Jones does not draw attention to them, and nor did the original writers. The cited descriptions of the nightmare experience seem to owe more and more to the imagery of Fuseli's painting from the 1820s onwards: a case of life imitating art. But the conclusion of Ernest Jones's book is *not* that the folk wisdom surrounding nightmares is mere mumbo-jumbo – on the contrary, modern medicine he says has in some ways unlearned folk explanations which are still very useful to the psychoanalyst. The conclusion is instead that, surprising as it may seem, if you go to your physician today complaining of nightmares, he or she is still liable to give you irrelevant advice about hygiene or indigestion or sleeping posture which goes right back to the "explanations" of the eighteenth century: 'the explanations of this condition still current in medical circles, and which ascribe it to digestive or circulatory disturbances, are probably further from the truth than any other medical views.'[29] Again, it is not that the Enlightenment hypotheses are completely off-beam: it is just that they confuse symptoms with deep causes. These superficial symptoms often happen to people without causing nightmares; and nightmares often happen without these superficial symptoms. Clearly a deeper explanation was needed.

Strangely, while Ernest Jones was rigorous in his interrogation of scientific and medical sources, he tended to be slapdash in his use of literature and visual art. He mis-dates and mis-reads the Fuseli painting, and he misquotes Erasmus Darwin: it should be 'squab' not 'squat' – a much better word – and the maid should be oppressed 'by sleep' not 'with sleep'. Be that as it may, in order to reach Jones's deeper explanation, we need to go back to the original reception of Fuseli's *The Nightmare*, among critics and commentators, at the time it was first exhibited.

The first ever review of the painting was in the London *Morning Herald* on Wednesday, 8 May 1782, the exhibition having opened at the Royal Academy,

27 Jones, *On the nightmare*, p. 256, part of the chapter 'The horse and the night-fiend', pp 248–73.   28 On other critical confusions surrounding *The Nightmare* at the time, see Frayling, 'Fuseli's *The Nightmare*', pp 11–15.   29 See, among many other references, Jones, *On the nightmare*, pp 13–14.

then in Somerset House, on Monday, 29 April. The review went straight to the confusion between "mare" and "mara":

> There is a wildness of conception in Mr Fuseli's picture of the Night Shade at the Royal Academy, which teems with that usual concomitant of genius, inaccuracy. He has introduced a mare's head into the piece, to characterise his subject. Now the personification of that disorder, which attacks the human frame in sleep, is borrowed from a word of northern origin; Mair or Mêre, a witch or sorceress. Shakespeare's Mad Tom [in *King Lear* Act III sc iv] mentions her in that character from some legendary ballad ...
> "St Withold footed thrice the wold,
> He met the Night Mare and her nine-fold;
> Bid her alight and her troth plight
> And aroynt thee, witch, aroynt thee!"[30]

So, according to this very first critic of *The Nightmare*, Fuseli had confused the man with the horse: the *Lear* reference suggests that the critic had been reading Dr Johnson's *Dictionary* on the subject. Johnson was still the authority in the 1780s, and could be depended on to cite interesting literary references as usage. He wrote:

> NIGHTMARE [night and ... mara, a spirit that, in the northern mythology, was related to torment or suffocate sleepers]. A morbid oppression in the night, resembling the pressure of weight upon the breast.
> Saint Withold footed thrice the wold
> He met the nightmare, and her name be told;
> Bid her alight, and her troth plight ...

'MARE', on the other hand, was a completely different word. It was 'the female of a horse'.[31]

The confusing thing for critics was that *The Nightmare*, unusually for Fuseli, did not make explicit reference to a specific literary or classical/mythological source: there was no subtitle and no clue in the title. Exhibition-goers were accustomed to paintings of specific dreams by various artists since the Renaissance, such as those experienced by Old Testament sages, Trojan warriors, Renaissance artists, or Shakespearean kings. However, a generic nightmare – The nightmare – perhaps set in the present day, was something new. Surely, given Fuseli's reputation up to now,[32] this must have a Shakespearean meaning – maybe to do with

30 The *Morning Herald*, 8 May 1782. 31 Dr Samuel Johnson, *A dictionary of the English language*, vol. 2 (London, 1755). 32 Fuseli's earlier exhibits at the Royal Academy, for example, had included visualizations

King Lear? The *Morning Chronicle*, of the following day, acknowledged that *The Nightmare* was a virtuoso performance, but was turned off by the painting's subject-matter:

> *The Nightmare*, by Mr Fuseli like all his productions has strong marks of genius about it; but hag-riding is too unpleasant a thought to be agreeable to anyone, and is unfit for furniture [i.e. as decoration] or reflection – *Qui bono*? [...] Yet surely a disagreeable subject, well executed, is preferable to the most engaging one ill described [...] [we have] another proof how artists sometimes lose themselves, and mistake their talents.[33]

'Hag-riding' – the review went on – could indeed be a reference to Mad Tom's song in *Lear*, or even to *Paradise lost* (6:ii) – a reference to the witch supposed to wander in the night 'lur'd with the smell of infant-blood'. So John Milton maybe – on the other hand, it could equally be a reference to the Queen Mab myth, as Dr Johnson had also written in his dictionary entry for the word "mare": Mab, the lascivious fairy queen who 'bestrides young folks that lie upright'. If so, the reference in the painting was likely to be to Mercutio's speech from Act I, Scene 4 of Shakespeare's *Romeo and Juliet*:

> And in this state she gallops night by night
> Through lovers' brains, and then they dream of love;
> [...] This is the hag, when maids lie on their backs,
> That presses them and learns them first to bear,
> Making them women of good carriage.

This debate in the journals of 8 and 9 May 1782 – which created an aura of mystery around the picture – may well have stimulated public interest in *The Nightmare*. The picture wasn't from any agreed literary source, or from nature – so exactly where did its nobility reside? What was its point? There was an immediacy about *The Nightmare* which the connoisseur Horace Walpole, for one, found 'shocking', and he wrote that single word in his copy of the Royal Academy catalogue next to the Fuseli entry.[34] But the publicity was working: over 6,500 people could have seen *The Nightmare* on Saturday 1 June and Monday 3 June alone – and they probably did. On Thursday 9 May, 2,713 people were recorded as visiting the Royal Academy exhibition, the highest figure for a single day of the entire run and even higher than the existing all-time record for daily attendances.[35]

So far the debate about the painting had concerned its "wildness", whether the subject matter was "disagreeable" or acceptable, and possible sources of inspiration

of scenes from *Henry VI Part II*, *Macbeth* and *Henry VIII*.   **33** *Morning Chronicle*, 9 May 1782.   **34** See Frayling, 'Fuseli's *The Nightmare*', p. 10.   **35** Ibid., pp 11–12.

in Shakespeare or Milton. The critical consensus seemed to be that Fuseli had per-
sonified an idea. The question was, what exactly *was* the idea? Where paintings of
visions were concerned, the critics seemed much more comfortable describing
visual conventions than explaining what all this might *mean*. It took a Church of
England vicar, the Revd Robert Anthony Bromley, Rector of St Mildred's in the
Poultry, to be the first to suggest that *The Nightmare* might, after all, be about sex.
In the first volume of his *A philosophical and critical history of the fine arts – painting, sculpture and architecture* (1793), Bromley included in his chapter on 'the qual-
ifications essential in the constitution of moral painting' an elaborate sideswipe at
Fuseli's picture. He didn't mention the artist by name but he didn't need to:

> the dignity of moral instruction is degraded, whenever the pencil is
> employed on frivolous, whimsical, and unmeaning subjects [...] *The
> Night-mare* [...] or any dream that is not marked in authentic history as
> combined with the inspiring dispensations of Providence, and many other
> pieces of a visionary and fanciful nature, are mere speculations [...] What
> good has the world, or what honour has the art, at any time derived from
> such light and fantastic speculations? [...] If it be right to follow Nature,
> there is nothing of her here. All that is presented to us is a *reverie* of the
> brain [...] mere waking dreams, as wild as the conceits of a madman. [A
> recent commentator] very properly calls these persons "libertines of paint-
> ing": as there are libertines of religion, who have no other law but the
> vehemence of their own inclinations.[36]

Bromley had evidently been reading the critics. But, in strongly implying that
Fuseli was among the 'libertines of painting', Bromley was breaking new ground.
Maybe *The Nightmare* was an example of the kind of libertine art which had been
exhibited in recent Paris Salons, or was known to be collected for private consumption by well-heeled connoisseurs and even the seedier members of the royal family.
A philosophical and critical history continued – at great and ponderous length – to
enunciate the principles that 'whatever is outré and extravagant can never be beautiful', and 'whatever is empty or poor of sentiment cannot instruct any persons'.[37]
Fuseli was furious. He took bitter offence at Bromley's attack on *The Nightmare*. It
was one thing to encourage a public reputation for eccentricity and even for being
"Painter in ordinary to the Devil" – Fuseli did that whenever the opportunity arose
– it was quite another to be publicly accused of being a libertine. Especially to
accuse someone who was as desperate to be accepted by the artistic establishment
as Fuseli himself was. So Fuseli wrote an ill-tempered and anonymous notice of

36 Revd Robert Anthony Bromley, *A philosophical and critical history of the fine arts*, vol. 1 (London, 1793),
pp 36–7, 56–61. 37 Frayling, 'Fuseli's *The Nightmare*', p. 12.

Bromley's book in the *Analytical Review* of July 1793 and then encouraged a debate at Somerset House which resulted in the Royal Academy cancelling its subscription to the second volume of Bromley's *History*. How could a commentator use 'so little delicacy' as to liken a living artist to a libertine? Whatever next?[38] Fuseli had been an ordained Zwinglian minister and preacher before he left Zurich for London, and quite apart from the social slur, Bromley's critique really stung him.

Apart from possible literary or mythical sources – or 'figures in art'[39] as he called them, which might have served as models for Fuseli, and there was much debate about these as well – there is another intellectual context which helps to clarify the contemporary meaning of *The Nightmare*, namely, the ways in which the painting could have been "read" at the time of its first reception. Fuseli was fascinated by visions and dreams, playacting and orating, larger-than-life super-heroes and curvaceous heroines, and painterly gloom, but in a quieter more private way he was almost equally fascinated by aspects of applied science and medicine. He was well informed about entomology and liked to study it over breakfast; he wrote a number of articles about insects for the *Analytical Review* (usually over the signature "R.R."); he made a surprising number of drawings of entomological subjects which he called 'his favourite study and amusement'; and he tended to lose himself in the close analysis of butterflies and moths when he was feeling particularly depressed. He also knew a great deal about the Linnaean system of classifying plants, insects and animals, and how 'his divisions and sub-divisions are crumbling every hour to dust', especially when viewed through the latest microscopes.[40] Ever since he first arrived in London in the mid-1760s, from Zürich, Fuseli had particularly enjoyed mixing in medical circles. On one occasion he surprised his friend the painter Joseph Farington when the conversation turned to the subject of madness. Instead of waxing lyrical about Lady Macbeth and King Lear, as he was expected to do, he talked statistics:

> Fuseli mentioned that a Medical man who attended Bedlam had said that the greatest number of these who were confined were *Women in love*, and the next class in respect of number was *Hackney* and *Stage coachmen*, caused it was supposed by the constant shaking exercise to which they are subject which affects *the pineal gland*.[41]

One of Fuseli's closest friendships in London was with Dr John Armstrong – notoriously waspish medical practitioner, poet and friend of John Wilkes – of

---

38 For the anonymous review, see Eudo Mason, *The mind of Henry Fuseli* (London, 1951), pp 278–9. For the controversy, see Joseph Farington, *The diary*, vol. 1 (eds) Cave, Garlick & Macintrye (New Haven, 1978–84), p. 165. **39** Fuseli's third Royal Academy lecture 'on Invention' about 'the judicious adoption of figures in art', printed in John Knowles, *The life and writings of Henry Fuseli*, vol. 3 (London, 1831). **40** On Fuseli and entomology see for example Mason, *The mind of Henry Fuseli*, pp 332–6, the source of the quotations on the subject in this paragraph. **41** Farington, *The diary*, vol. 6, p. 2288, entry for 2 April 1804.

whom the painter 'always entertained a high opinion', and who returned the com-plement by 'praising him in the Journals'.[42] In 1744, Armstrong had published his best-known poem *The art of preserving health* (it was often reprinted) a polemic in favour of regular exercise, moderation in all things, fresh air, honest toil, think-ing pure thoughts and eating sensibly.[43] In the long section devoted to *Exercise* (Book III), Armstrong wrote of nightmares:

> Oppress not nature sinking down to rest
> With feasts too late, too solid, or too full [...]
> Not all a monarch's luxury the woes
> Can counterpoise, of that most wretched man,
> Whose nights are shaken with the frantic fits
> Of wild Orestes; whose delirious brain,
> Stung by the furies, works with poisoned thought

Ways of avoiding nightmares, Armstrong went on, included going to bed early, avoiding rich food, engaging in 'pleasing talk' just before retiring and as a very last resort reading Homer aloud. Indulging in 'Sickly musing', 'hideous fictions' and nasty paintings, especially when alone, was not recommended. In the part of *The art of preserving health* which was about over-eating, Armstrong went on to cite the researches of a Dr John Bond who was soon to publish a full-length *Essay on the incubus, or night-mare* (1753).[44]

Bond claimed that this was the first-ever full-length work on the subject of nightmares, which it was not. Ernest Jones was to find on the library shelves six-teen earlier works dating from the period 1627 to 1740, mainly published in Ger-many and nearly all in Latin.[45] But Jones was to cite Bond more often than anyone. In his essay, Bond made the centrepiece of his argument the contrast between the old folkloric and moral explanations of the nightmare, with the new medical ones, which is why he was so useful to Jones. Bond began by dismissing superstitions 'that did not appear serious or probable', and explaining why he would confine himself instead 'the laws of animal economy'.[46] This was the enlightened position:

> I have therefore omitted an inquiry into the origins of many odd epithets
> and quaint names commonly given to this Disorder; such as Hag-riding,
> Wizard-pressing, Mare-riding, Witch-dancing & c [...] In our language it

---

42 On Fuseli and Armstrong, see Mason, *The mind of Henry Fuseli*, p. 127.   **43** John Armstrong, *The art of preserving health – a poem* (London, 1744), Book III, pp 84–6, Book IV, pp 108–9, the source of the quo-tation and subsequent references.   **44** Armstrong, *The art of preserving health*, Book II, pp 38–9. See also John Bond, *An essay on the incubus, or night-mare* (London 1753), pp 1–83.   **45** Jones, *On the nightmare*, p. 14.   **46** Bond, *An essay on the incubus*, pp 2–5.

is generally known by the name of the Night-mare; which strange term probably arose from superstitious notions which the British had, and perhaps still have, of it.[47]

The popular confusion between "mare" (female horse) and "night-mare" (bad dream) was, apparently, part of this superstition. Bond also excluded the thesis that 'the Night-mare is an imaginary Disease, and proceeds from the idea of some demon, which existed in the mind the day before.' Instead, he carefully listed the symptoms – people lying on their backs, having bad dreams, breathing with difficulty, experiencing a violent oppression on the breast and losing voluntary motion – and explained them all as relating to blockages in the circulation of the blood. In particular, he noted, nightmares occurred when the head was lower than the legs, when the victim had turned onto the left side, and when too much blood was flowing into the brain. So each of the folkloric explanations was 'really internal'. For Dr Bond, the kinds of people who were likely to have nightmares were relatively easy to classify:

> Young persons of gross full habits, the luxurious, the drunken and they who sup late, are most subject to the night-mare. Also Women who are obstructed; girls of full, lax habits before the eruption of the Menses.[48]

Clearly, the transition from theological or moral explanations to medical ones was well under way by this time, and the John Lockean tradition – dreams as 'waking Man's Ideas, though for the most part oddly put together' rather than 'the Soul [having] ideas of its own', according to the *Essay concerning human understanding* (1689) – had been thoroughly digested.[49] But still within this frame of reference, Bond's thesis about blood circulation was to be explicitly challenged by another Lockean, Dr Robert Whytt, in his *Observations on the nature, causes and cure of those disorders which have been commonly called nervous* (1765, repr. 1777). Whytt reckoned that Bond's conclusions were 'far from being satisfactory' – they begged many more questions than they answered – and proposed instead that the causes of nightmares lay not in the blood but in the stomach: indigestion, wind, excessive phlegm, eating too late, 'certain medicines or poisons' including nervous medicines, in short 'strange ideas excited in the mind in consequence of the disordered state of the stomach, not then corrected by the external senses as they are when we are awake.' Whytt agreed with Bond's list of symptoms – and his thoughts about 'a suppression of the menses in women' – but:

---

47 Ibid., pp 2–5, 24, 46–51, 79–82, the source of the rest of this paragraph.   48 Ibid., pp 46–51.   49 John Locke, *Essay concerning human understanding* (London, 1689), in *Works* (1714), vol. 1, pp 36–7.

neither a horizontal posture, sleep, nor heavy suppers, do ever produce the night-mare, at least in any considerable degree, unless the person be pre-disposed to it from the particular condition of the nerves of the stomach.[50]

Fuseli's painting *The Nightmare* clearly refers in many detailed ways to the con-temporary debate about the causes of nightmares and – in parallel – includes most of the folkloric explanations as well. The victim is sleeping on her back, turned to her left side, with her head below her legs and with a pressure on her stomach. On the bedside table is a jar of liquid, maybe a 'nervous medicine'. But the sightless horse and the mara are there as well – the superstitious notions, as Bond had written, 'which the British had, and perhaps still have, of it.'[51] Fuseli really enjoyed British superstitions, particularly the ones he'd seen enacted on the stage in Shakespeare's plays and most particularly imps, elves and fairies.

Like so many other aspects of *The Nightmare*, this medical debate even found its way into Fuseli's reputation. In the year he became a full Royal Academician, 1790, the *Public Advertiser* started a rumour that the artist's imagination did not spring from refinement of taste at all but from 'an animal process, and is brought about after regular intervals by Mr. Fuseli's eating raw pork for supper'.[52] This rumour was evidently still in the ether when one of his biographies appeared in 1830, three years after Fuseli's death; the biographer felt the need to dismiss it: 'The story of his having supped on raw pork chops that he might dream his pic-ture of the nightmare has no foundation.' On the contrary, wrote the biographer, Fuseli ate two frugal meals a day (the Armstrong diet, perhaps) and always avoided supper if he could.[53] But – he added, casting a shadow of doubt over the frugal Fuseli – the artist did once drop in on William Blake, probably around the time of the *Advertiser* allegation, and discovered him eating a plate of cold mutton: 'is *that* what you do it on?', Fuseli asked.[54]

By the time of this biography – Allan Cunningham's *Lives of the most eminent English painters* (1830) – there was a growing craze for books about geniuses, and the more eccentric the better. It had long become a mantra among Romantic writers to see dreams as gateways into the darkness (so that, as the German poet Novalis famously put it, 'world becomes dream; dream becomes world'). In pop-ular biographies a number of visual and literary artists were said to have induced their nightmares deliberately: the poet Southey was reputed to have used laughing gas, the novelist Ann Radcliffe indigestible food late at night, while others opted

50 Robert Whytt, *Observations on the nature, causes and cure of those disorders which have been commonly called nervous* (London, 1765), pp 315–18, the source of all the Whytt quotations above.   **51** See footnote 45. **52** *Public Advertiser*, 31 May 1790.   **53** Allan Cunningham, *The lives of the most eminent English painters*, vol. 2 (2nd ed. London 1830–3), pp 338–9, the source of the 'no foundation' quote as well; also Peter Tomory, *The life and art of Henry Fuseli*, pp 181–4.   **54** Tomory, *The life and art of Henry Fuseli*, p. 184, citing Cunningham.

for portions of undercooked meat after prolonged periods of vegetarianism. Not all of which had the desired result. The "romantic agony" could simply take the form of serious indigestion. Thomas De Quincey could not understand why Fuseli bothered to eat 'raw meat for the sake of obtaining splendid dreams'. 'Better' he suggested 'to have eaten opium'.[55] The rumour about raw pork gained some of its currency from the shocking *immediacy* of *The Nightmare*, and its concrete details: the image must have come from somewhere, and Fuseli was known to be very choosy about his sources. Where on earth did it come from?

Today, post-Freud and Ernest Jones, we can see that the painting is also and perhaps primarily about sex – although whether it is about submission, empowerment or voyeurism is still being hotly debated by art historians and critics. At the time, the thought that nightmares might have deep sexual connotations – and causes – whether openly expressed or disguised, was not yet thinkable. We have seen how the art establishment in the form of the Royal Academy ganged up on a hapless vicar who dared to imply that the painting might have had *something* to do with sex. Sigmund Freud's interpretation of Fuseli's *The Nightmare* has not been recorded. We know that, by his own admission, he derived far more pleasure from the subject matter of paintings, and the stories they told than from their 'formal and technical' qualities: 'I may say at once', he famously wrote in his essay *The Moses of Michelangelo* (1914), 'that I am no connoisseur in art, but simply a layman. I have often observed that the subject-matter of works of art has a stronger attraction for me than their formal and technical qualities, though to the artist their value lies first and foremost in these latter.'[56] So he would no doubt have related Fuseli's painting, at the level of subject-matter and story, to his own theory of dreams. Since Ernest Jones's conclusions, in *On the nightmare*, were based partly on *The interpretation of dreams* (1900), and partly on Freud's writings about angst and superstition, we can confidently speculate that he would have agreed with most of them at that stage in his career. And Freud would have been reminded of them every time he looked at the wall of his waiting room. For Freud, as we know, dreams were the 'guardians of sleep', the carriers of waking wishes or repressed desires which could not, for various reasons, emerge in any other way – usually wishes and desires from childhood. As a rule, these were in his view 'erotic wishes [...] and sexual desires', and they emerged through the freedom of the dream state in 'displaced' or 'symbolic' or 'condensed' or 'represented' forms.[57] Taking these ideas as his starting-point, Ernest Jones outlined the history of the explanations of nightmares pre-Freud which we looked at earlier, then added – following Freud – that in nightmares these erotic wishes and sexual

55 Thomas de Quincey, *Confessions of an English opium eater* (London, 1823), p. 118.   56 Cited in Anthony Storr, *Freud* (Oxford, 1989), p. 93, from the *Standard edition of Sigmund Freud's works*, vol. 13, trans. James Strachey & Alix Strachey (London, 1953–74), p. 211.   57 On Freud's *The interpretation of dreams*, with quotations, see Storr, *Freud*, pp 41–51.

desires were transformed into anxiety, and the more forbidden the sexual desire the greater the anxiety: nightmares embraced the terror which the sleeper feared the most, and had buried the deepest. In one way, this contradicted Freud's theory of dreams, which were supposed to be about wish-fulfilment, whereas for Jones they were about anxiety. How could they be about repressed wishes *and* anxieties, both at the same time? Well, said Jones, the *latent* content of the nightmare was wish-fulfilment – buried very deep – but the *manifest* content, the bit the dreamer remembered, was anxiety. That terror came, he said or rather asserted, 'from the deepest stirring of mental life, which was the primordial conflict over incest'.[58] This was an unacceptable desire 'of such vehemence, that it threatens to over-power the repressing force', and in general the more intense the repression, the more distorted, perverted or disguised the dream. So 'an attack of the nightmare is an expression of a mental conflict over an incestuous desire', which had indeed been repressed since childhood.[59] The folkloric explanations had a kernel of truth in them, said Jones, because they described in their own ways the symbolic lan-guage of nightmares – and 'the structure of myths and dreams are related in respect of the unconscious mechanism at work'. Hence Jones's chapters on the incubus, the vampire, the werewolf, the devil, the witch, beauty and the beast – and indeed the horse. The physical or organic explanations also contained a mod-icum of truth, provided one accepted that they were about 'one percent' rather than 'ninety-nine per cent' of the nightmare experience.[60] Incest was for him the key. He didn't attempt to prove this. He simply took it as fact.

Art historians, writing about Fuseli's *The Nightmare* since the publication of Ernest Jones's study, have tried to relate some of his ideas back to the painting itself. So we have one influential historian, H.W. Janson, agreeing that *The Night-mare* was really a displacement of the artist's sexual fantasies – about his friend's young niece, a girl called Anna Landolt who had recently married someone else: so the victim was a projection of the artist's dream-girl, while the incubus-demon took the place of the artist himself.[61] It may even have been a self-portrait! Since then most commentators have more or less taken it for granted that the fantasy in the picture is a sexual fantasy – with the mara as a form of grinning penis. A specialist in the study of sleep patterns, from the Department of Psychiatry at the State University of New York, has adopted a very different tack by arguing that the painting depicts several of the distinctive features of 'sleep paralysis', as distinct from nightmares and often confused with them: 'sleep paralysis' is an anxiety attack which happens just when one is falling asleep or waking up, and which is apparently accompanied by hallucinations of 'someone sitting on my chest'. '[*The Nightmare*] actually represents a specific phenomenon […] which long after the

---

58 Jones, *On the nightmare*, pp 42–4, the source of the next sentence as well. 59 Ibid., pp 42–4, 75–7. 60 Ibid., p. 52. 61 See, among many others since, H.W. Janson, 'Fuseli's nightmare', *Arts and Sciences* (Spring 1963), pp 23–8.

painting appeared was described in clinical terms and given its specific name.'[62] So it shouldn't be called *The Nightmare* at all. It should be called *The sleep paralysis*. Another specialist, from the Department of Neurology at McGill University, Montreal, has argued that nightmares in fact occur during confused states of arousal rather than dreaming sleep. For this scientist, the painting is evidence that Fuseli had a literal belief in nocturnal demons pressing upon the sleeper's chest, and at the same time illustrates the etymology of the word: 'the monster sitting on the patient's chest and the female horse (sic) leering in the background refer to the ancient Teutonic word *mar*, meaning devil, and the English word *mare*, which it suggests.'[63] And so on. Such analyses of the painting tend to be circular, self-reinforcing, and they tell us much more about the writer than the image. They look for reinforcement of their science in the painting.

Whether, every time he walked past it, Freud thought *The Nightmare* was about the repression of incestuous desires – or about ancient/medieval mythologies which interested him; about the metaphorical rather than the psychological – we do not know. His print may well have been one of his 'tools of thought, the kitchen utensils of his imagination', as Marina Warner has put it.[64] And *was* it entirely coincidental that in the summer of 1938 he settled in 20 *Mares*field Gardens, leaving the picture behind? Well, one thing is for sure. When Freud's patients arrived for their daily appointments at Berggasse 19 in Vienna, and sat in the waiting room looking at that framed print on the wall, they must certainly have known they had come to the right address.

62 See Jerome M. Schneck, 'Henry Fuseli, nightmare, and sleep paralysis', *Journal of the American Medical Association*, 207:4 (27 January 1969, pp 725–6), the source of the above quotations. 63 Roger J. Broughton, 'Sleep disorders: disorders of arousal?' *Science*, 159 (1968), pp 1070–8, on the 'nocturnal demons' and the etymology of the word "mara". 64 Marina Warner, 'Preface' to *20 Maresfield Gardens* (London, 1998), pp vii–ix.

Contributors

JOHN-PAUL COLGAN completed his PhD on post-Cold War nostalgia in the work of John Updike and Don DeLillo from Trinity College Dublin in 2005. He has previously published articles on nostalgia, commodity culture, and contemporary American fiction. After spending three years as a Teaching Assistant in the TCD School of English, he is currently Visting Assistant Professor of Twentieth Century Literature at South East European University, Tetovo, Macedonia.

DARA DOWNEY is currently in the final stages of reading for a PhD in the School of English, Trinity College Dublin. Her thesis deals with the relationship between representations of space, gender differences and hauntedness in its various forms in a select range of American supernatural and Gothic fiction from the mid-1800s to the present. She has published work on Stephen King and Shirley Jackson, as well as film noir and contemporary horror. Forthcoming publications include articles on Charlotte Perkins Gilman and Mary Wilkins Freeman, and on Richard Matheson's *The shrinking man* and Mark Z. Danielewski's *House of leaves*.

BILL DURODIÉ is Senior Lecturer in Risk and Corporate Security at Cranfield University. His main research interest is into the causes and consequences of our contemporary consciousness of risk. He is also interested in examining the erosion of expertise, the demoralisation of élites, the limitations of risk management and the growing demand to engage the public in dialogue and decision-making in relation to science. He has published widely on these topics and also recently featured in the BAFTA award-winning BBC documentary series produced by Adam Curtis: *The power of nightmares: the rise of the politics of fear*. Durodié is one of the initiators of the Manifesto Club.

CHRISTOPHER FRAYLING is Rector of the Royal College of Art, the only wholly postgraduate university of art and design in the world, and also Professor of Cultural History there. In addition, he is Chairman of Arts Council England, the largest funding body for the arts in the UK. An award-winning broadcaster and author, he has published sixteen books on art, design and film – including *Vampyres* (1992) and *Nightmare – the birth of horror* (1996) – and co-curated, in

2006, the major Tate Britain exhibition *Gothic nightmares – Fuseli, Blake and the Romantic imagination*.

FRANK FUREDI is a Professor of Sociology at the University of Kent in Canterbury. During the past decade Furedi's research has been oriented towards the way that risk and uncertainty is managed by contemporary culture. He has published widely about controversies surrounding issues such as health, children, food and new technology. His new book *Invitation to terror*, to be published in October 2007, explores the relationship between twenty-first century Western culture and its preoccupation with terrorism.

DAVID GLOVER is a Senior Lecturer in English at the School of Humanities at the University of Southampton. He is the author of *Vampires, mummies, and liberals: Bram Stoker and the politics of popular fiction* (1996) and co-author, with Cora Kaplan, of *Genders* (2000). His current project is entitled 'Literature, immigration, diaspora: a cultural history of the 1905 Aliens Act'.

KATE HEBBLETHWAITE is a postdoctoral research fellow at the School of English, Trinity College Dublin. She has an especial research interest in the interaction between nineteenth-century popular literature and developments in nineteenth-century science, and has published a number of essays on this subject. She has also prepared editions of Bram Stoker's *Dracula's guest and other weird stories* and *The jewel of seven stars* for Penguin Classics.

DARRYL JONES is Senior Lecturer in English and Fellow of Trinity College Dublin, and director of the MPhil programme in Popular Literature. He is author or editor of four books, including *Horror: a thematic history in fiction and film* (2002), and studies of Jane Austen and Robert Emmet, as well as numerous articles on nineteenth-century literature and on popular fiction. He is currently working on a study of mass death and catastrophe fiction since the Enlightenment.

ELIZABETH McCARTHY is in the final stages of reading for a PhD at Trinity College Dublin. Her thesis examines the aesthetic and cultural contexts of sexual violence and murder from the Romantic era to the present. She has published works on Romantic aesthetics and serial murder, the vampire body and politics of the guillotine in the French Revolution. She is the co-founder and editor of the online publication, *The Irish Journal of Gothic and Horror Studies*. She currently teaches in Trinity College Dublin.

BERNICE M. MURPHY completed her PhD at the School of English, Trinity College Dublin, where she is now an IRCHSS Government of Ireland postdoctoral research fellow. She edited the collection *Shirley Jackson: essays on the literary legacy* (2005) and is currently working on a book-length study of horror and Gothic-themed depictions of American suburbia from 1948 to the present day. She is also a co-founder and editor of the biannual online *The Irish Journal of Gothic and Horror Studies*.

DEAGLÁN Ó DONGHAILE is an IRCHSS Government of Ireland postdoctoral research fellow, based at the Department of English, National University of Ireland, Maynooth. In 2006 he was named Bruce Harkness Young Conrad Scholar of the Year by the Joseph Conrad Society of America in recognition of his essay, 'Conrad, the Stevensons and the Imagination of Urban Chaos', which is forthcoming in the collection *Conrad and Stevenson: writers of land and sea*. He is currently working on a book monograph examining terrorism in modernism and popular fiction.

MARK O'SULLIVAN is a writer. His novels for pre-teens and young adults have won awards in Ireland and France and been translated into several languages. His first adult novel *Enright* was published in 2005 by Blackstaff Press. He is married and has two daughters. He lives in Thurles, Co. Tipperary.

AMANDA PIESSE is a Fellow and Senior Lecturer at Trinity College Dublin, and Secretary to the Irish Society for the Study of Children's Literature. Recent publications include 'Character Building: Shakespeare's children in context' in *Shakespeare and children* (Oxford, 2007), two essays in *Irish children's writers and illustrators, 1986–2006* (Dublin, 2007) and 'Islands, Ireland and the changing state of writing for children' in *Treasure islands* (Dublin, 2006). She regularly contributes articles to *Inis*, the review magazine of Children's Books Ireland.

JIM SHANAHAN is an IRCHSS Government of Ireland postdoctoral research fellow at Trinity College Dublin, and is currently working on a book about the 1798 rebellion in nineteenth-century fiction.

Index

Titles of films are differentiated from titles of books by the inclusion of their release date.